At the Border of Empires

At the Border of Empires

The Tohono O'odham, Gender, and Assimilation, 1880–1934

Andrae M. Marak and
Laura Tuennerman

The University of Arizona Press
Tucson

The University of Arizona Press
www.uapress.arizona.edu

First paperback edition 2017

Printed in the United States of America
22 21 20 19 18 17 7 6 5 4 3 2

ISBN-13: 978-0-8165-2115-9 (cloth)
ISBN-13: 978-0-8165-3656-6 (paper)

Cover design by Lori Lieber Graphic Design, Inc.
Cover photo: OIA office, Sells, AZ. From the National Archives, Laguna Niguel.

Publication of this book is made possible in part by the proceeds of a permanent endowment created with the assistance of a Challenge Grant from the National Endowment for the Humanities, a federal agency.

Library of Congress Cataloging-in-Publication Data
Marak, Andrae M. (Andrae Micheal)
At the border of empires : the Tohono O'odham, gender, and assimilation, 1880–1934 / Andrae M. Marak and Laura Tuennerman.
p. cm.
Includes bibliographical references and index.
ISBN 978-0-8165-2115-9 (cloth : alk. paper) 1. Tohono O'odham Indians—History. 2. Tohono O'odham Indians—Cultural assimilation. 3. Tohono O'odham women—Social conditions. 4. Tohono O'odham Indians—Social life and customs. I. Tuennerman, Laura, 1966– II. Title.
E99.P25M37 2013
979.1004'974552—dc23 2012034715

♾ This paper meets the requirements of ANSI/NISO Z39.48-1992 (Permanence of Paper).

To our daughters—Elyse and Megan; Flannery, Delaney, and Rowan

Contents

Illustrations

Acknowledgments

This book began almost by accident when David Rich Lewis, in response to a manuscript I submitted to the *Western Historical Quarterly* on the Tohono O'odham and education in Sonora, suggested that I (Andrae) dig into the available archival resources in Arizona and California. Upon returning from my first trip to Laguna Niguel, I shared the several hundred pages of notes that I had taken with my colleague and mentor, Laura Tuennerman. I was not sure how to make sense of my findings, especially the role of the outing matrons. There was no comparative category of women working with the Tohono O'odham in Mexico. Laura is a specialist on the Progressive Era in the United States, and I knew that she had written about the settlement house movement in Cleveland. She suggested to me that the outing matrons had much in common with that movement, but was surprised to find just how Victorian they were in their sensibilities. Before long, making use of our shared interests but different training, we wrote our first conference paper together.

We presented four increasingly nuanced versions in 2007 and 2008 at the Second Annual Audrey-Beth Fitch Conference on Women's Studies, the World History Association Conference, the American Historical Association Conference, and the European Social Science History Conference. At the American Historical Association Conference, Sarah Deutsch approached us to offer us encouragement and suggested that we contact the University of Arizona Press about an advance contract for a "book," which we had yet to even imagine. It was at this point that we began to think seriously about a larger project, one in which we could explore the complex themes of imperialism, gender, and indigenous agency. One thing that we agreed on from the start was that we needed to place Tohono O'odham voices at the center of our work as much as possible. With the fortunate granting of a semester's sabbatical from California University of Pennsylvania, Laura had the time to write a first draft of several chapters of the book—and so we began.

We have been blessed with the help of many people and institutions in bringing this project to fruition. California University of Pennsylvania was extremely generous. We would especially like to thank the Department of History and Political Science, the Faculty Professional Development Committee, the College of Liberal Arts, the Honors Program, the Sabbatical Committee, and Academic Affairs for underwriting some of our research and most of our conference travel. A Pennsylvania State System of Higher Education research grant funded the majority of our archival research. This grant would not have been possible without the help of Lewis Honaker, Cheryl Vogrig, and the members of our internal review in the Office of Grants and Contracts. Cindy Speer arranged most of our travel, helped us to format and reformat our photos, and generally kept up our spirits. Bill Meloy helped us to chase down innumerable citations, Barb Sabo supported our prolonged use of library materials, and Diane Turosik managed to get us rare and hard-to-find books and other resources through interlibrary loan. The Division of Liberal Arts at Indiana University–Purdue University Columbus provided monetary support at the ending stages of the project, and Vicki Kruse was instrumental in navigating the ins and outs of the Indiana University–Purdue University system.

We made use of many different archival resources in both the United States and Mexico. In the United States we are grateful to archivists, librarians, and employees at the National Archives and Records Administration in Washington DC and Laguna Niguel, Special Collections and University Archives at Marquette University, the Presbyterian Historical Society Archives, the Arizona State Museum, Special Collections at the University of Arizona, and the Arizona Historical Society Museum and Archives. In Mexico our thanks go out to the folks at the Archivo General de la Nación, the Fideicomiso Archivos Plutarco Elías Calles, the Archivo Histórico de la Secretaria de Educación Pública, the Unidad de Información de Pueblos Indigenas, and the Archivo Histórico del Estado de Sonora. We owe special thanks to Norma Mereles Torreblanca de Ogario, Roberto Pérez Aguilar, Macrina Restor, Gwen Pattison, Alan Ferg, Lisa Jacobson, and Mark Thiel for making our archival work both successful and satisfying.

A number of scholars have read portions of our work, commented on our presentations, or otherwise provided us with important guidance. They include Carlos Salomon, Elaine Carey, Scott Morgenstern, John J. Dwyer, Stephen Lewis, Jeffrey Shepherd, Sam Truett, Engracia Loyo, H. Richard Friman, Peter Andreas, Paul Eiss, Sterling Evans, Brenden Rensink, Guillermo Palacios, Ignacio Almada Bay, Elsie Rockwell, Benjamín Alonso Rascón, Mark Wasserman, John Soluri, Dale Brennaman, Elizabeth Molnar, Francis Paul Prucha, and our incredibly helpful anonymous reviewers. A number of people in Arizona made exceptional accommodations for us. Thomas Sheridan shared his extensive knowledge of the Tohono O'odham and reminded us not to worry about the dry heat. Bernard Fontana opened up his home, and then responded to repeated questions of clarification regarding the history of the Tohono O'odham. Bernard Siquieros, the curator of education at the Tohono O'odham National Cultural Center and Museum, set aside time to meet with us. Most importantly, Reuben Naranjo Jr. has been a near constant companion on our journey, sharing his family history, tribal connections, knowledge, and the work of many researchers who are laboring to reconstruct the history of the Tohono O'odham in Sonora.

Tracy Ellen Smith designed our maps.

At the University of Arizona Press, Patti Hartmann and Kristen Buckles shared their enthusiasm for the project, gently reminded us to keep making progress, and stood by us when we ran into obstacles.

Portions of this manuscript have been published in other venues, but they have all undergone major transformations. Steven Danver was gracious enough to allow us to coedit a special issue of *Journal of the West* on American Indians and the borderlands of the West, where our article "'He Don't Show Us Much about Farming': Tohono O'odham Agency and Agricultural Priorities, 1910–1940" focused on OIA agency farmers. Jorge Alberto Trujillo asked us to contribute "Los vicios trasnacionales de los Tohono o'odham a principios del siglo XX" for the volume he edited for the Universidad de Guadalajara, *En la encrucijada: Historia, marginalidad y delito en América Latina y los Estados Unidos de Norteamérica, siglos XIX y XX*. Finally, Elaine Carey and Andrae Marak's publication with the University of Arizona Press, *Smugglers, Brothels, and Twine: Historical Perspectives on Contraband and Vice in North America's Borderlands*, contains our "Official Government Discourses about Vice and Deviance: The Early 20th Century Tohono O'odham."

We would like to thank our families—Angie, Flannery, Delaney, Rowan, Scott, Elyse, and Megan—who have sacrificed much so that we could work on this project.

At the Border of Empires

Introduction

As reformers—both missionaries and officials of the Office of Indian Affairs (OIA)—headed out to the American West at the turn of the last century with a new commitment to bringing this region more firmly under national control, they carried with them a desire to assimilate and acculturate the Native American tribes that occupied that portion of the country as part of the expansion of the American empire. The Mexican government, especially as it worked through the Education Ministry (Secretaría de Educación Publica, SEP) beginning in 1921, also viewed the Tohono O'odham living in Mexico's northwest as "proto-citizens" who were in need of "state tutelage" before they would be capable of assuming and attaining the comprehensive duties, responsibilities, and rights of full citizenship.[1] It is clear that notions of gender—ideals and norms—heavily shaped the actions of these reformers and the "subjects" of their policies and efforts. Indeed, teaching natives "proper" gender roles was seen as one key element in creating Indian citizens, though ideas of what "citizen" meant changed a great deal over the period covered here.[2] As such, reformers reflected the views of their larger society, modeling gendered behavior—sometimes in keeping with those views, sometimes in conflict with them—and negotiating with tribal members who brought their own views and ideals to the discussion.

It is worth noting here that the concept of "negotiation" we utilize is akin to the ways in which Gilbert Joseph uses the word "encounter" in his essay "Close Encounters: Toward a New Cultural History of U.S.–Latin American Relations." There he describes encounters as "a range of networks, exchanges, borrowings, behaviors, discourses, and meanings." Like Joseph we are interested in "the deployment and contestation of power" in areas of contact between Native Americans and the majority culture.[3]

Interestingly, we argue, it was at the edges of empire that local forces—individuals living well outside the metropole, be they missionaries, reformers, or Native Americans—had the most chance to impact the implementation of national policies.[4] We argue this even as we recognize that the US government (and to a much lesser extent, the Mexican government) brought significant resources to bear on the Tohono O'odham's ancestral homeland precisely *because* it was located on each nation-state's periphery. Many in the United States were interested in protecting themselves from the Mexican "other" (as well as from Asians and other undesirables), while Mexico was trying to protect itself from US cultural and economic imperialism.[5] Nonetheless, as Benjamin Johnson and Andrew Graybill argue, "Borderlanders . . . also used national states and their boundaries for their own purposes and sought to forge nations that reflected their own identities."[6] In many cases, they were quite successful.[7] In any case, we take Samuel Truett's advice in his seminal article "Neighbors by Nature" seriously; namely, it is incumbent on us to trace the flows of power from the borderlands back to the metropole and to recognize the often outsized impact that these linkages have had on the region.[8]

Following Jacob Torfing, we define hegemony as "the expansion of a particular discourse of norms, values, views, and perceptions through persuasive redescriptions of the world."[9] While the United States and Mexico used both public and private means to expand their cultural hegemony,[10] this hegemony was far from complete—instead there was a fair amount of negotiation, borrowing, exchange, and contestation.[11] In other words, we can view not what the leaders and policymakers wanted to happen, but rather how events played out in the lives of individuals mediated by any number of factors. Thus we arrive at the study of assimilation at the turn of the last century with a focus quite literally on gendering the periphery of empires.

In the 1880s the US government made sweeping changes in its approach to Native American relations, seen most clearly in the legislation known as the Dawes Act, which addressed the allotment of land to individual Native Americans in 1887, and in the funding of schools and the move toward compulsory education for Native youth. Inspired by ideas coming out of the developing social sciences, and embracing the spirit of the then blossoming Progressive Era, officials decided to adopt new policies and institutions such as allotment and government-funded and -run schools for natives to provide solutions for the "Indian problem." Progressive optimism led leaders to believe that now was the time to "fix" the problems, finally bringing Native people into the fold of the majority culture and the national economy. Assimilation, even Americanization though not full citizenship, was the key.[12]

To accomplish this, reformers needed to strike at what they perceived to be the roots of the problem—lack of education and a culture marked, as they say it, by laziness, vice, and improper gender norms—to bring a backward people into the modern era. They would offer services, policies, laws, and institutions meant to clear away old, traditional practices and replace them—through concerted educational efforts—with the values, morals, and practices of the majority culture. Viewed in this light, the Native American problem—and its solutions—mirrored those being addressed by reformers elsewhere in the United States. Similar efforts were taking place in US cities and colonies as reformers tried to Americanize wave after wave of recent immigrants and colonial peoples.[13] So too were Progressives addressing comparable issues for other nonwhites, as they attempted to transform African Americans into good workers and good citizens, assimilating them into the majority culture.[14]

In addition, in the United States, at the turn of the twentieth century, there was an increased focus on publicly funded education for all children. This expanded to include compulsory school attendance in almost all states and territories by 1900 and a growth in high school attendance overall.[15] With passage of the Smith-Hughes Act of 1917, a federal act that supported vocational training for those undertaking agriculture as a vocation, there was also more interest in—and funding of—vocational or manual training for working-class youth. One force behind this was growing concern over a diversifying population. As the country was flooded with immigrants, especially those coming from countries not commonly represented in the middle class, civic leaders faced questions about how to best Americanize and acculturate these newcomers.[16] Policymakers saw education as a major mechanism for achieving these goals. As Robert Wiebe has suggested, "As servants of the community, the public schools would simply have to inculcate its youth with a pure and narrow truth." This was true for both boys—who were viewed as future workers and citizens—and girls—who were viewed as "moral," the social conscience of the nation, and who would inculcate in their men the proper levels of thrift, cleanliness, honesty, and hard work.[17]

In the early twentieth century, ideas about assimilation and cultural change would be strongly shaped by the growth and professionalization of the social sciences. In particular, new professionally trained scholars began to question ideas about evolution and progressive human development—raising the question of whether or not assimilation and acculturation was inevitable or even achievable. Opinions varied, especially between sociologists who emphasized the environment as the major shaping factor of behavior and anthropologists who focused on ideas of racial difference and culture. With scholarly opinions varying greatly, leaders and reformers had a variety of theories to choose from.[18]

The US federal government, mostly through the actions of the Office of Indian Affairs, did not face this major reform task alone. They were joined by a rather varied group of concerned and generally reform-minded individuals and institutions, including the Catholic Church and the Bureau of Indian Missions, Protestant missionaries and groups such as the United Presbyterian Church's Board of National Missions, and female-led reform organizations such as the Women's National Indian Association and the Presbyterian Church's Women's Board of Home Missions. Scores of new federal employees who joined the OIA as teachers, farmers, field matrons, and other professionals attempted to implement new assimilationist policies. These individuals and organizations of the majority culture worked together, negotiated with each other, and sometimes fought among themselves as they pushed toward the end goal of changing Native American life forever.

Historian Jeffrey Ostler offers an apt description of these efforts in his work on the Sioux, suggesting that, "Armed with certain knowledge of their own superiority, boundless optimism in humanity's placidity, and unflappable confidence in their ability to direct social evolution, the 'friends of the Indians' launched the most comprehensive and sustained assault on Native ways of life in U.S. history."[19] We cannot take this assault—and the claim to the moral authority of the state by those in mainstream society with an almost unwavering belief in their superiority—unquestioningly.[20] Instead, like Philip Corrigan and Derek Sayer in their study of the formation of the English state as cultural revolution, we have tried to understand the ways in which moral authority of the powerful was not simply an unquestioned justification for actions, but also something that needed to be institutionalized through everyday routines and rituals.[21] The state, and a variety of functionaries who put life into policy through their actions—both routine and ritual—were necessary to undertake the assimilation process.

At this point in history, leaders decided on a program of assimilation that would no longer take the form of charity or handouts, and would not focus on relocation or separation of the tribes from society as past efforts had. Instead it looked to transform native lives, to change their very culture and economies to bring them into the mainstream. Men would become landowning yeomen farmers (and later wageworkers); women would become morally persuasive wives and mothers. Children would help in the transformation as well, leaving home to receive American educations, with firmly gendered foundations, and then returning to their tribes to help raise their family members in a modern world.

These efforts at assimilation were particularly gendered. As Katherine Osburn highlights in her classic work on Ute women, the OIA policies aimed at transforming native people were fashioned around majority-culture ideas of gender. She suggests: "A significant component of this plan was restructuring of gender roles according to middle-class Euro-American ideologies of 'separate spheres.' In this thinking, a man's primary social role was that of breadwinner while women's was that of homemaker."[22] Society, and the reformers who represented it on the front lines, viewed gender norms, relations between the sexes, and monogamous marriage as the very foundations of American society and were working to reassert, and in some ways remake, ideals of femininity and masculinity nationally.

Like any imperialist effort, these activities did not take place in a vacuum. The reformers had to face people, the "subjects" of their reform efforts so to speak, who already had strongly developed senses of culture, gender, and vocation. And certainly these individuals, the native subjects of reform, were active participants in the process of change. In some cases they were welcoming participants; in others they were either passive or active resisters of cultural domination and change. Most often a complex process of mediation took place as individual desires and personalities shaped the implementation of policy at the grassroots level. As historian Devon Mihesuah describes these mediations: "Native women have survived the 'good intentions' of women reformers in organizations such as the Women's National Indian Association and the Women's Home Mission Circle, groups that attempted to 'help Indian peoples by pushing for assimilation, education, and Christianization,' and Indigenous women continue to fight against stereotypes, abuse, and cultural appropriation."[23] Assimilation was far from complete; change was negotiated in many ways.

To situate the issue further, we look to historians of gender who have described the ways in which gender identity is fluid and contested. As Gail Bederman has suggested, "ideologies of gender are not totalizing. . . . Like all ideologies, they are internally contradictory. . . . Men and women are able to influence the ongoing ideological processes of gender, even though they cannot escape them." We must then look at gender identity as an evolving process rather than a "set of traits or sex roles."[24]

To better contextualize this book, it is useful to consider the changing nature of historical study of Native American assimilation over the course of several decades. There have been major shifts in historical studies on the topic in recent years that have made for a fuller understanding of the complexity of these issues. Challenging "conventional top-down narratives that depict Indians as bit players . . . or tragic victims," historians began in the 1970s to offer a "new Indian history" that depicts the assimilation process as a dialogue, however uneven, between those in the majority culture and the "subjects" of their policies.[25] For several decades our understanding of the process has been expanded by many excellent works that offer a better understanding of native agency, cultural exchange, and negotiated survival. For example, Marsha Weisiger's gendered analysis of Navajo pastoralism explores the process of cultural exchange and the tragic ways in which the BIA and the Navajo often misunderstood and spoke past each other.[26] Texts by Richard White, James Axtell, and others have explored exchange and contestation.[27] All of these have enriched our understanding of a process that was never complete. Notions of cultural hegemony have been replaced by important works that point to perseverance, selective adaptation, and tenacity in the face of authority.[28]

Recent historians, however, have begun to swing the pendulum back in the other direction. As Jeffrey Ostler has suggested, "Work emphasizing these themes has revealed the shortcoming of an earlier historiography that portrayed Indians as no more than victims of European domination and gave little attention to the voices of Native People." But he continues, "In so doing, however, the current generation of scholarship, taken as a whole, has deemphasized questions of power, ideology, and the state."[29] And the imbalance of power, between a federal government backed by courts of law, the military, and the police and individuals, families, and even tribes of Native Americans, was vast. As such, in this book we try to strike a balance—recognizing agency, choice, and negotiation but also emphasizing the structures that were in place through law and policy and its enforcement, which often gave government workers and missionaries alike the ability to significantly alter individual lives.[30]

The study of assimilation needs to be further nuanced around issues of the local and the personal. As Ann Laura Stoler has suggested in her seminal work on culture and colonialism: "how power shaped the production of sentiments and vice versa is a subject that still begs for more analytic attention. We need to dwell in the disquiets, in the antipathies, estrangements, yearnings, and resentments that constrained colonial policies and people's actions, compelled their fears, and shaped what they imagined they should but could not do."[31] In terms of power structures, forces of cultural imperialism, most specifically patriarchy and racism, and individual choice struck at the core of tribal life. However, the varieties of daily life also impacted tribal life at a grassroots level.

In this book, in the case of the Tohono O'odham, we have a version of the story of assimilation at the extremes.[32] The Tohono O'odham lived at the extreme edge of two empires—on the literal periphery of society. While their societies were certainly not untouched or pristine, having had contact with a variety of other cultures for centuries, they were geographically removed from the center of American and Mexican civilization. As a society bifurcated by an imposed national border, and lacking reservation status to identify a location all their own, their peripheral status was marked by disruption and at times invisibility to the majority cultures of the region. Some areas were close to the missions or to Tucson and were centers of dialogue and contested space. Others were remote, so far removed that even white priests refused to live there, and in return these communities refused admittance to whites of all sorts.

As Bernard Fontana has suggested, the very idea of tribal identity was a creation of whites. In his work *Of Earth and Little Rain*, he described the tribe as "a white man's invention," noting turn-of-the-century efforts to meld varied Tohono O'odham dialects and villages into one tribe. He explains that "Fomented by non-Papagos, these efforts resulted in the competing League of Papago Chiefs and the Good Government League." Both leagues were attempts at governance developed by non-Papago, and both failed to unify what were generally people with local identities. Even the Tohono O'odham tribal council that began to meet in 1937 initially failed to centralize tribal power.[33] As context here, one might consider the work of Benedict Anderson and the ways in which he argues that community identity and consciousness are imagined and indeed often purposely manufactured. Anderson invokes the point of Ernest Gellner that "'Nationalism is not the awakening of nations to self-consciousness: it *invents* nations where they do not exist.'"[34] Like gender and other ideologies, community or tribal identity is also negotiated and constructed.

Further complicating matters is the fact that the US–Mexico border was of relatively recent construction. The present-day border between the two countries was not finalized until the completion of a boundary survey begun after the 1853 Gadsden Purchase (known as the Treaty of La Mesilla in Mexico).[35] Even the Gadsden Purchase did not stop filibusterers from attempting—and failing—to annex additional parts of Mexico to the United States.[36] The border remained porous and a source for the possible passage of undesirable people, ideas, and vices.[37] On the US side of the border, OIA officials viewed the borderlands region as a source of trouble. For example, in 1916 Jewell D. Martin, an OIA superintendent, argued that it was necessary to provide telephone service to a proposed agency site in Indian Oasis in southern Arizona because "many stirring events may occur near the trouble zone of the boundary."[38]

In addition, Martin wrote to Dwight B. Heard, local chairman of the Arizona Council of Defense, offering the services of up to three hundred Tohono O'odham riders to patrol the border and deter the incursion of possible Mexican raiders during the Mexican Revolution after the US entry into World War I.[39] On the Mexican side of the border, the perceived threat was of a wholly different kind. Mexico's revolutionary and postrevolutionary leaders were in favor of continued US investment, especially in the industrial sector.[40] In fact, the overall amount of direct US investment rose during the 1920s as presidents Álvaro Obregón (1920–1924) and Plutarco Elías Calles (1924–1928) were in the process of reconstructing their shattered nation.[41] While both were interested in increased direct US investment in the Mexican economy, they had three larger concerns. First, they worried that there would be a backlash against increased foreign investment, especially in light of the fact that the Mexican Revolution itself was brought on, at least in part, by Mexicans' resentment of foreign businesses and their negative political, cultural, and economic impacts.[42] Second, they were uneasy about the possibility that the incoming American capital would bring with it US cultural imperialism. Third, with the passage of Prohibition in the United States, many centers of vice—including casinos, houses of prostitution, cantinas, nightclubs, cabarets, and bullrings—relocated from the United States to the Mexican side of the border.[43] These fears would eventually lead to the creation of a series of "frontier schools" meant to stem the tide of US cultural influences.[44]

The US–Mexico border was not the only border in the region. OIA officials also viewed the liminal spaces between the Papago and San Xavier Reservations and non-Indian communities (especially Tucson) as filled with a plethora of "vices." It was their job, they claimed, to protect the Tohono O'odham from these potential hazards. This was in keeping with the original intention of Indian removal and placement on reservations. William T. Hagan argues that when the United States adopted its reservation policy in the 1860s and 1870s, "there was almost unanimous agreement among the whites that this was the [N]ative American's best hope of survival." Indian and non-Indian mixing would be more detrimental than helpful, unless indigenous people were exposed only to those people approved by the government and thought to have the best interests of Indians at heart.[45] Tohono O'odham tribal leaders tapped into this trope at a meeting held in 1916 to petition the OIA to set up the Papago Reservation. For example, Benito Segundo, "governor" of Topawa, argued: "It is well known that if white men come in here they are not our relatives and soon differences will arise between us."[46] Outside influences of all sorts were viewed as disruptive, and yet forces from the majority culture were at work, even on reservations, pushing to shape native culture and life.

Time brought changes—and speeded up the process of assimilation. It allowed for more supervision of the tribe and increased contact between cultures. After the OIA set up the Papago Reservation in 1916, its official policy promoted vocational training of Tohono O'odham so that they could eventually assimilate into mainstream society. This move mirrored broader national trends discussed earlier.

Finally, on the issue of periphery, we argue as well that the Tohono O'odham were also on the periphery of our historical understandings. There is a scattering of historical works on the tribe, including recent works by Eric Meeks, *Border Citizens: The Making of Indians, Mexicans, and Anglos in Arizona*; Peter Macmillan Booth, "Creation of a Nation: The Development of the Tohono O'odham Political Culture, 1900–1937"; and Kenneth Dean Madsen, "A Nation across Nations: The Tohono O'odham and the United States–Mexico Border." In addition, historian Bernard Fontana has devoted his career to documenting tribal life and history. Nonetheless, much work, especially work focused on issues of gender, remains unwritten. This book, then, sheds light on an understudied tribe. It also provides an underutilized lens for understanding assimilation.

As a case study of assimilation efforts and a specific tribe, this book highlights struggles over gender roles, values and vice, the family and education, and even vocation that would forever change Tohono O'odham life but would, in the end, fall far short of the great success the optimistic US reformers dreamed about. It is thus the story of an uncompleted quest for full assimilation. This book examines the mediation between cultures, the individual personalities that sometimes shaped ideologies, policies, and events, and the real people who were impacted by change.

Our story begins in the 1880s and the years leading up to the Dawes Act, and ends in 1934 with the coming of the New Deal and the portions of that major reform effort that thoroughly changed the government's approach to Native relations. By the late 1920s, however, shadows of what was to come were cast by the findings of the Merriam Report, a government-sanctioned report that was highly critical of the work of the OIA in the twentieth century. Our period of study, then, was marked by change of policy and of circumstance; the goals and methods of the OIA were far from constant during these fifty years. We should acknowledge that a truly transnational history of the Tohono O'odham is needed; this is not that study. The Tohono O'odham make only ephemeral appearances in the records stored in Mexican state and national archives during the period that our study covers. Future researchers will need to conduct research at the municipal level in the many communities where the Tohono O'odham lived and worked. Of course, additional oral history research will also be necessary.[47] Nonetheless, we have tried to emphasize the transnational character of the Tohono O'odham where the source material allows. More importantly, we have striven to avoid oversimplifying the US and Mexican Tohono O'odham as two wholly different groups. As Guadalupe Castillo and Margo Cowan demonstrate in *It Is Not Our Fault: The Case for Amending Present Nationality Law to Make All Members of the Tohono O'odham Nation United States Citizens, Now and Forever*, the Tohono O'odham remain a transnational people today, and their ties across the US–Mexico border were considerably stronger in the past.[48]

In our first chapter we offer some necessary background on the tribe itself, its culture and its history and the history of Native American relations in the region long before the US government took a serious interest in this area. In the four chapters after that we examine the ways in which the US government—and others—instituted programs to eliminate "vice" among the Tohono O'odham and to encourage the morals of the majority culture as the basis of an Americanization process. In general the OIA viewed the Tohono O'odham as backward, prone to vice—or at least susceptible to it under the wrong conditions—and in need of civilizing. Specifically, in chapter 2 we analyze the practices that these governmental agencies engaged in to eliminate the use of alcohol, and to a less extent drugs, among the Tohono O'odham as they first came into substantial contact with the OIA in the twentieth century. In chapter 3 we look more closely at issues of household, marriage, and sexual morals as they impacted reform efforts focused on the tribe. The next two chapters discuss education and vocation as approaches to acculturation and Americanization. As such, the four middle chapters of the book examine the assimilation process through a focus on different policies and institutions with similar, shared goals.

In a final chapter we develop a comparative example of the gendered assimilation process by focusing on the experiences of the Tohono

O'odham living south of the border in Mexico. Though the subjects were arguably a single ethnographic group, as discussed above, the imposition of political boundaries bifurcated the tribe and would eventually lead to a major disjuncture in tribal experience. Although Tohono O'odham continued to pass back and forth across the border, living seasonally in different countries or at the very least visiting important ceremonial sites regardless of their national location, the imposition of "nationality" on members of the tribe who settled more permanently on one side or the other impacted the strategies they adopted as well as their eventual fate. By looking comparatively at the experiences of natives now living in Mexico, we can better understand the process of change on both sides of the border—and better understand how things could have been, and were done, differently.

In the end, then, we use a multipronged approach to understand the forced assimilation of the Tohono O'odham. We consider the imposition of majority culture on the tribe, but also the agency and actions of the natives and the negotiated realities that came to exist. We examine national policy, but are also mindful of the ways in which individuals, especially those living far from the metropole, often exercised a great deal of influence over individual lives—those of others as well as their own. We consider the economic aims of expanding the American empire to include this tribe, but also recognize the serious cultural forces at play in economic decisions. Above all we look at gender ideals as the key force in the process, considering not only gender as it applied to and shaped ideals of femininity and women's lives, but also as it redefined masculinity and male experience. Though the Tohono O'odham were a fairly small population living in a large territory well on the periphery of US society, they provide a case study that sheds light on the complex process of imperialism and colonialism as it affects the day-to-day lives of real men, women, and children. During this period of fifty-plus years, tribal norms interacted with—sometimes conflicting with, sometimes reinforcing—those of the larger "American society" in ways that significantly shaped policy and impacted tribal experience. This case study thus provides a lens for looking not only at Native American history but also at broader societal ideas about culture, femininity and masculinity, and empire at the turn of the last century.

CHAPTER ONE

The Early History of the Tohono O'odham

It must have been God's will that we are now here in this waterless country and he has shown us the way to live here.

—ALVINO GERNOMO, MINUTES OF COUNCIL WITH PAPAGO INDIANS AT INDIAN OASIS, 1916

Since they became convinced that Government was looking to their interests with a view of rendering them assistance, they have become very submissive and anxious to conform to any law which might be interpreted to them as necessary to their well being.

—R. A. WILBUR, OIA AGENT, ANNUAL REPORT, 1874

As mentioned in our introduction, the leading historian of the Tohono O'odham, Bernard Fontana, has suggested that "the 'Papago Tribe of Arizona' is a white man's invention."[1] Noted anthropologist Ruth Underhill argues that prior to contact with Europeans, "the Papago had no central government. Each village unit was autonomous and when two units occasionally joined, for war or games, the union was temporary."[2] Indeed, histories of the people we study in this book, the Tohono O'odham, suggest that the native peoples living in the western portion of present-day southern Arizona and northern Sonora were culturally, geographically, and linguistically diverse. In fact, it was not until after the Gadsden Purchase in 1853, which placed an international border through Tohono O'odham ancestral lands, and the arrival of a significant number of Anglos, that the distinction between the Pimas, who lived a sedentary lifestyle in the Gila Valley, and the Papagos (Tohono O'odham), their Piman-speaking neighbors who adopted a semisedentary lifestyle to the south in the Sonoran Desert, was "solidly established."[3] In spite of their speaking a common language with many local variations and dialects, great distances, difficult terrain, the international border, and a long history of village-level governance separated individual groups of Tohono O'odham from one another and from their Piman relatives (even as they were codependent). In fact, Peter Macmillan Booth argues that, ironically, the Tohono O'odham accepted a centralized tribal government in 1937 precisely to protect "village independence" and autonomy.[4] Historian Henry F. Dobyns noted in 1972 that "the pressures of White dominance, including territorial loss and reservation self-government, and the mechanization of transportation that allows rapid visiting among all Papagos have generated more social unity among these people today than at any time in the past."[5] While this is admittedly the end of our story, it seems important at the start to highlight the fragility, fragmentation, and contested nature of the idea of the Tohono O'odham as a unified people before briefly outlining some of their history.

Prior to the arrival of Catholic missionaries in 1687, the Tohono O'odham combined both secular and religious leadership in a single patriarch at the village level. The patriarch controlled special fetishes and knew a series of intricate "Wise Speeches" for important ceremonial occasions, especially those related to rain; he also adjudicated disputes between village members.[6] Between 1687 and 1711, Jesuit missionary Father Eusebio F. Kino made repeated forays into the Papaguería, where he found thousands of Tohono O'odham people living in scattered villages in the Sonoran Desert. Not only did he establish a series of missions, including San Xavier and Tucson, he brought with him "Old World seed crops, livestock, and infectious diseases."[7] The Spanish empire had arrived, but its Jesuit agents had to negotiate their continued presence. They did so by acting as "extension agents for European agricultural technology." The Tohono O'odham were quick to adopt winter wheat, horses, and cattle.[8]

The Jesuits continued their influence (but never dominance) in the region, introducing natives to Roman Catholicism by preaching in native languages and incorporating native dance and music into Christian practices.[9] When the Spanish government expelled the Jesuits in 1767, the Franciscans took their place. Around the same time as the Jesuit expulsion, the Spanish Empire under Charles III enacted the Bourbon Reforms, in part, as a means of better securing its claims in frontier regions like the Papaguería. This meant the establishment of a series of presidios (armed garrisons) in the region, including one in Tucson, from which the Spanish (as well as allied Piman and Tohono O'odham) soldiers engaged in forays against the Apaches.[10] The Franciscans used (and the government subsidized) their missions as a means to convince Native Americans—especially Apaches but also Pimans, Tohono O'odham, and others—to settle permanently, take up agriculture, and (in general) adopt Spanish customs.

By the time that Mexico won its independence from Spain in 1821, the Tohono O'odham had established a strong reverence for Saint Francis of Assisi (though they actually paid their respects to "a reclining statue of Saint Francis Xavier, the great Jesuit missionary saint and patron of all missionaries"),[11] took up an annual pilgrimage to Magdalena, Sonora, on October 4, and adopted a purely secular village chief or governor. According to Underhill, the new, more circumscribed governor's job was to "keep up the morals of the village, deal with offenders and talk with the Whites."[12] Mexico's independence brought additional changes to the region. The end of subsidies for presidios and missions convinced many Apaches to give up settled lives and return to raiding; in response, the Tohono O'odham "restructured their society to meet the Apache war machine and hold their ancestral territory with Mexican assistance."[13] By 1840, with the Franciscans unable to continue their mission work among the Tohono O'odham, Sonoran Catholicism, "a kind of Catholic religious practice without benefit of clergy," arose.[14] Among other things, individual villages built their own chapels, laymen put on the festival of Saint Francis Xavier each December 2 in San Xavier del Bac, and aboriginal practices morphed into Catholic ones, while retaining elements of both.

In 1853 the Gadsden Purchase led to the drawing of an international boundary with Mexico that ran directly through Tohono O'odham lands—making some tribal members "Americans" and others "Mexicans," though neither government granted them full citizenship.[15] Not only did the border remain porous, but, as David Lewis notes, the division of their lands between Mexico and the United States was so unimportant that it failed to show up on "the village calendar sticks—ironwood or saguaro staffs with carved mnemonic symbols, annual notations of significant events."[16] While these changes were unremarkable to the Tohono O'odham at the time—they "continued to live and to behave as if the boundary did not exist"[17]—it was the first step in moving portions of the tribe in different directions. For example, continued Apache raiding of Tohono O'odham and Anglo cattle (and occasional women and children) resulted in a coordinated defense north of the border, including the creation of a Tohono O'odham "standing army" of 150 mounted warriors to supplement Anglo efforts to repulse Apache depredations.[18] The naming of Indian agent Colonel John Walker in 1857 also reflected increased Tohono O'odham–Anglo collaboration north of the border, especially in and around San Xavier del Bac.[19] After the US Civil War (1861–1865), President Ulysses S. Grant adopted the Peace Policy. The policy, aimed at the eventual assimilation of Native Americans, "ended treaty making . . . made establishing

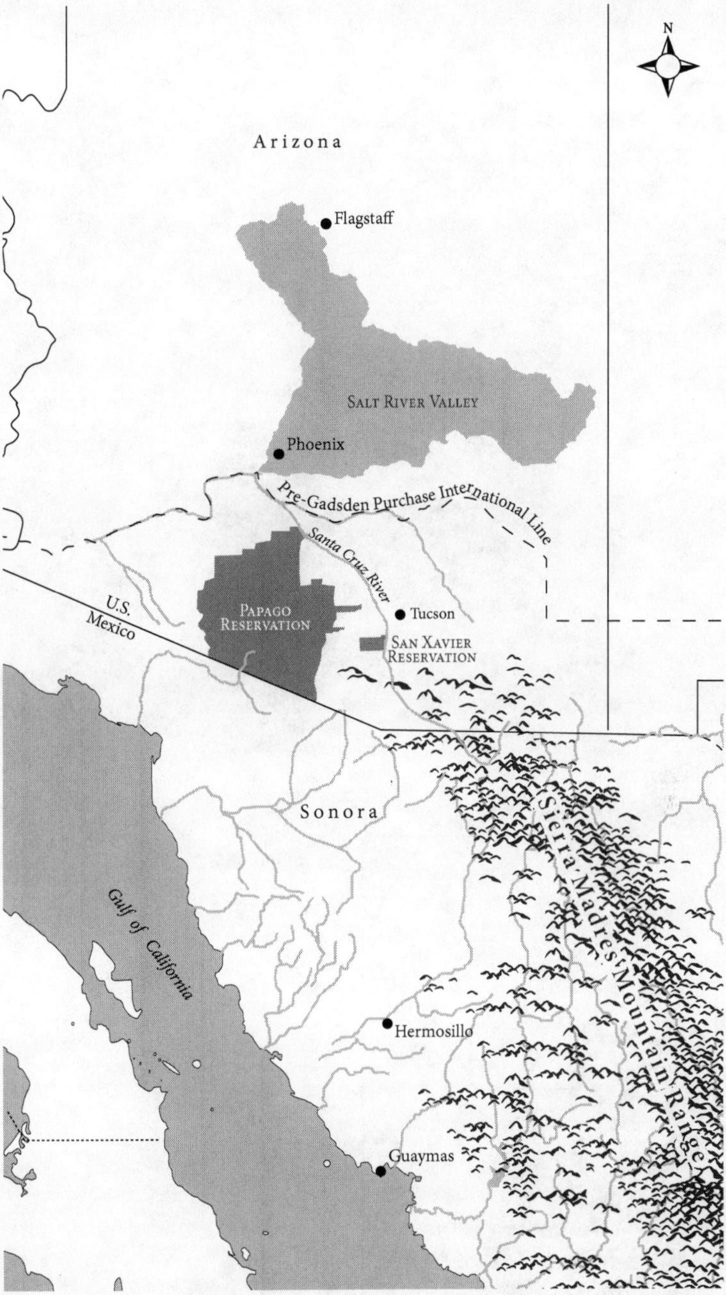

Figure 1.1 The Tohono O'odham and shifting national borders. (Map by Tracy Smith.)

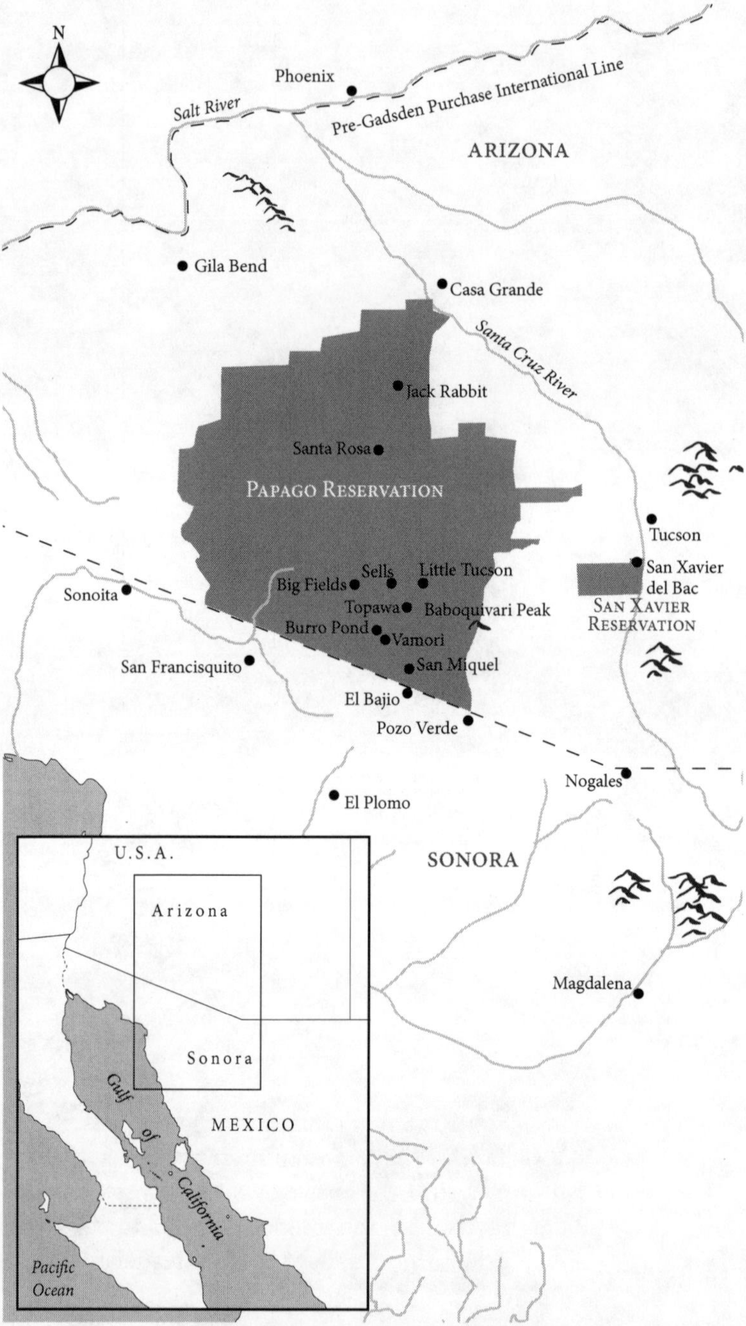

Figure 1.2 Tohono O'odham villages (inset). (Map by Tracy Smith.)

reservations a federal priority, and created the position of Indian inspector," which would be dominated by missionaries and military personnel.[20] The Tohono O'odham made a positive impression on Brevet Colonel George L. Andrews, superintendent of Indian affairs in Arizona Territory, who requested that reservation lands be set aside for them. He is worth quoting at length:

> The Papago Indians are and have been for years past the best, most industrious and most civilized Indians of Arizona; they embraced the Christian faith years ago and strictly adhere to it; they are and have always been on the most friendly terms with the Whites and Mexicans, many speak the Spanish language fluently; the tribe has from time to time rendered valuable services by scouting against the hostile Apaches and altogether no Indians of this Territory have a stronger claim upon the fostering care of the Government than the Papagos.[21]

But assistance would be tied to cultural changes. The letters of Indian agent R. A. Wilbur provide a clear illustration of government expectations: "I shall proceed to the Papago Country in a few days and explain to the Indians the conditions upon which they can expect to receive aid and assistance from the Government. Should I be convinced that they earnestly desire to abandon their nomadic life and settle in the vicinity of San Xavier I will proceed to purchase the necessary amount of seed wheat and barley, taking care that it is properly distributed."[22] Some Tohono O'odham, and some Anglos and Mexican Americans, did settle permanently.[23]

Others came from Sonora to settle temporarily in and around San Xavier during economic depressions, severe droughts, and periods of elevated Apache raiding only to return when things improved, suggesting that they viewed their relationship with Wilbur and the US government on very different terms. In fact, some of these migrations were surely part of what historian Peter Macmillan Booth calls "desert-river cooperative complexes," whereby desert villages made annual migrations to river-based settlements of their Akimel O'odham brethren. These relationships supporting these complexes were strengthened through intermarriage and trade.[24] In 1873, Wilbur arranged for Tohono O'odham children to attend school under the tutelage of two sisters from the Order of St. Joseph of Carondelet.[25] At the same time, the secretary of the interior assigned the agency of the Papago to the Catholic Church, then under the leadership of Bishop Jean-Baptiste Salpointe.[26] In 1874, President Grant, in part to protect the Tohono O'odham from non-Indian encroachment on their ancestral lands, used an executive order to create the San Xavier Reservation, in the process turning them into wards of the US government.[27] The Department of the Interior consulted with Bishop Salpointe and the Bureau of Catholic Indian Missions to replace Wilbur with Major John Coryn, a Catholic.[28] Coryn worked with the Tohono O'odham for a year, arguing that the Tohono O'odham were deserving of the federal government's attention by virtue of being "the most placable, quiet, law abiding and virtuous tribe in Arizona," thanks to "the watchful care the Catholic Church has bestowed upon them for the last two hundred years," while the nearby Pima were undeserving because "the vice of prostitution prevales [*sic*] to a great extent among their women, and a current report declares that such a thing as the practice of virtue is scarcely known among them."[29] His arguments backfired.

The OIA transferred jurisdiction over the Tohono O'odham from Coryn and the Catholic Church to the agency of the Pimas and Maricopas in Sacaton, which was being run by the Dutch Reformed Church, at least in part because the OIA determined that the Tohono O'odham needed little help.[30] The Catholic school run by the sisters closed, though Catholic officials did try unsuccessfully to get the federal government to continue funding it. In fact, through 1880, the Catholic Church set aside $2,500 each year for a day school for the Tohono O'odham, but conditioned their willingness to use it on the federal government assigning an Indian agent to the San Xavier Reservation.[31] The federal government had no interest in complying. As a result, the Tohono O'odham were left to their own devices.[32]

On the Mexican side of the border, where the Apache attacks continued to take their toll, events were taking a different course. First, the Mexican government made no specific efforts to work with the Tohono O'odham as a people. On the contrary, elites—along with a growing middle class of *gente decente*, or good, honorable people—pushed to eliminate corporate identities and communities—especially those of the Catholic Church, peasant pueblos, and indigenous groups—and replace them with wage laborers and capitalist yeoman farmers who, it was hoped, would view themselves as Mexican citizens and integrate themselves into broader Mexican society.[33] Mexican settlers—drawn to the region by the discovery of gold, silver, and copper as well as the expansion of the cattle industry—settled on Tohono O'odham ancestral lands and took control of many Tohono O'odham water sources.[34] This, coupled with construction of a railroad connecting the port city of Guaymas, Sonora, and the border city of Nogales, Arizona, which bisected their ancestral lands, severely limited Tohono O'odham options. They could fight to defend their lands, assimilate into mainstream Mexican culture, work for Mexicans but maintain their cultural separateness, intermarry with other indigenous peoples, retreat to the less hospitable regions of their ancestral lands, or—as they did after 1916—use the reservation on the US side of the border as leverage to push for similar considerations in Mexico.

As we will explain in chapter 6, the Tohono O'odham adopted a combination of these methods. These included engaging in "cattle rustling," migratory resistant adaptation through their now cross-border desert-river cooperative complexes, marrying into non-Tohono O'odham families and communities, permanent settlement in the United States, and living in small clustered communities on the fringes of newly majority Mexican cities and villages.[35] Given the unfavorable political conditions, the Tohono O'odham had mostly given up using military force to defend their lands and water sources by the time of the Gadsden Purchase. Nonetheless, when they raided El Plomo in 1898 to release one of their chiefs from jail, the *rurales*—a Mexican federal police force created by Porfirio Díaz to enforce his new export-led growth model based on "Order and Progress"—used the incident to harass and scatter the Tohono O'odham for over a decade, opening up more of their lands to settlement by outsiders.[36] Fontana argues that by the time ethnographer Carl Lumholtz arrived in the region in 1910, less than one thousand Tohono O'odham still lived in Mexico, while another three to four thousand had relocated to the United States.[37]

On the US side of the border, President Grant's Peace Policy came to an end for the Tohono O'odham in 1882.[38] It would be another five years before federal lawmakers passed the General Allotment (Dawes) Act, a statute that served simultaneously to open up Native American lands to outsiders and prepare Native Americans for citizenship.[39] Much like the Porfirian assault against corporate identity and landholdings in Mexico, the Dawes Act aimed to turn Native Americans—whom policymakers viewed as redeemable proto-citizens—into settled yeoman farmers (and ranchers). To do so it divided up reservation lands and distributed them to tribal members as individuals, heads of families receiving larger shares and dependents smaller shares. The lands were to be held in trust for at least twenty-five years while Native Americans transitioned, through federal education efforts and practice as farmers and stockmen, from being noble savages to US citizens.[40] When OIA officials deemed Native Americans ready for full citizenship, they would be issued fee-simple patents for their land, at which point they were free to keep it, sell it, or rent it.[41]

In the meantime, the OIA would sell, with Native American consultation, "surplus" lands to non-Indians to homestead and for the use of the United States's burgeoning railroad corporations.[42] In reality, allotted land was often too small to sustain Native Americans, and this practice disregarded the possibility of future Native American population growth; this was especially the case in the Southwest where much of the land was better suited to cattle raising and access to water was critical. It should be noted that although the principles behind the Porfirian program in Mexico and the Dawes Act in the United States were similar—that is, to turn purportedly backward people into progressive yeoman farmers—the approach and outcome was much different, a topic we will return to in chapter 6. On the San Xavier Reservation OIA officials allotted lands, 41,600 acres in all, in 1890, giving 291 male household heads: "20 acres of farm land and 50 to 80 acres of mesquite timber land." On average each received only ten acres of irrigated land.[43]

Although the allotment on the San Xavier Reservation created plenty of confusion over landownership, the OIA never took the next step of transitioning them to fee-simple patents so that lands could be sold.[44] It was right around the time that lands were allotted that three competing schools opened or reopened: (1) the Indian training school (or Escuela), a Presbyterian boarding school located between San Xavier and Tucson, (2) a Catholic day school in San Xavier run by the Sisters of St. Joseph of Carondelet, and (3) the Phoenix Indian School, a government-run off-reservation Indian boarding school that made extensive use of the "outing system," which generally placed Indian girls into the homes of non-Indians as domestic servants as part of their education.[45] Thus began a competition, with limited cooperation, between the Catholics, Presbyterians, and the federal government for the hearts and minds, and souls, of the Tohono O'odham.

The story of the early Presbyterian influence is important because their boarding school produced a sizeable number of Tohono O'odham fluent in English, giving them a leg up for reservation jobs when the OIA began hiring Native American employees in 1916 and a disproportionate influence on tribal affairs throughout the remaining time period of our study.[46] In the 1870s a German Presbyterian named Charles Cook served as a missionary among the Tohono O'odham's neighbors—the Pimas. His work attracted the notice of the Woman's Executive Committee of the Women's Board of Home Missions of the Presbyterian Church, who supported his work and his desire to start a school to serve the native population of the region. The mission board sent Mary Whitaker to Tucson, where, in the fall of 1888, she rented an old public school building, recruited Piman students, and opened the Escuela.[47]

For several decades the main focus of the Home Missions board remained on the Pima, although the Presbyterians did some work around San Xavier, including running a day school from 1887 to 1889. The first day school teacher, Dr. F. J. Hart, found it difficult to relate to the Tohono O'odham, the second, J. B. Douglass, was removed for alcohol abuse, and the third, J. N. Wilson, resigned after only eight months on the job. Isolation in the desert was not easy.[48] At the turn of the century Rev. W. H. Gill proposed working more broadly with the Tohono O'odham, noting critically that he believed the government was doing nothing to help them. He toured "Papago country"; naturally his travels took him into Mexico. Equally critical of the Catholics, he reported at the time that he found Tohono O'odham worshipping in old Catholic churches without "white" guidance. He reached out to these communities and even preached in some of these churches.[49] Gill noted at the time that there were few other Protestants working with the tribe, though the Mormons visited every other year.[50] As a missionary he believed there was much work to be done.

By this time the Tohono O'odham had learned of the Escuela through their contacts with the Pimas, and a few of their children began to attend the boarding school. Early students included a student named Jessie who was the daughter of Chief Pablo. The first Tohono O'odham student to graduate from the school at Tucson was José Xavier Pablo, who completed his studies in 1903, and eventually went on to be an interpreter for missionaries and anthropologists, the first ordained elder of the Presbyterian Church from the Tohono O'odham tribe, a US government employee for the OIA, and the self-appointed Tohono O'odham spokesperson with Education Ministry officials in Mexico.

There were frequent changes in superintendents, as many went on to other missionary fields and at least one left to become the president of the University of Arizona. The superintendent of the Tucson school from 1895 to 1903, Rev. Frazier S. Herndon, left the school to go live among the Tohono O'odham and engage in mission work. Herndon had begun his work at the Tucson school as a blacksmith, then became an industrial teacher, assistant superintendent, and eventually superintendent. Upon leaving the school in 1912, he opened a school and a small chapel in Indian Oasis (Sells) with his wife, who ran a Sunday school for the Tohono O'odham—as well as Mexican and Chinese children.[51] In 1914 he moved his school to Vamori near the Mexican border and opened up a Presbyterian church in nearby San Miguel; establishing his church in San Miguel allowed him to successfully minister to the nearby Tohono

O'odham settlement in Pozo Verde.[52] Herndon worked with early converts to translate portions of the Bible into Tohono O'odham, held occasional night school for Tohono O'odham parents, and sponsored major camp meetings in Sells, San Miguel, Topawa, and Vamori.

Beyond focusing on the Tohono O'odham villages, Herndon made trips into the countryside beginning in 1904, generally traveling with José X. Pablo as translator and with musical instruments to conduct services throughout the territory.[53] In addition, in the absence of an OIA field matron in Tucson—at this time their outing system focused its efforts in Phoenix—Mrs. Herndon supervised Tohono O'odham girls who worked in the city, filling a role similar to that of the matrons.[54] All of this Presbyterian mission work, the churches, schools, and eventually social services were supported by various organizations of the church, including the board of Home Missions, the Women's Board of Home Missions, and the board of the Church Erection Fund.[55] While some donations came from the local synod, much of the funding came from out of state. Missionary societies, church groups, and individuals from East Coast cities like Philadelphia and New York City provided most of the funds, along with at least one major gift from philanthropist Mrs. Russell Sage. Prior to 1894, the Tucson school was also run as a contract school and thus received significant funding from the federal government.

The Catholic Church also continued its efforts to educate the Tohono O'odham. For example, church officials ran a day school for the Tohono O'odham at San Xavier del Bac from the early 1890s to 1910 without subsidies from the federal government. Despite the lack of federal funding, they began to provide the federal government with quarterly reports on school employees, students, and their attendance in 1900.[56] Church officials spent much of the first decade of the twentieth century trying to fend off the threat of non-Catholic schools and pushing to give Indian parents the right to send their children to the school of their choice. For example, Bishop Granjon argued that the federal government need not provide additional schooling in San Xavier del Bac given that the Catholic Church was running a religious day school for 126 locals and would be willing to expand to accommodate more students if necessary. In fact, he argued that having only a Catholic day school added to local harmony and the Tohono O'odhams' good behavior.[57]

The OIA began its close relationship with the Catholic Church in 1910 with the transfer of the religious day school at San Xavier del Bac under the federal umbrella.[58] Interestingly, the OIA arranged for the three sisters who ran the school to be transferred to the federal payroll without taking

Figure 1.3 Tohono O'odham girls' first communion, 1916. (Courtesy of Department of Special Collections and University Archives, Marquette University Libraries, #11225.)

the required examination. For their part, church authorities looked forward to collaborating with the OIA because Indian agent Henry J. McQuigg would take on the responsibility of enforcing school attendance, redirecting the usual parental criticism related to children's attendance from the church officials to the federal government.[59] However, they did fear losing local support for their schools if word got out that they were now working for, and were subsidized by, the government and so initially worked to keep their relationship secret.[60] McQuigg, a Catholic, worked with Bishop Granjon to increase Tohono O'odham ties with the Catholic Church; both McQuigg and Granjon, the first more than the latter, feared that the work of Reverend Herndon coupled with the return of Tohono O'odham from non-Catholic boarding schools would lead significant numbers of Tohono O'odham to fall "away from their old . . . religion"; Granjon, however, believed that many of them might simply be "belly-converts" and easily recoverable if the Catholic Church could deploy more resources in the region. One major issue, beyond the Church's limited resources, was that Bishop Granjon did not think secular priests could handle the hardship and isolation of the desert; thus, he pushed the Franciscans to begin administering to the Tohono O'odham, "even if only on regular visits."[61]

The next few years saw increasing involvement by the OIA, the Presbyterians, and the Catholic Church. The federal government set aside small plots of land in 1911 (adjusted in 1912) at Indian Oasis (Sells), Baboquivari, and San Miguel. Meanwhile, Reverend Herndon baptized Chief Pablo, setting off alarm bells within the Catholic bureaucracy, who feared that the baptism would result in a massive conversion. The Franciscans agreed to minister to the Tohono O'odham, but Bishop Granjon resisted their request to have San Xavier del Bac ceded to their control, suggesting that they be placed instead at Jack Rabbit, a remote location in the most northern reaches of the future Tohono O'odham reservation. He argued that through his offices the Tohono O'odham at San Xavier "are already being attended to. . . . If you [the Cardinal] want the regular clergy to act as missionaries, then they need to go where the Papago that are not being attended to are." Bishop Granjon also argued that the Dawes Act would result in the doors to the San Xavier Reservation being "thrown open" in the coming years, resulting in the dispersal of the Tohono O'odham and undermining the "raison d'etre for the Franciscan Community there."[62] The Franciscans responded with a litany of Bishop Granjon's failings, noting that both the Mormons and Presbyterians had made major inroads with the Tohono O'odham. Bishop Granjon went so far as to respond to the pressure of the Franciscans by denouncing their intentions to set up shop at San Xavier from the altar at Sunday mass, prompting Indian agent McQuigg to note that the bishop's stance was in fact undermining the Catholic Church's efforts on the reservation, especially in light of the fact that Reverend Herndon was at the moment in the planning stages of opening his chapel and school in San Xavier. Eventually, demonstrating the power of nonlocal power players, the Bureau of Catholic Indian Missions decided to withhold money from the bishop until he turned the San Xavier del Bac mission over to the Franciscans.[63]

Eventually Father Bonaventure Oblasser, a Franciscan, took on the task of erecting a series of day schools for the Tohono O'odham. He would be a permanent fixture during the remaining time of our study. Oblasser worked closely with Indian agent McQuigg to select the locations and arrange Tohono O'odham assistance in constructing them. They started construction immediately in Little Tucson, Topawa, and San Miguel, began planning for a school in Nine Mile Village (south of Casa Grande), and planned to expand into Coyote, Burro Pond, Gila Bend, and Santa Rosa when additional funds became available. Given the fact that so few

Figure 1.4 Bishop Navarette at San Xavier del Bac Mission, 1928. (Courtesy of Department of Special Collections and University Archives, Marquette University Libraries, #12222.)

Tohono O'odham had access to day schools, Oblasser and the OIA agreed not to compete with one another by building day schools in the same locations; in turn, they agreed to keep the government informed of their work.[64] In spite of the agreement not to compete, Catholic officials often feared that the Presbyterians were working to solidify their early advantage. Sister Mary Aquinas complained that the Presbyterians went so far as to take advantage of the Tohono O'odham preference for Catholicism by dressing as priests or nuns when recruiting for their schools.[65] It is hard to know the veracity of this claim. What can be verified is that Reverend Herndon, in collaboration with Sam Cachora, one of his early converts, tried to create the first ever pan-tribal organization, the Good Government League (GGL), in 1911.[66]

Presbyterian Tohono O'odham from the southern reaches of the future Tohono O'odham reservation dominated the GGL. The GGL, which often claimed to speak on behalf of all Tohono O'odham, pushed for the allotment of reservation lands, the end of sectarian—that is, Catholic—schools, an increase in government day schools, and the construction of a government boarding school at Indian Oasis (Sells); their agenda split the reservation along religious lines even as it demonstrated the broad support among the Tohono O'odham for increased government aid.[67] Oblasser and his Catholic allies worked to counter the pro-Presbyterian aspects

Figure 1.5 San Xavier del Bac Mission, ca. 1929. (Courtesy of Department of Special Collections and University Archives, Marquette University Libraries, #11222.)

of the program by mobilizing Tohono O'odham Catholics across the Paraguería.[68] In 1914, the GGL ceased to function as such, being transformed into the Papago Farmers Association, which served as the first truly pan-tribal organization on behalf of Tohono O'odham land rights.[69] By 1916 the Catholic missionaries had six Tohono O'odham schools and thirty-two churches, ministering to thirty-nine separate settlements; the only place that they had failed to establish a foothold was in the "Southern Papago Missions," the location where the Presbyterians had strongest support.[70]

Perhaps surprisingly, Herndon and Bonaventure would work closely with government officials and members of the Tohono O'odham Nation to push for the creation of the Tohono O'odham Reservation, which was realized in 1916. Their teamwork began in a rather roundabout way. In 1914, Commissioner of Indian Affairs Cato Sells assigned the superintendent of the Gila River Indian School, Frank A. Thackery, to take charge of the "Indian labor problem in the Salt River Valley, *particularly as it relates to the growing cotton industry* among the white farmers." Sells told him to

> cooperate with the white farmers . . . with a view of finding suitable employment for Indians *who may have no means of properly utilizing*

> *their own labors*. You should particularly endeavor to effect a stable system in the employment of Indian labor with a view of building up a *large and permanent market for such labor*, and of such class as will be *justly remunerative to them* and will otherwise contribute to their support and civilization. You are authorized to supervise the wage scales and system of employment of Indians by white people and the settlement of wages due and to adjust disputes or other difficulties arising between the Indians and whites in connection with such employment.[71] [emphasis in the original]

Thackery was already known as a defender of Native American land and water rights, standing up against the railroad interests, as well as "prospective settlers and land-grabbers."[72] In the process of overseeing the allocation of Tohono O'odham labor, Thackery became convinced that the planned allotment of Tohono O'odham lands would not solve the tribe's issues.

He put together a "committee of eight" to study the condition of the Tohono O'odham and advocate for an executive order setting aside additional lands for them. Thackery, McQuigg (Indian agent at San Xavier), Reverend Herndon, Father Oblasser, Herbert V. Clotts (assistant engineer for the OIA), C. R. Oldberg (superintendent of irrigation for the OIA), and two influential Tohono O'odham, Joshua Cachora and José X. Pablo, made up the committee. They also had the backing of Arizona's newly booming cotton industry as well as its first ever governor, George W. P. Hunt, a populist Democrat backed by "miners, railroad workers, farmers, and small businessmen."[73] Oblasser noted later that Thackery advised that the purpose and actions of the committee needed to remain secret until after the executive order was decreed because "most inhabitants of the newly formed state, and especially those of Tucson, did not realize the extent of the Indian holdings."[74]

Based on research by the committee of eight, which examined documents showing the extent of Tohono O'odham lands when the early Spanish missions were established, President Woodrow Wilson created the 3.1-million-acre Papago Indian Reservation with the signing of Executive Order 2300 on January 14, 1916. The territory came nowhere close to restoring their ancestral lands. Some of those lands were south of the US–Mexico border and thus out of the US government's jurisdiction. Other lands would later be set aside as the Organ Pipe National Monument, placing a higher value on an admittedly majestic species of cactus than on the Tohono O'odham residents. Some areas, especially those rich in ores, remained in private hands or were set aside as part of the public domain, while others would be turned into a firing range to train US soldiers. Perhaps most startling, government officials did not grant the Tohono O'odham rights to the minerals that were inside reservation boundaries until 1955.[75]

In spite of these shortcomings, Thackery's push for secrecy was prescient. The backlash, led by local Republicans, the Tucson Chamber of Commerce, and Democratic congressman Carl Hayden, was severe. Editorials in the *Tucson Citizen*, the *Arizona Republican*, and the *El Paso Herald* complained that the Tohono O'odham already had more land than they needed through allotment, that reserving even more land for them would strip Tucson of the ability to raise the taxes necessary for modernization, that the Tohono O'odham were nomadic (i.e., uncivilized) and not likely to ever settle down, that undeserving Mexican Tohono O'odham had migrated to the United States to take advantage of the reservation, that the reservation valued Indians over whites, and that the real purpose of the reservation's creation was to prevent Mexican and American cattlemen from using the lands.[76] Thackery moved to limit the impact of the backlash. He met with 141 Tohono O'odham leaders in Indian Oasis (Sells) in September to publicly collect their testimony attesting to the merits of the reservation. They noted, among other things, that if those who were against the reservation had owned the land as long as the Tohono O'odham had, they too would be willing to fight to defend the land and that it should not be forgotten that they had played a major role in defending the region against Apache assaults.[77] The *Arizona Daily Star*, which did not outright reject the reservation, noted several advantages: (1) the federal government would now be responsible for Tohono O'odham health and education expenses, (2) federal expenditures on the reservation would benefit local non-Indians, (3) the federal government would invest in roads and other infrastructure, and (4) the value of the land given over to the Tohono O'odham was (for tax purposes) nearly worthless.[78] President Wilson had it both ways by maintaining the majority of the reservation while setting aside a jagged 475,000-acre strip across the middle of the reservation that preserved Anglo cattle grazing lands and provided "ready access to the Ajo mines" for non-Indians.[79] The "strip" would not be returned to the Tohono O'odham until the late 1930s.[80]

Overall, from the creation of the Papago (Tohono O'odham) Reservation to the beginning of the Indian New Deal in 1934, the OIA, the Catholics, and the Presbyterians slowly increased their local footprints, leading to increased internal divisions within Tohono O'odham villages, but also broader pan-tribal alliances. The OIA encouraged and supervised off-reservation work for the Tohono O'odham, men in the cotton industry and women in the homes of Tucson and Phoenix's Anglo middle class. The OIA promoted a modernizing and civilizing program focused on developing on-reservation large-scale farming and ranching for men and proper in-home womanly work for married Tohono O'odham women. More importantly, Tucson served as an unsupervised locus for cultural contact and learning. As Fontana has argued, "by the 1930s Papago Indians had become irreversibly tied to non-Indian cash economy for their livelihood," even as other major aspects of their culture survived.[81]

Up to now, we have given a rather straightforward, and brief, narrative history of the Tohono O'odham, one that we hope will provide ample context for the following chapters. But we would be remiss if we did not note that the desert is a key feature of Tohono O'odham history. We will not be the first to note that the land inhabited by the Tohono O'odham is a harsh one—a dry and mountainous desert that has strongly shaped, and continues to shape, the tribe's lifestyle, farming, and food ways. The earliest history of the Tohono O'odham is difficult to document for archival-based historians like ourselves. Thankfully, the Tohono O'odham also have a strong oral history tradition. From this tradition we know that the Tohono O'odham have laid claim to a large region in the current southwestern United States and northwestern Mexico since the beginning of time. We also know that Tohono O'odham understandings of their own history are deeply interwoven with their oral traditions as well as with their understanding of and connection to geographical space.[82] The Tohono O'odham creation story, as recorded by Bernard Fontana, provides us with some sense of these connections.

> Elder Brother, Earth Magician, and Coyote began their work of creation, each creating things different from the other. Elder Brother created people out of clay and gave them the "crimson Evening," which is regarded by Papagos as one of the most beautiful sights in that region. The sunset light is reflected on the mountains with a peculiar radiance.
>
> Elder Brother told the Papagos to remain where they were in that land which is the center of all things.
>
> And there these Desert Indians have always lived. And from his home among the towering cliffs and crags of Boboquivari, the lonely, cloud-veiled mountain peak, their Elder Brother, I'itoi, spirit of goodness, who must dwell in the center of all things, watches over them.[83]

Place is also a key to the Tohono O'odham identity, and claims to the Papaguería were often repeated in more modern times. For example, in 1918 John F. Truesdell, assistant to the US attorney general in Denver, Colorado, began an investigation of an alleged 1880 contract signing over large tracts of land to a non-native, Robert F. Hunter. The land in question was about two million acres, nearly half of the Tohono O'odham reservation at the time. Preparing for a case that eventually went to the US Supreme Court, Truesdell interviewed natives about the nature of land and land rights. His reported findings were all on the same theme. One man reported, "I do not know anything about a grant. The Mexicans never had any land to give us. From the earliest times our fathers have owned this land which was given to them by the Earth's prophet. His grant is of greater importance than any that could be made by the Mexicans. This is the reason we do not want to give up our land, it was given to us by the strongest powers." Another interviewee suggested similarly: "Nevertheless we are the original owners of Salt River Valley. We have been so from time immemorial."[84] Alvino Gernomo of Big Fields made a similar statement in defending the creation of the Tohono O'odham reservation in 1916, stating that "it must have been God's will that we are now here in this waterless country and he has shown us the way to live here."[85]

Oral traditions repeated generation after generation provide a similar view of the connection between land and people. In the 1940s, one tribal member recounted a story told to him by his grandfather. The story tells of the beauty of sunrises and sunsets, but also of the problem created by the sun being too close to the earth—everything was dry, nothing would grow. Because the people complained, the sun went away. After a time, they welcomed the sun back "because the Indians could grow no food. They didn't care how hard they would have to work" as long as he came back, but they asked him to make it cooler, so the sun brought his nephew with him who kicks "a red ball of dust so it would be cooler."[86]

Just as this land was contested and ever shifting in its boundaries and ownership, so too were the lives of the Tohono O'odham who lived there. Their identities, lifestyles, and cultural boundaries faced successive waves of challenge from outsiders and modifications and modernizations from within. The US government, the Catholics, Presbyterians, and others engaged in programs to eliminate "vice" among the Tohono O'odham and to encourage the morals and gender identities of the majority culture as the basis of an Americanization process. It is to the story of those efforts, and of Tohono O'odham responses to them, that we turn in the next four chapters.

CHAPTER TWO

Vices and Values

Fighting Against the Influences of the "Wrong Sort"

One girl gave a party one night for the children and their fathers and mothers of these children that were to leave for Riverside school. They asked me to come to, which I did. They served hot tamales and coffee. The Indians would have had a very nice time among themselves and no drinking, but when the Mexicans and Yaquis heard the music, they came from all around lining up from three to five rows and more around the yard, venturing in after a dance was over they would elbow some of the Indian boys out into the dark and get them to take a drink. The Mexicans among themselves would take the bottle out of each other's pocket and drink, then put it back, not caring whether we saw them or not.

I stayed until after one O'clock a.m. and by that time there were so many drunk men that some of the girls were glad to come home with me. The rest of the Mexicans and drunk Indians stayed until 6 O'clock in the morning. I had heard the Indians tell how much drinking was going on at the dances, but it was worse than I expected to find.

—JANETTE WOODRUFF, OIA MATRON, QUARTERLY REPORT ON THE OUTING GIRLS, SEPTEMBER 30, 1924

Whoever established this liquor drinking for us, did so that we might ask for rain. That is its purpose. For we have no rivers and therefore must obtain rain.

—PAPAGO MAN, SANTA ROSA

In the early 1930s, ethnographer Ruth Underhill interviewed a Tohono O'odham woman named Chona and produced an autobiography based on those interviews. In this work Chona tells of the manufacture and consumption of cactus wine (also known as *tiswin* or *nawait i'ita*)—a process completed at the beginning of the tribal New Year as part of a ceremony to bring rains to the desert.[1] One striking thing about the autobiography is that in the parts covering her youth in the 1840s and 1850s, before sustained contact with whites, there are no other mentions of drinking, though Chona did speak with great enthusiasm about gambling and in passing about illicit sexual behavior.

In the sections covering the later decades of her life, Chona refers to a number of societal changes taking place around her. She and her family members began to wear "clothing"—pants for the men and skirts for the women—rather than breechcloths. They allowed a priest and not the tribal medicine man to name their firstborn child. She made her first trips out of the desert and into the city, to Tucson, perhaps in the 1870s or 1880s, and purchased manufactured cloth and her first pair of shoes.[2] In the only real reference she makes to whites, she states: "There were white men here and there on our land by that time, as there never had been. So our men began to learn to drink that whiskey. It was not a thing that you must drink only once a year like our cactus cider. You could drink it any time, with no singing and no speeches, and it did not bring rain. Men grew crazy when they drank that whiskey and they had visions."[3] Implicit in this statement were a number of major shifts for the tribe in terms of alcohol use. Cactus cider, manufactured by the tribe itself from the fruit of the saguaro cactus in late July, was fermented and then consumed ceremonially in early August, as part of a long event full of singing, dancing, and visiting. The ceremony was highly ritualized and required tribal members, though drunk, to maintain proper behavior.[4] Jose Antoin and Mattias Hendricks, Tohono O'odham informants for Frances Densmore, an ethnologist with the Smithsonian Institute, noted that the tiswin mixer, the winemaker, invoked favor on the ceremony by asking: "Do me the favor to bring good wind and clouds and rain, and to keep the people from bad behavior after they have drunk the wine."[5] Whiskey, on the other hand, the product of the majority culture, was always available and was not constrained by the same sorts of societal expectations. And as she said, drinking it had no impact on the rain—only on the minds and lives of the men and women who consumed it.

Though Tohono O'odham commentaries on alcohol are rare, in the twentieth century tribal member Peter Blaine described drinking among Tohono O'odham men and stated that alcohol harmed tribal life. Again his focus was on the consumption connected to the larger culture rather than that associated with tribal traditions. He suggested that "modern" life had brought problems to the tribe as fewer men worked and more wasted their time in town drinking. Though his report postdates the period of our study, it is worth noting his belief that the Tohono O'odham were harmed by the introduction of outside influences into their traditional practice.[6]

Finally, Tohono O'odham James McCarthy, though never a drinker himself, also described the cactus wine drinking festival of his youth as a community event with little negative outcome, but later described problems related to more "mainstream" alcohol consumption by the 1930s. He described, for example, a fire that claimed three lives and destroyed a Tohono O'odham home in 1939, caused by drunkenness. McCarthy was appointed a private policeman for a local mining company in the late 1930s, with his job specifically focused on curbing Tohono O'odham drinking because it negatively affected productivity. He reported, "Our people were getting worse from drinking wine and tequila. Some of our boys were bringing a lot of tequila across the border from Sonoita, Mexico . . . the company was losing money because the men got drunk and couldn't work."[7] Increased contact with the larger society on both sides of the border, and the incursion of mainstream "vice," culminated in long-term changes in the Tohono O'odham community and its attitudes about vice.

In 1917, Jewell D. Martin, superintendent of the Sells Indian Agency in southern Arizona, told his supervisor that Tucson "is not a fit place for Indian girls to work after returning from boarding schools . . . [since] many of them do not have the moral stamina to withstand the temptations to which they are subjected."[8] Two years later, Janette Woodruff, an Office of Indian Affairs (OIA) field matron, remarked that almost all of the Tohono O'odham girls under her supervision attended the Catholic fiesta in honor of San Francisco de Xavier (Saint Francis Javier) in San Xavier del Bac Mission about nine miles southeast of Tucson. But she allowed them to do so only after the "Sisters very kindly fitted up a room to keep the girls that had no parents there over night."[9]

These two cases highlight the challenges faced by the OIA as they tried to move the Tohono O'odham further into larger society, primarily in the twentieth century, and they highlight the OIA's approach to the issues. As government workers pushed to assimilate the Tohono O'odham into the larger American society, they expressed real concerns about the impacts of the larger society on the natives. As Superintendent McCormick wrote in 1923, "Morally these Indians compare with any white people. This has not come to them through civilization."[10] In other words, McCormick recognized that prior to the civilizing efforts of whites, the Tohono O'odham had their own moral order. Lower-class whites—especially males—and members of races perceived as less laudable—especially Chinese and Mexicans—posed a real threat to the Tohono O'odham, whom the OIA viewed as backward, prone to vice—or at least susceptible to it under the wrong conditions—and in need of civilizing.

Figure 2.1 Women harvesting saguaro cactus fruit, 1941. (Courtesy of Department of Special Collections and University Archives, Marquette University Libraries, #00067.)

The OIA's assumptions about vice were also highly reflective of the gender norms of the larger society, norms that the reformers themselves generally embraced unquestioningly (even if they failed to live up to them). Based on these norms, "good" girls avoided temptation and raised the morals of others. "Bad" girls, by comparison, gave in to their passions and were propagators of vice. Thus, like white women in the larger society, Tohono O'odham women were viewed as potentially reforming/redeeming influences within the household, if properly instructed and advised. There was hope that Tohono O'odham women could and would be the moral guardians of their homes, a topic that will be covered extensively in the next chapter. Notably, while they were not stereotyped as dangerously sexual, as was the case for example in prevalent views of African-American women at the time, they were viewed as weak and corruptible and in need of protection from men of all races, who were seen, in the best cases, as base and in need of "female" influence and, in the worst cases, as dangerous and even criminal.

An OIA field matron described one good girl, Marie, like this: "I am glad to say that she has been a good girl. I have not seen her out late at night, or associating with women of doubtful character. I have never known her to drink intoxicating liquor, or to act in a manner other than decent and honorable. . . . I have never seen her associating with men, but on the contrary, she seemed to [be] inclined to be alone, or with her sisters when away from her home."[11] Bad girls, on the other hand, gave in to urban temptations and were ruined. One superintendent wrote of two female cousins who "got into bad company" while working in Tucson. Though they were sent home to the reservation, both returned to the city—one walking sixty-five miles. They were jailed for drunkenness on several occasions, and both ended up unmarried but pregnant. Both girls were eventually sent away (probably placed in the home of a Catholic or Presbyterian non-Indian to do domestic work) to Benson in neighboring Cochise County, as they were viewed as "unfixable."[12]

Reformers believed that Tohono O'odham men had their own issues. Here we see a very racialized view of masculinity, where one's place in the society's racial order was reflected in adherence to gender ideals. As Gail Bederman has suggested in her study of manliness and civilization, "Gender, too, was an essential component of civilization. Indeed, one could identify advanced civilizations by the degree of their sexual differentiation. . . . [C]ivilized white men were the most manly ever evolved—firm of character; self-controlled; protectors of women and children. . . . [S]avage men were emotional and lacked a man's ability to restrain their passions."[13] Like the women, Tohono O'odham men were weak—open to temptation—and alcohol was seen as the largest potential danger. All other problems—sexual exploits, physical altercations and abuse, and economic and personal irresponsibility, including gambling—were likely to result from alcohol use. As Superintendent McCormick reported in 1923, "Drunkenness is about the most serious violation of the law on this reservation."[14] Reformers and government workers believed Tohono O'odham males could live moral lives within the mainstream culture, so long as they too were protected from corrupting influences.

In an era dominated by Prohibition—and thus the belief that the government should create a "physically rejuvenated, morally superior nation" and protect the population from the evils of alcohol by outlawing it—attitudes toward alcohol and Native Americans are hardly surprising.[15] Within the racial attitudes of the day, and widely held popular beliefs that nonwhites were less "civilized" and less "evolved," the view of natives as almost childlike and in need of supervision or "parenting" further contributed to this view.[16]

The OIA view that vice was rampant in Tucson was also reflective of a shift to a more "fluid definition of respectability" by working-class women in the early twentieth century that coincided with the rise in industrialization and urbanization nationally. It centered on newly arisen social settings such as coed high schools, dance halls, cars, movie theaters, and amusement parks, less parental supervision, and new depictions of sexuality in media and publications. Though middle-class ideas of respectability had not changed, the new working-class norms were accepting of some female sexual self-expression and assertiveness. Many adults felt that this new popular culture was creating confusion in the moral order and would result in eventual ruination.[17] Thus exposure to the "lower" classes was seen as exceptionally risky for the Tohono O'odham as they moved into closer contact with the majority society.

OIA officials felt that it was incumbent upon them either to prevent Tohono O'odham women, and to an extent men, from taking advantage of such social milieus or to chaperone them if they did. Matron Woodruff reported: "There were delinquencies among the Indians as a matter of course. . . . White teachers tried to build up ideals, but the proximity to low standards sometimes created a situation that was destructive to the general morality of the community."[18] Woodruff and other field matrons repeatedly expressed concerns about protecting the Tohono O'odham girls from exposure to potential vices in Tucson—making sure girls did not go unsupervised, did not accept gentlemen callers in their own rooms, and did not drink or attend wild dances. The girls were a risk to themselves if exposed to the wrong sorts of influences.

Tohono O'odham men needed supervision and protection too—especially from bootleggers who made alcohol readily available.[19] In the early twentieth century Prohibition was generally the law of the land, aiming to cut alcohol off at its source, and the threat of legal prosecution was used to try to scare native men away from alcohol consumption. While men were not chaperoned, major dances and events were often "supervised" by outsiders in the hope of restricting certain types of behavior.[20] When they were not, as described in the quotation that opens this chapter, a great deal of alcohol found its way into Tohono O'odham hands.

The tribal members themselves also grappled with problems related to vice and the intrusion of a majority culture and lifestyle into their own. Some sought the assistance of officials and the legal systems to protect them against the harms brought about by excessive drinking and extra-marital sexual encounters. Others actively chose traditional tribal approaches to things like sexuality and ceremonial drinking—either living in ways that ran counter to the mandates of the larger society or getting caught up in the legal net put in place to discourage certain types of behaviors and becoming labeled as criminal. Almost all tribal voices suggest some type of negotiation between traditional and majority culture that involved selective choices about which values and actions to adopt and which to ignore.

For some Tohono O'odham, resistance presented itself in the form of avoidance. Some natives recognized the threats of the larger society and wished simply to be left alone. This is most clearly seen in the response of the village headman Konerone in the Ge Aji section of the reservation northwest of Sells. Konerone's followers pulled the stakes of OIA engineers as they undertook the survey for land allotments. Later, Konerone convinced his followers not to use a newly drilled well and helped them smash in the windows of a newly constructed school, all in hopes of maintaining Tohono O'odham cultural ways. Their resistance to assimilation culminated in their fleeing "to the mountain villages" to avoid contact with outsiders.[21] José X. Pablo, a Tohono O'odham graduate of La Escuela who would later work for the OIA, also championed these sentiments even as he acted as an agent for change, suggesting that the Tohono O'odham "are asking for nothing except to be let alone to pursue their own way in peace without aid from the Government or anyone."[22] Tohono O'odham tribal leaders and members shared the OIA's fears about the influence of outsiders—but they differed in their solution to the problem.

To understand the interaction between the Tohono O'odham and the larger nation on issues related to vice, two things should be recognized. First, like reformers all over the nation during the Progressive Era, the OIA believed that vice was a serious problem for the Tohono O'odham and for the larger nation that incorporated them. Vice was a moral issue and needed to be addressed if citizenship was to be achieved someday, and also a societal issue in that it was the root cause of many larger problems such as poverty and marital difficulties. Secondly, and more importantly, again like so many of their Progressive Era peers, the OIA believed that the problems of vice were related to society and environment and could be fixed. While optimism and growing professionalism spurred the OIA on, these ideologies served as the force behind much of Progressive reform.[23]

They did not dismiss the Tohono O'odham as unsalvageable; they did not declare them biologically unfit and unfixable. Here the government was drawing a fairly distinct line between those cultures that could not be fully Americanized, specifically Asians and at times Mexicans, and those who could be brought into the fold, such as Native Americans, African Americans, and recent European immigrants.[24] They did not generally argue, like those in the eugenics movement would, that race biologically determined the social standing of the Tohono O'odham permanently.[25] Indeed, one Presbyterian account suggested, "The changing of the racial traits of a people is an extremely slow process, and we cannot expect the Indian to make the advance in a few years that required other races possibly a thousand years to accomplish. A contrast of conditions only a decade ago with what they are today would convince the most skeptical of the evident progress that has been made in every line of endeavor."[26] Another chronicle of Presbyterian work written in 1905 suggested: "The Indians can be civilized, and many of them have been through the influence of our schools. But we must not expect them to jump from savagery to our stage of civilization in one generation."[27] Progress might be slow, but it was racially possible.

Though there are few overt statements about the comparative evolutionary position of the Tohono O'odham, and thus their ability to be Americanized, there are hints throughout governmental and missionary records of the racial views of the majority culture. For example, many OIA officials stationed at the Sells Indian Agency viewed the Mexican and Chinese denizens of the borderlands region to be worse than the Tohono O'odham, worrying that the Tohono O'odham often acted like children, while Mexicans and the Chinese were actually deviant. For example, Woodruff argued that "the proximity to low standards [i.e., Mexicans] sometimes created a situation that was destructive to the general morality of the [Tohono O'odham] community."[28] In another case Woodruff blamed a lack of home and mother, and not racial failings, for a girl's inappropriate sexual behavior, writing, "I have another little girl, a Papago, that has been keeping company with a married man. He has made her believe that he is going to get rid of his wife and marry her. It is a pitiful case as the girl has no mother and no home."[29]

In her work on women reformers in the American West, Peggy Pascoe highlights the ways in which women engaged in home mission work at the turn of the last century challenged the biological determinism of the era to view their clients as "fixable" or "salvageable." According to Pascoe, these women "argued that race should be no barrier to educational opportunity or to participation in religious activities" and that acculturation was possible, if the morality of the major culture was taught, reinforced, and embraced.[30] To bolster this argument, these women highlighted the fact that while the evolutionary "gap" between the races was quite small, environmental forces played a strong role in keeping certain races in backward positions.[31] Thus, both individual moral failings, and larger communal sources of vice, needed to be addressed if "progress" were to be made—but progress was indeed possible.

Similarly, Presbyterian reformers held out great hope for the Tohono O'odham under their "influence." The secretary of La Escuela wrote, "The Indian children are naturally religious and respond readily to Christian influence and training."[32] And one school superintendent described the work of La Escuela as such: "The school has succeeded best in the fact that it has been a real character builder. The Bible instruction and the Christian training given in the school have been the greatest factors in lifting the Papagoes out of superstition and ignorance and placing it on the road to Christian civilization."[33]

Very much in line with the voluntary reformers described by Pascoe, OIA officials—both male and female—adopted a mixture of efforts aimed at protecting, disciplining, and educating the Tohono O'odham to bring them in line with the dominant culture of the day. The government officials pushed for acculturation—to bring the Tohono O'odham under the reach of the civil and moral codes. As such, a movement into the mainstream—rather than the passing of laws to separate out and further restrict members of this tribe—was seen as the cure for all that ailed them. This suggests both a strong belief in the power of the existing culture and a willingness to believe that the Tohono O'odham could be successfully incorporated into that mainstream culture.

Figure 2.2 OIA office, Sells, Arizona. (Courtesy of the National Archives at Laguna Niguel.)

Policymakers firmly moved away from nineteenth-century views of vice as being intrinsic to individuals, a personal moral failing, to the more progressive or modern view that there were both societal causes of and cures for these problems. Clearly, some failings continued to be personal and moral, but even these, if approached correctly, might be fixed. In the eyes of government officials, the Tohono O'odham had moved from being permanently damned to being wayward children (or proto-citizens) in need of guidance and redemption. As the Supreme Court described Native Americans in their consideration of citizenship, they were on the road toward "advanced" civilization, but currently in "a state of pupilage."[34] In very paternalistic ways, officials looked to protect and educate their native charges, moving them toward a better life within the mainstream society. This assumed that a better life was a mainstream life, one constructed and measured by middle-class white America. It also assumed that eliminating racial and ethnic difference was not only desirable, but also in everyone's best interest.

In addition, while there was "no clear racial order among monolithic groups labeled Anglo, Mexican, and Indian" and identity remained flexible and contingent, whiteness and ethnicity did matter. Historian Eric V. Meeks remarks that the denigration of nonwhites (i.e., white supremacy) was "built into the very identity of Arizona from its inception."[35] For example, Mark C. Anderson, using political cartoons published in US papers during the Mexican Revolution (1910–1917), incontrovertibly demonstrates that the depiction of Mexicans as backward, racially limited, and morally decrepit was part of a much broader cultural understanding that Anglos had about their southern neighbors.[36] Similarly, Anglos viewed Native Americans as not measuring up to their white counterparts. Nonetheless, among progressive social workers, government employees, and missionaries, "racist ideology was not expressed as hatred but rather as paternalism."[37]

Susan Yohn argues that missionaries, for example, were in fact "antiracists" because they understood that race and culture were socially constructed. Even so, "they believed their own mores and habits to be superior and expected their clients to be transformed."[38] Hence, social workers believed that they would be able to assimilate people of color, just not as equals. To assimilate them, their culture and character would have to be corrected (using Anglo ideals of manhood and womanhood as blueprints). Nonetheless, as Evelyn Nakano Glen notes about social workers' views of Mexicans, people of color were assumed to have limited aspirations, and so could be left in their current humble place in society regardless of any changes they made.[39] Such racialized paternalism had the potential to be highly limiting (economically and in terms of mobility) and thus potentially as damaging as racialized hatred. As Marsha Weisiger has shown, the OIA's paternalistic attempts to eliminate overgrazing on the Navajo Indian Reservation had disastrous consequences. The agency never took the time to truly understand the Navajo or listen to their concerns. Its actions resulted in the impoverishment of the Navajo, the near destruction of their flocks, and their dependence on "trading-post credit, federal largesse, and whatever wage work they could find," not only producing the opposite effect that OIA officials had aimed for, but also seriously harming Navajo culture and cultural practices.[40]

To better understand the balance between societal and individual causes—and the OIA and Tohono O'odham mediation and negotiation that took place around issues of vice—it is useful to now turn to a consideration of two specific areas of vice that received the greatest focus in the Tohono O'odham community. In this chapter we will examine efforts focused on the use of alcohol, and in the next we will turn to sexual misconduct, including cohabitation, seduction, and adultery. Whether looking at governmental policy, reports accounting for time spent, or legal records, no other issues of vice are as prominent as these two; they were the focus of acculturation and reform efforts. It is notable that these are the two vices most frequently written about, since another vice—gambling—appeared most frequently in native records of traditional Tohono O'odham life.[41]

Approaches to and negotiations over alcohol and sexual misconduct tell us a great deal about both racial/cultural and gender assumptions.

In the case of alcohol, the answer, over all other "fixes," in keeping with the policy of the day in the larger society, was restricting access to liquor. Prohibition reached the Tohono O'odham even before it was the law of the land nationwide. Most generally the focus was on identifying and prosecuting bootleggers—suppliers of liquor who were most likely not members of the tribe. This focus came directly from the top in the OIA, where Commissioner Sells had publicly stated in 1914, "I believe that the greatest present menace to the American Indian is whiskey. It does more to destroy his constitution and invite the ravages of disease than anything else; It does more to demoralize him as a man and frequently as a woman; It does more to make him an easy prey to the unscrupulous than everything else combined."[42]

Public drunkenness, most commonly at religious celebrations and festivals, was the focus of most of the legal action taken by the OIA. Records are full of reports of the use of police, often Indian policemen, to "observe" public events to watch for public drunkenness. The report from OIA farmer A. M. Philipson to Superintendent McCormick in 1924 was typical of those found in OIA records. "Jose Leon Flores, the Indian Judge here, asked me to write to you and ask to have Hugh Norris or some other good policeman here on the evening of the 23rd and on the day and evening of the 24th. The Indians intend to have a little celebration of San Juan's Day and Jose is afraid Policeman Encinas will not be able to look after the liquor dealers and users properly."[43]

Generally the problem was not viewed to be the Tohono O'odham themselves, but rather the bad influence of other groups who furnished liquor at dances and other events. Field matron Woodruff described a party she attended and noted, "The Indians would have had a very nice time among themselves and no drinking, but when the Mexicans and Yaquis heard the music, they came from all around lining up from three to five rows and more around the yard, venturing in after a dance was over they would elbow some of the Indian boys out into the dark and get them to take a drink." Under the influence of these outsiders, the Tohono O'odham became quite drunk. Woodruff recalled, "I had heard the Indians tell how much drinking was going on at the dances, but it was worse than I expected to find."[44] Where Prohibition failed, moral guidance was the preferred approach. One La Escuela superintendent suggested in 1934: "Since repeal, moral conditions on all our reservations have been growing worse. Many Christian Indians feel that something myst [*sic*] be done about it and as a result, all of the camp meetings stressed the importance of high ideals and Christian living in combating the present evil tendencies."[45] Moral guidance and protection were key approaches for a variety of reformers among the Tohono O'odham.

Records suggest that officials were more worried about suppliers, especially the corrupting influence of bootleggers from the lower orders, than they were about those who drank. Frequently those found drunk were set free, unpunished so long as they identified the source of their alcohol. For example, Philipson reports:

> I sent Matias Encinas over to Pina Blanca, the village in the south west corner of this reservation, last Saturday and Sunday to watch for drunks during the Feast there. . . . Francisco . . . , Lottio . . . and Jose . . . , all Papago Indians of this reservation came there drunk. Matias arrested them and brought them to San Xavier where a hearing was held at my office by Indian Judge Morino on Tuesday evening. They all plead [*sic*] guilty and told where they purchased the liquor. It was decided to turn them loose provided they point out the place and the man from whom they purchased the liquor.

The bootlegger himself did not get off so easy. Indeed, Philipson adds, "I took Matias and Lotio . . . and Jose . . . to Tucson yesterday morning, Commissioner Edwin F. Jones sent a man from the Prohibition Officer's quarters with the Indians after the Mexican. They arrested him and he plead [*sic*] not guilty, but Comm. Jones put him under $500.00 bond to appear before the Fed. Grand Jury."[46]

Perhaps it is not surprising that the greatest concern was over "Mexicans" and other working-class individuals who might attend tribal events and corrupt the Tohono O'odham. As Philipson reported in 1928: "Juan Davis, one of our San Xavier Indians, just came to tell me that there will be a dance in the San Xavier Village on the night of April 3, in celebration of 'Feast of the Holy Cross.' As these dances usually draw a rough crowd of Mexicans and other bootleggers, we would be pleased if you could send a brace of Indian Policemen in to be present at this celebration."[47] Tribal members were viewed as corruptible, susceptible to the lure of vice, but outsiders—especially nonwhite others—were seen as the real criminals and sources of danger.

In another case, Philipson discovered that, in spite of Prohibition, some of the Tohono O'odham were purchasing lemon extracts from a Chinese vendor and getting inebriated. Superintendent T. F. McCormick tasked

Philipson with rounding up the men because "as long as they were drunk they deserve being punished."[48] Again the real danger came from outside the tribe, in the form of "nonwhite" suppliers of liquor.

The location of Tohono O'odham land in the borderlands—literally on the Mexican border—put this group at considerable risk. Patrolling the border was a big job for the OIA and the native police force they employed. One assistant commissioner complained, "The Reservation borders on the Mexican line for fifty miles and this Mexican country being 'wet' a considerable amount of 'tequila' and 'mescal' is smuggled across onto the Reservation and from now on a closer watch than ever will have to be kept on the Border if this liquor traffic is to be handled in the proper way."[49] Tribal members often crossed the border, whether for attendance at religious festivals or for agricultural and familial reasons. Indeed, George J. Harris, a Bureau of Immigration official, noted that "No regulatory measures could possibly be devised on this border in any way affecting the freedom of movement of the people living on the border."[50] But traffic across the border also opened the tribe up to the threat of imported vice, though it is worth noting that contemporaries praised the lack of crime and disorder given the location of the tribe. As one report to the Board of Indian Commissioners suggested, "Considering the size of this reservation and its location along the Mexican border there is very little disorder. A few arrests are made now and then for drunkenness. The three Indian police who are kept in the south end of the reserve and the three officers of the border patrol who watch the roads leading from the international boundary have kept down smuggling and the use of intoxicating liquor."[51]

It was not just geography that made the case of the Tohono O'odham special. There was also the issue of alcoholic products aimed more specifically at the tribe based on its customs and those of neighboring tribes. In some cases special legislation aimed at specific "native" projects. The state of Arizona, for example, passed a law "making it a misdemeanor for any person to sell or furnish or cause to be sold or furnished to any Indian of whole or mixed blood any tulapai, tiswin [cactus wine] or corn beer or to manufacture, cause to be manufactured or aid in any manner in the manufacture of or in the sprouting of corn or any other cereal for the purpose of manufacturing tulapai, tiswin or corn beer."[52] As historian Robert Perez notes, the outlawing of the ceremonial use of alcohol was a small part of a broader "assault on aboriginal spirituality and ceremonial practice."[53]

An interesting part of the story of vice and Prohibition efforts comes to light when one examines the fate of those caught drinking, often discussed in reports on work completed on the reservation. In the cases where charges were not dropped, the offenders were generally sentenced to physical labor. In a fairly typical case, Philipson brought Antonio before the Indian judge. Because Antonio claimed he could neither remember where or from whom he purchased the alcohol that resulted in his arrest for public drunkenness, the judge sentenced him to ten days of labor under Philipson's watch.[54] In December of that year, in a report on irrigation projects, Philipson noted, "We had four prisoners doing time for being drunk during the San Xavier Fiesta, they did the following: 65 man days and 11 team days, on the ditch repairing job."[55] Similar reports suggested prisoners were used for short periods of time to build roads and repair ditches.[56] While there is no indication that the procuring of unpaid labor was the main motive behind anti-vice campaigns, there is little doubt that the OIA and the reservations in general benefitted from this forced unpaid labor used to build and repair infrastructure.

There is very little connection between the images we get of alcohol use from the official records of the OIA and reports of consumption furnished by native sources. While the OIA focused on laws and punishment, and on the problems of public drunkenness, as described in the beginning of the chapter, the Tohono O'odham generally described liquor in relation to traditional ceremonies—especially the ceremony connected with the coming of the rain. In her anthropological study of the tribe first published in the mid-1930s, Ruth Underhill discussed mostly homemade cactus wine consumed as part of a community-wide celebration meant to bring about the rain. She reported no quarreling as a result of intoxication, though a great deal of cactus wine was consumed over the course of several days.[57] Underhill described the process of making cactus wine, sharing it with neighbors, and of "making themselves beautifully drunk, for that is how our words have it. People must all make themselves drunk like plants in the rain and they must sing for happiness."[58] There were no mentions in her accounts of policemen, arrests, or even disorderly conduct. This type of alcohol consumption was described by the tribe as ceremonial, even sacred.

Indeed, Peter Blaine offered a rare account of government intervention in ceremonial drinking in an undated account. He recalled: "The government tried to stop the wine drinking ceremony on the main reservation. The Presbyterians tried to stop it, too. . . . It was south of Santa Rosa that many ancient ceremonies were carried on. No police could ever stop their ceremonies. The superintendent, Mr. Elliot, called a special officer to stop the doings out there. But it was not stopped." He went on to recount a trial of three tribal members over the issue of cactus wine and, as an interpreter, described the outcome: "I was asked to speak for them, to explain to their lawyer about the religious aspect of the ceremony. The lawyer had thought the wine feast was just for getting drunk or selling. I told him the wine was for ceremonial uses. He pulled out a law book and found that ceremonial wine use could not be stopped. No way! . . . The case was finally turned over to the jury. They were out about 15 minutes and decided 'not guilty.'"[59] If ceremonial drinking was viewed by officials at all, they seldom mentioned it in records or reported attempts to interrupt its practice in any major way. Official focus remained on Catholic festivals and other public events attended by multiracial crowds.

We know even less about the ways in which the Tohono O'odham viewed nonpublic recreational drinking. One comment made by Peter Blaine, however, may provide some insights. Blaine noted that when he took a job with the Civilian Conservation Corps in the 1930s, he told his superiors that there was one job that he refused to do, that of arresting anyone for drinking alcohol: "I like my drinks now and then myself, so why turn in one of my buddies. . . . I'd have to arrest myself."[60] How much recreational alcohol consumption flew under the radar of governmental officials and religious reformers remains unknown, but it was probably substantial and accepted by a wide range of actors.

Other native references to alcohol or legal prosecution are lacking, so it is difficult to know how the prohibition campaign was viewed by those it was focused on. However, when we move to the issue of illicit sexual relations in the next chapter, we will find some tangential references to the social costs of drinking and other vice, and can view the complexity of the issue.

Reformers conformed to broadly held notions of gender and race, at least in the case of their clients. In their views, men were prone to vice, especially drinking, which was seen as both a factor in other social problems and a vice in and of itself, and needed to be kept in check by the existence and enforcement of laws. The connection between drinking, social problems, and poverty was made by one Presbyterian reformer, who recalled of Sells, "Drunkenness, fighting and gambling were very common through the village among both men and women and these conditions contribute to the extreme poverty that was prevalent there."[61] Women, more moral by nature, could help to improve the overall society, but they too were weak and needed supervision and protection from base and lower-class influences. Like children, the Tohono O'odham needed paternalistic guidance as they moved into larger society and were exposed to, and ideally adopted, the culture and values of the larger society. A mixture of legal actions and moral suasion options were utilized to both encourage "good" behavior and punish bad, in hopes of protecting the Tohono O'odham from the vices of the larger society, and the threat of race-mixing, as they transitioned into modern society and evolved culturally.

CHAPTER THREE

Marriage and Morals

The Solution to Vice and the Key to Americanization

Answering your letter relative to Lewis . . . , son of Felix . . . and Manuella . . . , who is living with an Indian girl at Salt River Agency illegally, I am enclosing the 'Consent to Marriage of Minor' signed by the parents of Lewis . . . today. Lewis has a pretty bad reputation, but I hope he will do better since he has taken a wife. (May they live happily ever after.)

—A. M. PHILIPSON TO E. S. STEWART, JANUARY 27, 1927

Papago Bride and Groom; On their wedding morning the groom received the sacrament of baptism and during the nuptial mass made his first communion. Under his arm the groom carried the marriage certificate and several beautiful holy pictures given them for the home by Father Bonaventure, who married them. The honeymoon trip ended at their home a short distance away, where they partook of a wedding breakfast of beans & tortillas.

—(MISS) MARIE ROHRET, *INDIAN SENTINEL*, VOL. 4, NO. 2 (1924)

When she was in her teens sometime in the 1850s, a Tohono O'odham girl named Chona was told by her father that her parents were arranging a marriage for her. Her father indicated the chosen boy, but it mattered little. She did not know the young man personally; however, she recalled: "I knew who the marriageable young man was. It was the medicine man's son. I had never spoken to him; I had never spoken to any young man except relatives and of course we do not marry relatives. But my breasts were getting large, now. That is how we know when a girl should marry. 'They ought to be used for something,' we say."[1] Had she known the young man—and not liked him—it would not have mattered. Chona made it clear that she would have never questioned her father, or later her younger brother who arranged her second marriage.

Traditionally, Tohono O'odham parents arranged the marriages of their daughters. Finding a proper mate often involved years of careful scrutiny as the parents searched for a boy with a reputation for hard work and a family with whom they wanted to create bonds of reciprocity. Generally, after the parents proposed the potential marriage to the boy's relatives, the boy would come to the girl's house and spend four nights there. If things went smoothly, the girl would leave with the boy and take up residence with him in his parents' house. Only after they had had several children would the couple move out and build a house of their own.[2]

Traditionally, Tohono O'odham men were allowed to have more than one wife, and the parents of girls often preferred to marry off their younger daughter(s) to the same boy on the grounds that if the marriage between the boy and their eldest girl was working out well, then there was little reason to take a chance with another potential spouse. Also of importance was the fact that if a couple "did not want to stay together, they could be divorced merely by deciding to separate." Younger children usually returned with the divorced girl to her parents' house, though older boys often decided to stay with the father.[3] Chona experienced both of these "traditions" in succession, as her first husband took a second wife more than a dozen years into their marriage. At this point, in the middle of the nineteenth century, polygamous marriages were already less common in the tribe; however, as a medicine man, her husband was expected to have multiple wives.

Chona nonetheless found this arrangement unacceptable and returned to her parents' home. Initially her hope was that her husband would abandon his new wife and reclaim her. However, within a matter of days her uncle found her a second, much older husband, who had great wealth and was a widower. This marriage was viewed as an excellent match because he was well able to provide for Chona and indeed provided her with the first store-bought goods she had ever owned. That she "did not love that old man" and was not even fond of him mattered little. She stayed with him for decades, having two sons by him early in the marriage.[4]

Other Tohono O'odham reported on similar arranged and informal marriages, and separations, well into the twentieth century, suggesting the lasting utilization of a system of marriage that relied heavily on family and loyalty but also allowed for flexibility and change over time.[5] However, with the incursion of outside influences—reformers pushing civil marriage—and the encroachment of modernity, changes in tribal relations also occurred. Marriage became, for reformers and tribal members alike, an area of contestation, assimilation, and resistance. Records show at least a small number of civil marriages among the tribe in the first decades of the twentieth century.

Figure 3.1 Papago home. (Courtesy of University of Arizona Libraries, Special Collections, University of Arizona, Cooperative Extension Service, Photographic Album of Activities in Pima Co., 1922–1930, AZ-520.)

Tohono O'odham reports also indicate some changes. On the one hand, James McCarthy described his own marriage in 1929 to Emilia, a Tohono O'odham from Sonoyta, Mexico, as informal. They met in his mother's household and began living together in a marriage that lasted fifty-five years but was not "legalized" until 1944 with a church wedding. On the other, though family had some role in the match, this marriage was not traditionally arranged and contained none of the family negotiations seen in more traditional marriages. A then thirty-four-year-old McCarthy stayed in his mother's house, with his new wife, while his mother simply moved elsewhere.[6]

Throughout her account of her life, Chona spoke often of the gendered division of work. Women ground corn, carried water, and were to follow the directions of their husbands. If they traveled or attended dances, it was upon the invitation of their husbands. Otherwise they worked surrounded by other women in the household—first their mother, sisters, and even grandmothers, then their mother-in-law, sisters-in-law, and other female relatives. Upon Chona's marriage the advice offered to her was: "Stay home, don't run around. Do your work, carry the wood, cook something whatever there is. Any work you see, you do it."[7] Indeed, being "industrious" was a highly recommended quality in a marriage, but there was no expectation that a woman would do men's work or vice versa. The only exception Chona mentioned was that of a "man-woman," her husband's brother who preferred to be a woman and placed himself in the female part of the household during working hours.[8]

Thus, Tohono O'odham had well-developed marriage traditions and clear conceptions of household management and gender division of work.[9] Not surprisingly, however, as white missionaries and government workers came in closer contact with the tribe, they showed disapproval of native traditions and set out to bring tribal members into the larger society through acculturation along "proper" gender lines and legal marriage arrangements. Even as they did so, they also felt that the existing Tohono O'odham culture needed to be protected from the influence of outsiders. As mentioned in the last chapter, Superintendent McCormick had written in 1923 that the tribe had its own moral code. For example, "In earlier times any one found guilty of adultery was put to death. Our greatest trouble now is with the girls who leave the reservation and work out in towns as domestics."[10] Here we examine government attempts at protecting and guiding the Tohono O'odham in the realms of marriage and sexuality and the thinking behind those attempts, and consider their relative successes and failures.

In July of 1920 field matron Janette Woodruff wrote:

> One of the helpful attainments of civilization among the Indians, is when the Commissioner urges us to enforce the marriage law among them. Sometimes it is quite a task on the Supt. and employees to reason with some of them, and talk to them in a quiet way, and have them get married. I notice after they are married they seem so happy together, and are rather proud to think and know they are trying to start out in life right. Many of them come with their own free will and tell me they want to get a marriage license.[11]

In the process of Americanizing or "civilizing" the Tohono O'odham, legally sanctioned marriage was viewed as a strong civilizing force. Indeed, marriage was naively viewed as the societal institution that could and would correct much of what was wrong in native society.

As Nancy Cott has described in her work on marriage in the United States as it related to a variety of groups, "'Civilizing' meant instituting faithful monogamous households, turning Indian men into farmers motivated by the work ethic, and urging Indian women toward norms of modesty and domesticity."[12] Creating stable households was the first step toward the assimilation of adults; developing domesticity and appropriate vocation would come next. It is helpful then to first focus on issues related to household formation—marriage, modesty, and domesticity. Later in this book we will examine other strategies for assimilation, including education and vocation.

The definition of marriage adopted by the OIA and other reformers was very specific—for them marriage was heterosexual, monogamous, lifelong, and sanctioned by law. This definition was not unlike the one promoted by missionaries throughout the West in the nineteenth century, and by a variety of reformers and government officials nationally in the twentieth.[13] As Cott describes in *Public Vows*, authorities embraced a very specific definition of marriage: "lifelong, faithful monogamy, formed by the mutual consent of a man and a woman, bearing the impress of the Christian Religion and the English common law in its expectations for the husband to be the family head and economic provider, his wife the dependent partner."[14] Marriage was patriarchal, consensual, and Christian.

Embraced by the larger nation, this image of marriage, Cott argues, was viewed as more than a crucial social issue; it was seen as the institutional base of the nation itself, providing a gendered social structure and a basis for the economy. Whether addressing Mormon polygamy or marriage in the "Indian way," reformers worked to bring those involved in "deviant" forms of marriage into the fold. For Native Americans in general, and the Tohono O'odham in specific, becoming part of the majority culture could not happen unless a specific view of marriage was embraced. Cott suggested that native marital practices were seen as a threat to American political sovereignty, "For if monogamy founded the social and political order, then groups practicing other marital systems on American soil might threaten the polity's soundness."[15] Marriage in the "Indian way," viewed as impermanent and immoral, was a major roadblock to civilization.

But why was marriage viewed as such a crucial part of the civilization process? Ideally marriage provided the basis of order and authority in society. It locked men and women into a family unit that created social and economic stability; it proscribed a gendered interdependence based on strongly held gender norms, and it protected married individuals (and perhaps others) from vice. Key to this last goal, within a marriage, properly trained women, who were by their nature believed to be more moral and civilized than men, could exercise control over their husbands and households. Vices like illicit sex and seduction could be avoided, and men's more base urges to drink and gamble could be modified. Finally, in somewhat unclear ways, marriage alleviated concerns over racial mixing and misogamy, but only when marriageable people married the appropriate partners. In return, marriage provided social and financial stability to women and their children, assuring them support and allowing them legal remedies when abandoned. As such, marriage was believed to be the near perfect institution for ushering tribal members into the larger society. This reinforces Ann Laura Stoler's contention, which we will elaborate on in a moment, that sexuality, and the morality that circumscribed it, were at the base of colonial power relations. As another field matron, Mary Stewart, suggested—in the face of couples married "in the Indian way," something viewed by most reformers as no better than simple cohabitation—intervention by matrons to bring about civil marriages meant that "immoral relations are corrected. Marriages are brought about in legal form, where Indian marriages are practiced."[16] "Correct" unquestioningly meant legal and majority-culture morality determined the shape and form of marriage as an institution.

Early on in her pathbreaking study of sexuality and imperial power, Stoler explains: "In 1929, one of the principal architects of French colonial educational policy, Georges Hardy, warned a group of prospective functionaries that 'A man remains a man as long as he stays under the gaze of a woman of his race.'" She continues by pointing out that

> the statement is compelling on several counts. Both declarative and imperative, it threatens, prescribes, and assures, succinctly capturing a set of assumptions and anxieties about life in the colonial tropics for European men and the European women recruited to follow and care for them. Its conditional clues signal a caution: racial vigilance and virility were domestic and household affairs, and vulnerabilities of body and mind were tightly bound to the conjugal and sexual arrangements in which Europeans lived.[17]

In a similar fashion, this strong preference for civil marriage found among missionaries and OIA officials, and a belief in its efficacy for addressing a whole host of social and cultural issues as part of the Americanization process, provides us with a clear view of the gender ideals and assumptions held by those who embraced this "standard" view of marriage. It also points to the way in which monogamous legally binding relations were favored by the majority culture and were in fact viewed as crucial to the advancement of Native Americans as a race, while in turn racial purity and security were assured through the adoption of intraracial monogamous and lasting marriage.

Looking specifically at Native Americans, in this case in western Canada, historian Sarah Carter has examined the issue of why marriage reform played such a crucial role in the West. She argues that white expansion into the West was in fact justified by claims of "saving" and "civilizing" the tribes already there; claims of saving native women from slavelike marriages were common among leaders and reformers.[18] Nineteenth-century anthropologists added credibility to this claim, describing monogamy as "the highest form of marriage enjoyed by the most 'civilized' people of the world."[19] For example, noted anthropologist of the Seri and Tohono O'odham W. J. McGee argued in 1898 that "primitive peoples" at the "barbaric" level of human development practiced a lower level of marriage based on the capture of nontribal warriors and/or females, leading to low levels of intertribal acculturation. When barbaric people entered the next highest phase of development, one based on barter and the understanding of the private ownership of land and water, intertribal harmony and acculturation, it was argued, would be achieved. The assumption was that at this stage marriage would be based on the exchange of gifts. The final phase, enlightenment, reflected the highest possible level that humanity could reach and was best understood as reflecting mainstream American society, where marriage was freely entered into. Since these stages of progress reflected "the law of normal growth, and indeed of cosmic progress," it was believed that as Native American civilization "evolved" so too would the native view of marriage.[20] Social science clarified and justified the superiority of the majority culture's view of marriage over all other variants in addition to suggesting that marriage itself could serve as a crucible for acculturation.

OIA workers and other reformers working with the Tohono O'odham, then, were in good company as they worked to inculcate specific views of masculinity and femininity and to move all couples towards legal, monogamous marriage. The proper acculturation of women was an especially important first step if women were to play their role as civilizers within their marriages, their households, and their communities. For those who still believed in eugenics, feminine virtue and chastity was the key to racial purity.[21] For nearly everyone, women in the US West and Southwest were viewed as genteel civilizers and helpmates. As Elizabeth Jameson notes,

"Women were to shape national morality from the privacy of their family hearthsides, leaving public action to men."[22] This belief ran through many areas of nineteenth-century reform and well into the Progressive Era. Women as municipal housekeepers was a common theme among urban and political reformers. Indeed, an entire group of women's suffrage supporters argued that women should vote because they were more moral than men and would thus improve politics.[23]

For the OIA, the workers most firmly charged with addressing issues of marriage and morality were the field matrons. As will be discussed in greater detail in chapter 4 on vocation, matrons were hired to work with the tribe throughout much of the period under study here. Mixing together concerns about vice and desires for proper vocational roles for women as housewives, field matrons focused expressly on championing monogamous, legal marriage. In the face of dangerous influences, and out of a desire for Tohono O'odham women to serve the role of civilizer common among her white peers, matrons often reported on their attempts to get girls married and to discourage informal marital arrangements, generally described as "living in the Indian way." Frequently the aim was to put in place a legal union where couples were cohabiting or when children were involved. In some cases this could be difficult, as in the case of a girl named Julia who was living secretly with a young man. While her father wanted the matron to compel them to marry, the courts did not want to grant a marriage license to a couple under the age of eighteen when pregnancy was not involved. The matron then appealed to her superior for help getting a license issued.[24] While we do not know the outcome of this case, it is worth noting that the girl's family used the OIA as leverage to advance their agenda. We need not assume that the family's agenda—pushing for the marriage—coincided with the OIA's broader agenda—assimilating the couple into mainstream society.

In many other cases where the concern was over sexual exploitation of women, a topic we will return to later in the chapter, the solution was almost always legally sanctioned marriage, unless the man involved was non-Tohono O'odham. There are even indications in the records that superintendents were (illegally) performing marriage ceremonies when a justice of the peace was not available.[25]

Lisa Emmerich, the leading scholar on the field matron program, has chronicled a national shift in the program, over time, from a focus on acculturation to a focus on public health. While this shift was undoubtedly taking place among the Tohono O'odham, it was equally true that field matrons there held on to notions of Victorian womanhood longer than studies of the program nationally might indicate. While the records are filled with progressive notions about education and health programming, they are also replete with stories of trying to bolster a morality that was viewed as superior by the dominant culture in protecting females from corruption.

To supplement existing literature on the field matron program, then, and to gain a new perspective on the nature of its work, it is useful to contextualize the program within the realm of Progressive Era reforms. While there is no evidence of cross-fertilization of ideas, when viewed in the context of the Progressive Era, the activities of the field matrons bear a striking resemblance to those of settlement house workers and suggest a context, other than federal government policy, for understanding these women and their activities—one that was avowedly both domestic and gendered.

Perhaps most striking is the notion of the house itself. The most basic idea behind settlements was the notion of residency. Reformers went to live among their clientele, meeting with them and serving them in the setting, not of an office, but of a house. Matrons too lived and often worked in homes, conducting much of their business within their residence. At first glance it might seem that residential space and reform were well separated. One matron reported the following on a prospective house:

> This house has ample room so that I may equip an office, in which to transact business with Indians, and white employers, and thus hold the remainder of the house private as a dwelling for myself and family. It stands alone, and our Indian friends would not disturb a neighbor in calling upon me. This is desirable. There is a garage with room for two cars. It can be locked to protect the cars therein. The house is modern. It is in fair order excepting the bath room, which is small, inconveniently located, and somewhat of a makeshift, but it will suffice.[26]

However, additional records suggest that many spaces besides the office were shared by matrons and clients. Matrons reported on girls visiting and even entertaining in the matron's home.

Woodruff complained: "In some of the homes [where the girls are employed] the girls had no place where they might receive men callers, so I urged them to bring all their friends to my house."[27] She also noted that on their days off working girls often spent time at her home, where Woodruff furnished food for them and they sometimes helped with the cooking. "It was a splendid thing for the girls to have this day off and a place where they were free to pursue their own individual interest, a place they could

Figure 3.2 San Miguel Mothers' Garment Making Club, 1926. (Courtesy of University of Arizona Libraries, Special Collections, University of Arizona, Cooperative Extension Service, Photographic Album of Activities in Pima Co., 1922–1930, AZ-520.)

call home. Some skimmed over the papers and magazines that I provided; some brought their sewing and asked me to give advice and help; others, under my guidance, prepared numbers for literary society, and a few preferred to do nothing but relax and visit."[28] Mrs. Herndon, wife of the Presbyterian missionary, reported on similar uses of her home—utilizing the manse as a social meeting place for Tohono O'odham girls working in Tucson.[29]

In several almost comical passages that both suggest her own prejudices and the uses of her house by natives, BIA matron Libbie C. Light expressed concerns over sharing her bathroom with the Tohono O'odham: "There is but a single toilet room in the house. Indian applicants waiting for work, are often required to use it. As it is required for the use of myself and husband, I am compelled to clean and sterilize it after it has been used by Indians, as I consider it unsanitary after use by them. This is a most objectionable condition to me, and I am sure that you will consider it to be so. A house with a second toilet for use of Indians should be provided," and "I urge the house with *two* bath rooms and toilets, one for my private use, and one for the use of the Indians. This is entirely necessary. I submit that it is asking too much of me to be required to use the toilet that is used by Indians, who come from the camps, and the village seeking labor, and who sometimes wait for hours at a time, until, by inquiry over the telephone, I have found a place for them."[30] There were even cases where girls seeking safety stayed overnight in the homes of matrons.[31]

At the matrons' homes the girls not only found space to rest but also highly gendered educational opportunities—something that will be touched upon in the chapters on education and vocation as well. Reading materials were available with the hope of cultivating literary tastes. Matrons also provided instruction in crafts and household skills, with particular emphasis on sewing, sanitation, and food preparation. Notably, as was the case in most settlements, matrons' homes generally favored the culture of the matron, with education viewed as part of the acculturation process. Food preparation focused on making light bread or pastries.[32] In the case of recreation, matrons provided equipment for activities such as tennis or volleyball.[33] Other "appropriate" leisure activities included reading—with an attempt to cultivate "literary taste"—and the playing of musical instruments. There was even instruction on the "tasteful adornment" of the home. As matron Mary Doyle reported, "Among the week's events there is probably none more worthy of note than the distribution of reading matter among our young men, as you are well aware the cultivation of literary taste in the young serves not only to instruct and amuse, but proves an effective moral agent as well."[34]

Within this context of educating women to their proper gender roles, the strong interest of the government—and its workers—in marriage rates takes on new meanings. Indeed, one of the major tools that the matrons used to overcome Tohono O'odham vice was civil and monogamous marriage. In an astounding 1917 report, Superintendent Jewell D. Martin suggested, "it would be immeasurably better even for the girls to be sent back to the Papago desert to become wives on the desert farms and ranches than to run the risk of falling prey to the half-educated young Indian men who are in and around Tucson and . . . who do not as a rule wish to marry because they can have more spending money without a family to support."[35] The fact that Martin was willing to give up any chance at assimilating a Tohono O'odham woman into the urban labor force, the bedrock of OIA efforts described in chapter 4, in exchange for protecting her from the vice of unassimilated Tohono O'odham and Mexican men is significant. This is especially the case given the fact that OIA officials and other reformers generally had a positive moral view of Tohono O'odham men.

In this sense, OIA policy (or at least the people who put it in action) vis-à-vis marriage favored a view of women that was in many ways conservative and traditional, focusing on Americanization specifically by pushing gendered norms and expectations that favored marriage and the protection of moral virtue rather than women's rights, independence, vocations, or careers.

Matrons often reported on their attempts to get girls married and to discourage "living in the Indian way," described in some detail at the beginning of the chapter. Matrons often aimed to move a couple into a legal union when they were living together or when children were involved. OIA officials also worked to co-opt the sanctioning of Tohono O'odham marriage and divorce proceedings. Superintendent Jewell D. Martin noted that Mattias Hendricks, the Tohono O'odham leader of Vomari, had been "dabbling in divorce business" and other things that "he had no right to do." Martin tried to convince Hendricks to become an OIA-sanctioned judge, but when that failed, he appointed as judge "a returned student of the rather intelligent competent class, who can read and understand the regulations and to whom I personally gave careful and detailed instructions in his duties."[36] Sadly, we lack the necessary sources to know how locals in Vomari reacted to the OIA's attempted usurpation of traditional Tohono O'odham power.

Though the student appointed by Superintendent Martin—and other natives—may have supported civil marriage, this was not an issue to be left in tribal hands. The support of marriage from outsiders was viewed as both useful and necessary, though it was not always successful. Clearly, matrons viewed marriage as a sign of civilization and believed that individuals who embraced marriage were better off than those on whom it was forced. Although the reports of all of the matrons working with the Tohono O'odham contain evidence that they believed that civil marriage alone would solve most couples' problems and give them a proper moral grounding, none demonstrate this more clearly than those of Janette Woodruff. What perhaps frustrated her most was when she offered marriage as a solution to Tohono O'odham couples but was rebuffed. For example, when Frances had a child out of wedlock with "big Joaquin," Woodruff offered to have them married. Joaquin responded by telling her that they already were married in the Indian way. When Woodruff tried to press the issue, Frances laughed at her. Woodruff tried on two occasions either to get the sheriff to take Frances and Joaquin to court and force them to get married or to bring the Catholic priest out to perform a ceremony in order to "make an example of them."[37]

Civil marriage was encouraged as an appropriate moral choice, fitting with larger societal norms. As such, it was seen as a step toward civilization for members of the Tohono O'odham. But perhaps most importantly, it was seen as a way of maintaining stability—social and economic—within the Tohono O'odham community. Civil marriage protected women and men from vice and provided for the financial support of women and children.[38]

In the end, however, there is evidence of Tohono O'odham ignoring the advice of officials related to marriage and sexual impropriety, or resisting it in one way or another.[39] While the records contain evidence of civil marriages and domestic training, these are cases held out as examples. The efforts of the OIA hardly routed out traditional practices. In some cases where marriage was resisted, it was forced. For example, A. M. Philipson reports on one case where he arranged and forced a marriage between a girl and a boy she had been seeing. Even after she requested not to get married and instead to go away to school, the marriage was completed.[40] In many cases, however, as suggested by the case of James McCarthy at the beginning of the chapter, traditional marriages in the "Indian way" continued well into the middle of the twentieth century.

In other cases majority culture sexual standards were simply ignored by Tohono O'odham, as in 1914 when Minnie Estabrook reported sending girls to the doctor "for a physical examination to either confirm or contradict the rumors regarding their condition."[41] Reports of other "bad" women exist as well—with "bad" being defined as having children and having never been married.[42] Nonetheless, OIA officials remained optimistic, and clung to their views on civil marriage as a civilizing force and their high hopes for female moral suasion. In 1927 Philipson wrote, with some irony, of one such case: "Answering your letter relative to Lewis . . . , son of Felix . . . and Manuella . . . , who is living with an Indian girl at Salt River Agency illegally, I am enclosing the 'Consent to Marriage of Minor' signed by the parents of Lewis . . . today. Lewis has a pretty bad reputation, but I hope he will do better since he has taken a wife. (May they live happily ever after)."[43]

Vice, in terms of sexual improprieties, was of great concern to reformers, who thought it was made worse by the exposure of Tohono O'odham to the lower classes of the larger society. One superintendent wrote, in response to a complaint about a Tohono O'odham man engaged in sexual relations with a woman other than his wife:

> Jose stoutly denies criminal relationships with any other woman though personally I am inclined to doubt his word. There is anything but a

> desirable condition existing among those young returned students who find work in Tucson. This is not strange. The surroundings are not different there from those to be found in any other city of Tucson's size, but there has been much vice rampant there, and it is quite natural that many of the young Indians should yield to its influence. I think I am right in affirming that there is less illicit carnal intercourse among the Indians even in Tucson, per capita, than among either of the three other races there, but of course this is no excuse for laxness on our part so long as there are preventable cases existing among the Indians.[44]

While alcohol seemed the primary concern of the agency farmer and the police force, the issue of potentially fallen women and seduction was of central concern to agency field matrons. Indeed, as one agency worker suggested, women were needed specifically for this job. An unknown worker reported, "There are a number of Papago young women who are becoming loose in their morals and a scandal to the other girls. Lately I have sent some home and talked with others but a capable woman should be sent to do this. Supt. F. A. Thackery informs me that two Indian girls have recently had illegitimate babies there whose father was either white or Mexican living in Tucson. So far, the Papago girls have stood off the temptation in Tucson better but there are many of these beginning to succumb."[45] As with the cousins who were discussed in the previous chapter, temptation and bad influences were of great concern as Tohono O'odham women moved into the cities to work.

OIA field matrons were part of a much broader trend of the professionalization of social work during the Progressive Era. Initially many of the individuals working with the poor, recent immigrants, and Native Americans were volunteers or untrained professionals. Missionaries (in the case of the Tohono O'odham, both Presbyterians and Catholics), charity workers, and others often were motivated by compassion to perform "good works." Over time, even among missionaries and volunteers—and certainly among professional social workers—there was a shift toward viewing charity work as a science. This included a move toward efficient, professional standards.[46] It also moved many reformers to demand more involvement from the state—in addition to the private sector—with a growing focus on social justice and social welfare.[47]

The move toward scientific professionalism did not mean that workers were able to move completely outside of their own culture and moralities; most remained bound to their middle-class sensibilities. Nor did it mean that they demanded equality for their clients. Instead, they insisted that they receive more acceptance, tolerance, and understanding—but also the necessary intervention to keep them on the right path. Most importantly, it was accompanied by a shift toward viewing social problems (i.e., vices) not as the result of individual moral failing, but rather as having societal causes that could be addressed and fixed.[48]

Field matrons working for the OIA arbitrated domestic disputes, offered marital advice, and undertook a wide variety of efforts to safeguard the moral character of the young women they worked with. OIA matron Mary Doyle, a Catholic nun, for example, reported on a young girl named Maria whom she directly supervised for two years. Maria had "lax morals" and had ended up in court. However, with time and supervision, Doyle reported: "There has been a vast improvement in her since she has resided with us. For some time after she came here people regarded her with great coldness and disdain; but she has raised herself in their estimation to a remarkable degree by her edifying conduct and quiet, pleasing manners. She is employed in domestic work and sewing, and has lately taken up the study of music."[49] The types of behavior that field matrons considered appropriate were consistently discussed in their reports, where they worried about protecting women from "influences," which included other women of bad reputation, men, and drink.[50]

While marriage was seen as the final solution for problems, short-term efforts focused on protecting girls from being led astray and influenced by the wrong sorts of people prior to marriage. There were great similarities here to other imperial views, as in the English case where historian Philippa Levine has noted that "fears and laws around sexuality almost invariably focused on the control of women. . . . Whether it was a fear of the sexualized woman who had stepped beyond male authority or whether, conversely, it was a fear that the traditionally meek women would be sexually violated by lawless and lustful colonials, these anxieties made sex a key site of imperial fear, concern and action."[51] Openly sexual women were viewed as deviant and in need of control and intervention. Less openly sexual women were assumed to be weak and vulnerable—the potential victims of seducers.

Thus matrons frequently worked with the police and other governmental officials to address immoral behavior. At times, they also looked to the girl's own family and community to take control of her. One matron wrote to a father about his daughter's bad conduct, describing her as "drunk, indecent, ugly and blasphemous." The matron suggested, "I think you are aware that your daughter, Carlotta . . . , has been guilty of bad conduct recently. I regret to inform you that her deportment has become exceedingly bad, and it will be necessary to take measures to bring her to justice unless you, yourself, or other relatives can control her actions. . . . You are requested to take charge of her and KEEP HER AT HOME."[52] In this case, family supervision was preferred to legal action. If family supervision failed, however, the matron suggested that local officials place Carlota in "an institution or prison."[53]

While matrons and families worked to preserve the girls' good names, the matrons faulted white employers for not protecting Tohono O'odham as well as they should. Matrons reported their interest in finding suitable homes for working girls, "where their environments will be of an inspiring nature, rather than in places where the living conditions do not tend to promote their best interests."[54] Records report of tensions with employers who did not provide the proper supervision of their maids. Outside housing was a particularly contentious problem, since employers could not properly supervise girls living outside the main house during their time off.[55] This particular conflict with employers suggests that the matrons continued to be concerned with moral issues, particularly with protecting virtue, while they attempted to meet employment needs; the latter was clearly viewed as being intimately connected to the former.

As an interesting counterpoint, there also seemed to be some expectation coming out of the Tohono O'odham community that matrons would promote morality among those under their supervision. Woodruff, in her report on working girls in 1927, suggested: "Looking at the situation from another side, the Indians think I should stop the dancing and drinking among them. I can realize how the Indians feel to have their children come to town and be led away by the evil that is carried on in the village."[56] Moral protection loomed as a large concern for the matrons and for at least some of the native population themselves. Although this was the case, we should emphasize that tribal support for moral behavior (and for the outing program in general) did not necessarily mean support for the overall assimilation campaign. For example, Marie, a Tohono O'odham girl placed in a Hollywood, California, home through the Catholic Church's outing program, wrote to one of her friends in hopes of gaining her assistance in running away so as to reunite with her previous employer, a Mrs. Ganahl. Marie complained that her current employers compared her to and treated her like "a colored maid" and said that she had "a black face" and therefore did not "know anything." Marie was motivated by more than her mistreatment. She wanted "to go someplace where I can get 30 dollars a month and help Father Bonaventure a little more on everything and my folks and also get my new clothes my new shoes see."[57]

Hence, Marie's goals were not assimilationist in nature, but rather economic. Her focus on using the extra money that she would earn for her family and the local church also strongly reflected Tohono O'odham values stressing kinship and community cohesion.

Often one vice was seen as contributing to another, and thus to protect women (and men), matrons sought to limit things like alcohol, gambling, and even the playing of pool. A superintendent, writing about a married native man who had gotten a girl pregnant, reported, "Jose is what is commonly known as a pool-room bum and spends nearly all the money he can get hold of in the pool-rooms." He then suggested, "All the Papagos should be run out of the pool-rooms if possible."[58] As historian Regina G. Kunzel notes, while young men and women probably viewed pool halls and other areas of heterosexual sociability such as movie theaters as places of "autonomy, romance, and pleasure," reformers viewed them as locations of "promiscuous sexuality and inappropriate *delinquent* behavior."[59]

Because of the importance of addressing vice issues in the community, even the OIA's farmers were engaged in anti-vice work aimed at potentially fallen women and matters of the home. For example, A. M. Philipson intervened in the case of Maria and Jose, who had a common-law marriage and a nine-month-old daughter together. Jose had been staying out late, and when Maria accused him of seeing another woman, Jose kicked her out. Maria turned to Philipson in hopes that he could make Jose support her financially. Philipson, with the help of the local Indian judge, did her one better and managed to convince Jose to let her return home, but demanded that they "secure a marriage license and be legally married."[60] In another case, OIA officials tried to force Lupa to marry (probably because she was pregnant, though the record never says so explicitly), even though they were uncertain whom she had been dating. After local officials arranged Lupa's marriage to Joe, one of several men she had been dating, Lupa approached Philipson to see if he could get her out of the marriage by arranging for her to go away to the Sherman Institution in Riverside, California. He refused to accept her application.[61] The refusal fit in with a larger pattern—that of refusing to place Tohono O'odham women with children in the homes of white families even if the woman had another family member to watch after her children. Of course, this fit in well with the Victorian notion that women should work outside the home for cash only until they had children, after which they belonged back in their home.

Returning again to the autobiography of Chona, we find the most explicit information about illicit sexual relations in several passages about "wild women." Chona first hinted at the idea of women deviating from expected sexual behaviors when she suggested her own fear of being with a man. Her mother responded by saying, "It's right to be afraid of men. All good girls are."[62] Good girls also never talked to men alone—they traveled in groups when they went to gather fruit or water, protected by older women. While "good" girls were afraid of men and sexual relations and never talked to men alone, "wild" girls courted both. Chona suggested, for example, "Sometimes there would be boys there (at the pond) watering their horses. The wild girls would throw gravel at them, then laugh and run."[63] Wild women also went alone to dances, and sometimes did not come back home at night. They "went about painted every day," emphasizing their breasts with paintings of corn ears, birds, and butterflies.[64]

While Chona's narrative suggests her own emerging adolescent thoughts and dreams about boys and sex, she also makes it clear that her parents carefully supervised her and instructed her in proper behavior. But she did report other cases that varied from the norm. Her son, for example, met with a wild woman when he was a teen. Here "wild women" were described as "women who run about without husbands and sleep in the arroyos." This particular wild woman also had additional sexual partners without any appearance of family-arranged marriage, wanted money to buy things, and wanted the son to give up planting and go to town to seek a different life. She also "would not wait and do things at the right time" and apparently engaged in sexual relations during menses, something that was believed to kill the power of medicine men.[65] But all these types of sexuality, while outside of the tribal norms, were dealt with in one way or another by the tribe itself and were not seen as problems brought about by the outside world, except perhaps by contact with a cash economy.

While relations between tribal members could often be addressed through families and "rectified" through marriage or enforcement of other anti-vice laws, seduction and in some cases adultery were separate and vexing issues. One report from an unknown OIA employer noted, "I have to-day sworn out a warrant and complaint on a felonious charge against a white man who is alleged to have seduced a 16 year old girl who expects a baby in two or three months. I expect to be able to locate the white man and sincerely hope to put him in prison and also institute a civil suit."[66] In the case of "inter-racial" seduction, legal action, and not marriage, was the solution. While cohabitation, or informal marriage, between members of the same race was a moral violation, "seduction" was a crime.

However, the law was not as reformers might have wished when dealing with cases involving adult women. Superintendent McQuigg sought the advice of an attorney in a case of seduction only to find out that while a moral affront was undeniable, no actual laws seemed to apply. The lawyer reported,

> Owing to the age of the said Ada . . . , we cannot proceed against Pynes for Statutory Rape, Seduction or Contributing to the Delinquency and Dependency of a Minor; as the legal relation of Parent and Child does not exist between Pynes and the child, we cannot proceed against him for Non-Support of Child; and as we have no Bastardy law in Arizona, we cannot be proceeded along this line. It does not appear from the facts disclosed that he arranged for any transportation for the woman for any immoral purposes, and therefore could not be prosecuted under our White Slave law.[67]

A similar complaint was made by A. M. Philipson as late as 1933 when he wrote in his weekly report:

> We are again reminded of the lack of adequate Federal Laws for Indian People on Indian Reservations by the case that came up before our Indian Judge on Nov. 28th. The Indian, a married man with a family of four living children was found guilty of seducing a 13 year old Indian girl and getting her with child. There is no Federal Law covering such cases, consequently, the Indian Court is all we have to punish this culprit. This court gives him six months in jail and $5.00 a month to pay toward the support of the child.[68]

That "seduction" was immoral, even criminal, behavior was clear; that it could be properly addressed through the courts was a more contentious issue.

In typical turn-of-the-century style, when law failed to address a problem, moral suasion was seen as the solution. As one superintendent suggested:

> As you are probably aware, there is no law against adultery among Indians. They are under US law, and there is no federal statute touching the point, so it is not possible to hale [haul] one into state or federal court and mete out summary justice as in the case of a citizen. There is however a regulation which will permit us to handle such cases in the Court of Indian Offenses, and this it is my custom to do, where evidence is sufficient to warrant one's being held it obtainable.
>
> I can and will arrest Jose and have him imprisoned and fined if either my employees or myself or others can get sufficient evidence

> against him to sustain a case; and we will make special effort to do so, in view of your statement as to the probability of his having criminal association with another woman. But while I think I can keep him from open flagrant adulterous living and shall undertake to do so, still I doubt if any but moral suasion can be used to extract alimony or separate maintenance funds from him. It would be ever so much better if he and Florence could be reconciled and could live together in peace.[69]

Moral guidance and suasion were seen as the keys to both acculturation and the destruction of vice. Here again the focus was on the power of marriage and reconciliation to undo vice and provide happiness.

While OIA officials were addressing Tohono O'odham vices, they often had issues of their own. Such was the case with farmer A. M. Philipson. The record is unclear as to exactly when Philipson became a widower—an efficiency report filled out by his boss in May 1920 listed Philipson as married even though, as we will see below, he had accepted female boarders in February of that year. In March 1921, Philipson wrote to Superintendent McCormick in hopes of receiving a favor. Because it reflects the social values of mainstream society (or at least the potential undermining of those social values) as well as those that the OIA was trying to impose on the Tohono O'odham, his letter is worth quoting at length:

> I would like to ask a favor of you for my own personal protection relative to the Donsemore Sisters occupying part of my quarters since Feb. 19th. I did not think of it this way at the time or I would have asked it then before permitting them to come in here. You can see what a position it places me in, knowing what I told you about my domestic affairs. I have absolutely no way of denying any charge that might be brought against me for allowing strange women to occupy my private rooms. Now the favor I ask is this, Please write me a letter or order dated Feb. 19th, 1920 directing me to allow these women to occupy the rooms they are occupying. Such an order from you will, I think, put me in the clear before the court should an attempt be made to sue this charge against me. I do not know that anything of the kind will be attempted, but in case it would, I want to be on the safe side.[70]

While there is no way to tell for sure, apparently Philipson had invited female boarders into his home prior to the death of his wife. Philipson feared it becoming public.

Another Tohono O'odham case suggests inappropriate behavior by an OIA male employee as well. Janette Woodruff reported the scandalous behavior of H. H. Glover, a supervisor of construction, whom she had left in charge of her house while she was out of town. She wrote: "Upon my arrival home one girl that came from Sacaton reported to me that she stayed in my house the night she came. That Mr. Glover let her in, and in the night when he came home later he wanted to co-habit with her. She says she firmly resented [resisted], and he went away back to his own room."[71] Fortunately this girl, new to the city and its temptations, had thwarted Glover's intentions.

These cases are not surprising. Historians have found others involving charges of immorality brought against OIA officials, especially by women in the service who claimed a place of "exalted moral position and sexual purity."[72] Historian Margaret Jacobs, for example, discusses this issue in her work on the Pueblo. The reforming women she studied often focused internally, as well as externally, aiming to clean up the OIA—both by stopping the traffic in liquor to the Indians and bringing an end to sexual immorality within the OIA—for example, conducting campaigns against superintendents for sexual immorality within the ranks, evidenced by workers having syphilis. In a somewhat parallel example, Eileen Findlay has looked at marital reform efforts in Puerto Rico at the turn of the century. In her work she has suggested that reformers encouraged marriage for Puerto Ricans in part out of hopes of protecting white males from temptation.[73]

Frequently interracial sexual activity was viewed as seduction, a crime perpetrated upon weak and often young women by immoral men. The records document numerous fatherless "white" babies, the assumed product of seduction. In 1915 field matron Minnie M. Estabrook reported: "I went with the police last night at 11:45 p.m. to the Perry home in Tucson and found the house maid, Marie . . . , in bed with a white man named Troutter. They were both arrested and pled guilty "to a charge of illicit cohabitation." He was sentenced to 60 days jail or a fine of $60 and her to 30 days jail or a fine of $30. She paid her fine and was released.[74] It is unclear why, in this particular case, both parties were arrested and tried—just as it is unclear who the white man in question was. But interracial sexual activity, even if consensual, was seen as dangerous and needing to be addressed.

Assimilation did not, in the minds of reformers, necessarily mean equality and most certainly did not call for a breakdown of racial separation. Like many other states, Arizona had already passed antimiscegenation laws to protect "whiteness," in 1865 and again in 1901, forbidding the intermarriage of whites with blacks, "Mongolians," and Native Americas, and later their descendants.[75] At the time, one OIA official reported that intermarriage had not been particularly common for the Tohono O'odham, a tribe that had long existed far on the edges of the empire. In a 1917 annual report on the tribe, Jewell Martin suggested, "There is a statute prohibiting intermarriage between Indians and whites but even before the statue became operative there was practically no mixing of the races. The Papagos are all about full blood. They intermarry with the Pimas a little but otherwise their amalgamation with other races is confined to some half dozen cases where they have intermarried with Mexicans or Yaqui Indians."[76] In reality, there was a good bit of interracial marriage, especially with the transnational Yaqui, going on beneath the OIA radar.[77] To accommodate this change in practice, the Tohono O'odham created a new clan, the Ogol or Judum (Bear) Clan. Membership in the clan was available only for the descendants of Tohono O'odham women who married Mexicans and Yaqui (but not Anglos). Exogamous marriage for men with Yaqui or Mexican spouses seemed to have no impact on clan membership.[78] It is possible, however, that governmental officials were unaware of, or simply did not care about, the extent of interracial marriages, so long as they did not involve whites or did not occur in urban centers. It is also possible that many government officials could not tell the difference between Mexicans, Native Americans, and mixed-race people.[79] But evidence certainly exists. For example, in James McCarthy's autobiography, he records two relatives marrying interracially—a brother to a Mexican woman and a niece to a "colored man."[80] In his writing, at least, he passes no judgment on either marriage and mentions no intervention from reformers and officials in either case.

Regardless of Martin's claims, sexual exploitation of Tohono O'odham women by white men—and perhaps men of other races—was a growing concern as these women moved into the cities and thus into closer contact with white society. Interestingly, historian and Sonoran Tohono O'odham Reuben Naranjo Jr. claims that both Anglos and Mexicans married Tohono O'odham women on both sides of the US–Mexico border as a means of laying claim to mineral deposits, primarily gold. He argues that in spite of the creation of the Ogol Clan, these patterns of intermarriage remained a *secreto a vozes* (an open secret) among tribal members.[81] In spite of the intermarriages, Tohono O'odham remained closely tied to their tribal identity. As for the OIA, reformers seldom highlighted intermarriage as a concern or even possibility, though white men were represented in the legal records as sexual exploiters alongside native or Mexican men.

There is some evidence that OIA officials were concerned over what they viewed to be the unfair treatment of the children of these marriages—mixed-blood natives. Malcolm McDowell wrote to Superintendent McCormick looking for examples of virtuous Tohono O'odham with mixed ancestry:

> I am getting together some data to refute the lying statement, so often made, that a mixed-blood Indian has in him all the vices of both the races and the virtues of neither. It is astonishing that a lie of this kind continues to live but it does and is repeated so often that the word "mixed-blood" has become almost a term of opprobrium. My attention was drawn sharply to this falsehood by a young lady in Washington who is about three-eighths Indian and five-eighths white and I promised her I would do what I could to nail the lie.
>
> You know and I know that wherever we go in the Indian country we find mixed-bloods who are the leaders in progressive thought and action and who are the equal of their all white neighbors in the arts, sciences, professions and in commerce. I have a number of concrete examples of the big part which mixed-bloods are taking in the affairs of their communities but I want more.[82]

At least one official questioned whether intermarriage with whites was a bad thing.[83] When writing to Superintendent McQuigg in support of a law allowing superintendents to issue marriage licenses, E. B. Meritt responded to McQuigg's suggestion that intermarriage restrictions be changed, stating,

> As for endeavoring to procure a change in the law of the State which prohibits intermarriage between Whites and Indians, you are advised that the Office believes that it should not interfere in this matter, which is one concerning which the State has a full right to exercise such authority as it sees fit. However, the practice of intermarriage between Indians and Whites is carried on in many other States and, so far as the Office knows, it has not resulted to the detriment of society.[84]

While making clear that intermarriage was not an issue for the federal government, there seems to have also been a belief here that it was not necessarily an evil.

However, this reference to intermarriage is unique in the records we consulted. The main concerns about protection of racial purity and racial difference that appear in government records are those aimed at the reformers themselves—as OIA leaders expressed rather nonspecific concerns about white female workers living in isolated areas away from their racial peers. They are nonspecific in the sense that it is never entirely clear whether they were worried about white workers being corrupted or simply lonely in the absence of white society. What is clear is that the OIA and other reformers believed that females, unlike males, could not thrive in racial isolation. This fear motivated some rural schools, for example, to hire only male teachers or to seek "white" women as companions for their teachers if they were female. Local Catholic leader Father Oblasser expressed a similar concern and found it necessary to hire "white" companions for white female workers in isolated areas. He reported: "The ladies teaching at Cowlic and San Miguel prefer a white lady as companion. So I am using the $45 salary to pay the companions, and will have the Tertiaries of Cleveland and Spokane supplement the salary to equal that of their companions."[85]

But in a broader sense, concern over white women on the frontier created a complex issue for the OIA as there was a strong belief that women workers were needed to reach native women. Many in the government believed that white male officials simply could not interact with native women in the way that white female officials could. A report from the Board of Indian Commissioners, for example, urged the creation of community centers on the Tohono O'odham reservation, but noted the importance of woman-to-woman instruction: "Through them the women of the tribes could and would be reached and led to improve their homes and better their living conditions and I am firmly of the opinion that the sooner the Indian women are energized by a progressive influence the sooner the Indian problem will be satisfactorily solved. And Indian women can only be reached through other women."[86] Thus the OIA would need to balance its goals of addressing vice with its overall gender and racial concerns.

An interesting and contrasting view of gendered marital relations is available when we consider the lives of the field matrons themselves, who were predominantly white single women living in fairly isolated tribal areas. Historians looking at empire and racial relations have frequently documented the way in which, when women were present, the structure and rules of the society around them took on new importance. Field matrons, along with teachers and the wives of OIA officials, discussed more fully in chapters 2 and 4, were frequently the only white women on the Tohono O'odham reservation. Ann Laura Stoler describes studies of European colonial racial and gender relations as follows:

> More recent attention to the structures of colonial authority has placed new emphasis on the quotidian assertion of European dominance in the colonies, on imperial interventions in domestic life, and thus on the cultural prescriptions by which European women and men lived. From an earlier focus on how colonizers have viewed the indigenous other, more work is beginning to sort out how Europeans in the colonies imagined themselves and constructed communities built on asymmetries of race, class, and gender.[87]

Along these lines, field matrons and the wives of missionaries set up their own homes as models of white civilization—prescriptions of proper domestic life. And whether they were calling for white companions or requesting private bathrooms, they expressed a desire for racial separation even from those they were civilizing. Yet there is a great irony here, since most matrons, as single working women, were not truly living the lives they prescribed. Not unlike other female reformers in the West, perhaps best described by Peggy Pascoe, these middle-class, often Protestant women, were trying to bring female moral authority to western cities. But as Margaret Jacobs has pointed out in her description of the origins of the field matron program, these women were not what they preached—they were not married, domesticated ladies; rather they were single career women.[88] Jacobs suggests that

> even the OIA's job description for the field matron reflected in part the ways in which the notion of separate spheres had broken down. Although the OIA expected its female employees to demonstrate femininity and self-sacrifice, it also defined the work of the field matron as a "skilled and demanding job requiring hardiness, self-sufficiency, and a large degree of professional autonomy." As such, the vocabulary chosen celebrated traits more appropriate to the notion of the male sphere. In addition, rather than employing married women who could model appropriate female behavior, the OIA at first preferred to hire single women as field matrons.[89]

Indeed, the matrons to the Tohono O'odham were social service professionals who made careers of selling what they, in most cases, did not themselves embrace. Whether that irony was appreciated by the matrons, and impacted their actions, remains unclear.

The native views of matrons are even sketchier. There are scant mentions of matrons in native sources aside from casual comments, such as that by Blaine, who mentions in passing that Woodruff was, for example, a nice woman. He recalls that she "helped the girls get jobs cleaning in homes in Tucson. Her home was always open to anyone. She used to live on south Sixth Avenue. I remember her pretty well, because all the young Indian girls used to go to her place to have their gatherings. She checked the town after 8:00 o'clock to see that the Indian girls were away from the city. I went to her place with a group for a party, one time. I guess it was a wedding dinner that was there."[90] So if the tension between the ideal and the life of the matrons was a cause of concern among, or even noticed by, tribal members, it is not evident in existing records. And while the government offered solid criticism of the matron program nationally in the Merriam Report, their concern was not over the matrons as professionals but rather the reverse:

> The Service is notably weak in personnel trained and experienced in educational work with families and communities. The result is the almost total absence of well developed programs for the several jurisdictions specially adapted to meet local conditions. For many years the Indian Service has had positions for "Field Matrons" employed especially to work with families, but the salaries and the entrance qualifications have been so low that the competent field matron able to plan and apply a reasonably good constructive program is the rare exception. . . . At present the plan is to replace field matrons with public health nurses as rapidly as possible. This action will be an improvement because the vast majority of field matrons are untrained for their work.[91]

Written at the end of the 1920s, this report emphasizes the importance of trained professionals over the assumption that white women, by their nature, were the role models native women needed. Yet in other ways the report was quite traditional in its views of gender—showing its cultural biases on issues of domesticity and marriage. Native women's cultural "progress" was measured by their ability to sew well and the presence of "a women's magazine or mail order catalog" in their homes. As for marital relations, according to the report, women were failing to do their proper duty: "Apparently little pressure is brought to bear upon the husband by the wife to increase the income, or upon the wife by the husband to disburse it more wisely. . . . Husband and wife will therefore take no responsibility for each other's actions, for if they refrain from advice they are left free to quarrel by slurring each other. Mutual distrust is evidenced by the custom of the wife's accompanying the husband everywhere."[92]

Not only were wives and husbands interacting in improper ways, but the "Indian" family was not yet meeting the standards of the model white family. Specifically, the report complained that native families were less likely to be "two-generation (husband, wife and children) families" and continued to be "less stable," as practices of informal separation, remarriage, and polygamy were still common.[93] Though not specific to the Tohono O'odham, this report certainly indicated that by 1928, after decades of effort, the OIA had not brought native marriages in line with the standards of the majority culture. As Susan Carter summarizes in her own work on gender roles and marriage, "Ultimately, the state had the capacity to disrupt, but not utterly transform, Aboriginal marriage and domestic life; their technologies of control were limited."[94]

Field matrons viewed civil marriage for native women, if not themselves, as an important civilizing institution. It provided solutions to numerous "problems" in the Tohono O'odham society. For example, it was based in patriarchy and thus encouraged proper gender roles that included dependency for women and a role as head of household for men. It also demanded monogamy—thus ideally protecting both men and women from vice and corruption. Indeed, in terms of moral supervision, when all else failed and evidence of lax morals manifested in the form of a pregnancy or even unruliness, marriage was seen as the solution to clean up the messy realities of life. Unfortunately from the reformers' point of view, reality continued to be messy; and while their records reported their "successes," many failures went unrecorded. In fact, most failures probably went unnoticed by OIA and church officials. In many cases native men and women chose to shun civil marriage, sticking with tribal traditions, and men and women, reformers and natives alike, continued to transgress.

CHAPTER FOUR

Schools and Gendered Education

Assimilating Tribal Youth

I just received word that Antonio Chico has taken his three children out of school (San Xavier Day School) and started for the Magdalena Feast, He is going by way of San Pedro and coyote village, they say, and will be in that section for two or three days, perhaps you could have a policeman from out there intercept them and bring them back. . . . We are having quite a bit of trouble about absentees, some having gone to Santa Rosa to gather their crops out there, they say.

—A. M. PHILIPSON, FARMER, TO MR. MCCORMICK, SUPERINTENDENT, SEPTEMBER 9, 1922

Tohono O'odham tribal member James McCarthy, born in 1895, offers an intriguing tale of his experiences with Indian schools in his autobiography, *A Papago Traveler.* His story is representative of a number of trends seen in the negotiation between government and church officials and tribal members over the education of youth—something viewed by officials as crucial to the "civilization" and Americanization of tribal members, but viewed by the Tohono O'odham with a great deal more resistance and skepticism for a variety of reasons. McCarthy recalls that around 1900, "When I was about five years old, my parents had not sent me to school. Then one day the big Papago policeman, Hugh Norris, came and told my folks that I had to go to school."[1] His enrollment, however, lasted only a year; then he moved to Tucson where, he recalled, there were not many schools and children simply did not attend. Then in 1906 Norris once again visited the family to demand that McCarthy go to school in Phoenix. Although he lacked shoes and the clothing to make the trip, he was sent by train to a boarding school. McCarthy provides a fairly detailed description of his reactions to school as a child, including a strong sense of embarrassment over having his hair cut and his familiarity with strict punishments meted out to students, especially to those who ran away.[2]

In spite of the strong efforts to keep children in school, McCarthy and several friends ran away. He returned home and eventually enrolled instead in a reservation day school through third grade. While there is no indication how typical McCarthy's experiences were for the Tohono O'odham, by the end of his formal education, McCarthy had attended five different schools—boarding and day—sometimes leaving a school of his own accord; sometimes simply completing the educational offerings at that site; and sometimes transferring back and forth between various schools. Some schools, like the Santa Fe Indian School, he seemed to particularly enjoy. There he attended with his nine-year-old brother—though he reported they saw little of each other. What he most enjoyed was picking a trade—farming—and excelling in that pursuit. He also found this particular school welcoming because there were a lot of other Tohono O'odham there; while he frequently talked about feeling a sense of brotherhood with students from other tribes, he welcomed the sight of his own kind.[3] In the end he left this school as well and eventually enrolled in a school of his choice, the Albuquerque Indian School, before his final return by force to the Phoenix Indian School, an institution he attended three separate times.

McCarthy's account of his time in school provides several interesting insights. It is notable, for example, how little choice his family seemed to exercise. Officials frequently made school decisions for him, and his family seemed powerless in the process. Indeed, he described losing touch with his family, forgetting about home and family in his years away at school where he never received letters or visits or other types of contact from family members. His mother welcomed him home when he ran away, but otherwise seemed totally uninvolved in schooling decisions.

On the other hand, McCarthy himself showed a great deal of agency throughout his time in school. He ran away from schools he did not like and sought those he did. Especially as he got older and acquired an interest in sports, he was able to broker his own deal to attend a school of his choice and eventually extended his time in school by a year to do the same. His love of sports, specifically baseball, seemed to be the single thing that kept him in school and that made the school experience particularly meaningful for him. There were financial benefits to schooling as well, since, once he was a teenager he was able to secure paid summer jobs through the school—agricultural jobs in other parts of the country that he was well prepared for because of school curricula.

Also worth noting is that McCarthy appears to have lived in an entirely masculine world. He writes only of male friends and coworkers at school. While he established a cross-tribal identity, bonding with boys from other tribes in ways he never would have had he stayed on the reservation, he reports virtually no interaction with females of his tribe or any other. On a related cross-cultural note, he recalls spending a summer living with a Japanese family, working on their farm, developing ties with that family as well. An unintended consequence of his school experience seems to have been exposure to, and an interest in, other cultures—though at the time his ties to the majority culture, acculturation per se, were less obvious.

Thus it is clear that as a child, McCarthy showed a great deal of agency and action during his time in school. Rather than passively following the path laid out by those in authority, he used a combination of running away, befriending teachers and officials, and developing skills in sports to take control of his education. In her article on student actions and resistance to authority in schools, K. Tsianina Lomawaima writes about resistance to control and "strategies Indian children devised to undermine federal objectives" at other schools. While McCarthy's strategies were quite different from those Lomawaima reports on, they suggest the same type of navigation within the existing structure by Tohono O'odham youth in order to shape their own experiences.[4]

In her article on the "Save the Babies" campaign, a public health initiative, historian Lisa Emmerich compares this difficult attempt at changing culture among natives to the work done in Indian schools. She states, "In the Indian school system where coercion guaranteed compliance, de-Indianization continued at a steady, albeit slow, pace."[5] Indeed, a great deal of the research on Indian schools—both day and boarding—has suggested that the policies there were indeed strict, coercive, and effective: changing children's names, clothing, and hygiene habits and along the way slowly bringing them under the influence of "American" morals and cultural ideals.[6] Jeffrey Ostler describes those heading up this effort, and the larger campaign for assimilation, in a succinct and moving way: "Armed with certain knowledge of their own superiority, boundless optimism in humanity's plasticity, and unflappable confidence in their ability to direct social evolution, the 'friends of the Indians' launched the most comprehensive and sustained assault on Native ways of life in U.S. history."[7] Whether one reviews OIA school policies, specific curricula, or the writings of teachers, what emerges is a fairly consistent focus on Americanization, defined and tied closely to concepts like patriotism and gender appropriate work. Indeed, we find evidence of what Vicki Ruiz describes as,

Figure 4.1 Girls of San Xavier del Bac, 1916. (Courtesy of Department of Special Collections and University Archives, Marquette University Libraries, #11223.)

"Targeting women and especially children, the vanguard of Americanization place their trust in the rising generation."[8] Change the children and ideally the future Americanization of the tribe would be assured.

And yet at the grassroots level, when one looks at the experiences of Indian schools and Tohono O'odham such as McCarthy, the real failures of the system to achieve its goal—that is, the education and acculturation of all Native American children—are striking. However, while schools were not highly successful among the Tohono O'odham in moving boys into the wage-labor economy—a clear goal of education in the twentieth century at least—they did, somewhat inadvertently, move girls, even as they became wives and mothers, into the paid workforce. Reports on the tribe were full of concerns about poor attendance and lack of resources, and native sources document frequently undependable attendance, lack of efficacy, and at times unintended consequences from the interaction between natives and schools. OIA employees, even farmers and field matrons, spent a great deal of time enforcing agency regulations that required parents to enroll their children in OIA schools under the threat that those out of compliance would be tried by an Indian judge. The local superintendent argued: "Physical disability is the only excuse for these children not enrolling" at boarding schools in Yuma, Phoenix, Riverside (in California), or at local mission schools. The threats used—ranging from jailing (where they would be forced to engage in hard labor, usually for the agency farmer), fines of up to ten dollars, and sending children away to boarding schools without the parents' consent—give some sense of the parental reluctance to comply. In one case, the Indian judge's own sons were arrested and held overnight for failure to attend school.[9]

Still, in the face of coercion, for a variety of reasons and in a variety of ways, tribal members often utilized schooling options on their own terms and toward their own ends. They also made decisions about attendance based on their own needs, pulling children from school to travel with the family for agricultural work or for the observance of traditional festivals. As the OIA farmer A. M. Philipson reported to his superior in 1922, in the letter quoted at the beginning of this chapter, absenteeism was a serious problem.[10] In fact, some entire villages refused to cooperate with government agents and missionaries alike. For example, when Father Bonaventure went to Cababi in 1914 in hopes of setting up a Catholic day school, Chief Katode told him that he could not build a school, using the scarcity of water as an excuse. Father Bonaventure had assumed that Cababi would be a good location for a school, since the majority of the residents had had their children baptized. Nonetheless, not a single parent spoke up in favor of a school. Father Bonaventure asked the OIA to send out Hugh Norris, an Indian policeman, to dislodge Chief Katode, but when that failed, he, the Presbyterians, and the OIA simply moved on to greener pastures, setting up schools in other locations—Covered Well in the case of Father Bonaventure—that were more accommodating.[11]

Of course, not every village and its residents was so direct in its refusal, and many found some value in the schools. A. M. Philipson, who served as the agency farmer on the Tohono O'odham reservation, started his career with the OIA in the Tucson area at the Tucson day school. In 1916, he asserted that the OIA had set too high of a standard for Tohono O'odham assimilation. He argued that there were two underlying reasons for the inability of the Tohono O'odham to assimilate rapidly. First, many of their parents were "almost devoid of civilization," and as a result "the majority of them [the students] are very, very backward and very slow." Second, most students did not attend school until after the fall harvest and left again in March "to go back to their ranches with their parents."[12] In other words, while many parents valued the schools and sent their children to them, they prioritized the maintenance of their preexisting patterns of economic subsistence over education. Great tension thus existed between the government's desire to send native children to schools and the Tohono O'odham's priorities, which often favored things other than school attendance.

In addition, those running the schools were frequently mired in issues of politics and religion—and were often blinded by cultural bias—in ways that detracted from their ability to achieve their goals. As a result, schooling as a method of cultural assimilation and social control had at best mixed results, and the government itself, in the form of the Merriam Report in the late 1920s, expressed serious concerns about the impact of schooling on family, community, and individuals. Nonetheless, the US government strongly supported schooling as a path to Americanization, and eventually, citizenship. And the Tohono O'odham were believed to be worthy of walking that path. As George Hunt, governor of Arizona, wrote in 1914, in requesting a bill to support Tohono O'odham schooling: "The Papago Indians are entitled to a great deal of credit by virtue of their excellent industrial and moral standing among tribes of the Southwest. I am of the opinion that the least which the government can do is to extend these Indians reasonable facilities for the acquiring of additional training for citizenship, which they are desirous of obtaining."[13] Progress was not to be easy or assured, but in this view education was the key to civilization. As Haddington Brown wrote in a history of the Tucson Indian School in 1905, "The Indians can be civilized, and many of them have been through the influence of our schools. But we must not expect them to jump from savagery to our stage of civilization in one generation."[14]

The earliest US government mention of schools set up for the Tohono O'odham dates to the 1870s when the US special Indian agent, local rancher, and medical doctor R. A. Wilbur reported on the construction of a schoolhouse at San Xavier del Bac and the hiring of two Spanish-speaking nuns from Tucson to serve as teachers.[15] These reports suggest that the agent believed "the Indians are greatly pleased with the school and are all eager to send their children, as from their long association with the whites they fully appreciate the benefit of an education."[16] Notably the school was both Catholic and Spanish speaking, reflecting the fact that the "whites" mentioned were Catholic missionaries rather than Anglo pioneers.[17] In 1874 some success was reported for the school in the special agent's annual report. By the end of a nine-month term, eighty-nine children were in attendance, and while the curriculum at the school is not described in full, it is clear that it was gender specific, with girls receiving instruction in sewing and cooking.[18] That same report, however, hints at one source of conflict that would continually shape school policy in the region, and nationally, namely tension between Protestant governmental officials and Catholic leaders. Here Agent R. A. Wilbur expresses strong concerns about Catholic leadership, suggesting that "some time ago the fact was forcibly impressed upon me that the bishop and priest had a larger interest in securing the . . . labor of the Indians than in any spiritual good they might be able to confer upon them."[19] The report was replete with complaints against Catholic clergy, who were accused of misrepresenting Wilbur's character to the Indians and trying to keep the natives in "a condition of vassalage and servile bondage." This was probably the result of the fact that some Tohono O'odham were attached to the mission. Archbishop Salpointe noted that

> the Indians were perfectly free to work for themselves or for the church, to cultivate their own fields or the church land, with the difference that the former had to look for their maintenance, while the latter were supported by the mission. Those who worked for the mission were dependent on it for food and clothing, not only for themselves but for their families. For that purpose provisions were stored in the mission house, or convent, and distributed in due time.[20]

In addition, the agent claims, correctly, that "these priests are not American citizens," suggesting that their efforts undermined his own more nationalistic ones and thus were not in the national best interest. Notably he contrasts these priests with the "American catholic priesthood as we find them in the older states"; Catholics might be all right, but foreign-born ones were a risk to his agenda.[21]

Not surprisingly, even in this early period, schools, as perhaps the single civic institution in the territory at the time serving natives, were a major source of conflict between the Catholic missionaries and the civil authority. Wilbur suggests that the priests had "openly declared war against the humble school system which the Governor of the Territory had succeeded in getting into successful operation," and that the Catholic leaders had "publicly stated that they will not rest until they have uprooted every germ of the free education so planted. They have shown in every way that they are not in sympathy with the genius and spirit of American Institutions."[22] Thus a tension over control of Indian schools and the educational process, and assumedly curriculum, had begun in the Tohono O'odham territory by the 1870s.

While this conflict seems to have roots in specific regional personalities (i.e., the background of the individual priests), it reflected a larger national

Figure 4.2 Children at San Xavier del Bac Mission. (Courtesy of Department of Special Collections and University Archives, Marquette University Libraries, #11338.)

story as well. Writing of a period only a few years later, Hoxie describes "the beginning of a new era in federal Indian education." He argues that "over the next fifteen years congressional appropriations for native schooling rose from $75,000 to over $2 million." He emphasizes that "Native American education became the province of people devoted to applying modern techniques to the job of 'civilization,' and Indian schools—once an embarrassing rhetorical flourish on treaties and appropriation bills—became an integral part of the government's assimilation program,"[23] with a focus on inculcating youth in the culture of the majority. Certainly the government, and its officials on the ground in various territories, had a clear agenda in mind. However, as historian Francis Paul Prucha has noted, lack of official government schools created an opening for Catholics to go after federal contracts—expanding rather than reducing their influence in the area of Indian schools.[24] Thus both Catholic missionaries and the US government, supported by Protestant leaders, were involved in—and sometimes at odds over—the education of native children.

The local contours of this struggle are hard to identify for the remainder of the nineteenth century, as reports on schools for the Tohono O'odham are sparse. However, it is clear from Presbyterian records, as mentioned in an earlier chapter, that the Woman's Executive Committee of the Women's Board of Home Missions of the Presbyterian Church supported the formation of an Indian school in Tucson, known locally as "La Escuela," in the fall of 1888.[25] While the school originally served primarily the Pima, probably because they did not engage in seasonal migration and were therefore easier to gain access to, Tohono O'odham children also attended. This school was run as a contract school and thus received significant funding from the federal government. The Presbyterians also worked around San Xavier, including running a day school briefly toward the end of the nineteenth century.[26] The Presbyterians seldom mention the Catholic leaders in their records. However, the US superintendent of the Indian schools, Dr. Daniel Dorchester, writes about Superintendent Billman, who ran the Tucson school until 1894: "I regard it as one of the very best and most successful of the Indian Contract Schools. One of its advantages is that the Indians have faith in Superintendent Billman. In spite of the fact that the Papagos are Catholics and Mr. Billman a Presbyterian, there has been no trouble between them over religious matters, but a strong mutual confidence."[27]

We can achieve a somewhat clearer understanding of the ongoing struggle between Catholics and Protestants over control of the schools by looking at records from the early twentieth century. Once again Prucha provides context for the local issue in his description of the larger national conflict. In the introduction to *The Churches and the Indian Schools*, he summarizes the issue as such: Catholics did not support government schools; they believed they would "pervert the faith—and sometimes the morals as well—of the Catholic Indian children." Conversely, according to Prucha, "the system of Catholic mission schools on the Indian reservations, established to spread the Catholic faith among the Indians and to preserve the faith of those converted by earlier missionaries, became a major obstacle to a universal public school system maintained by the federal government for the Indians."[28] Major struggles, motivated by a desire for universal school attendance, over the location and nature of that education were waged for several decades.

In Arizona, practicality seemed to dictate policy from an early date. Catholic leaders and the government negotiated to meet schooling needs at the least cost, avoiding competition where possible. For example, when the US government turned over Tohono O'odham schooling to the Catholic Church in 1873, Archbishop Salpointe informed Special Indian Agent Wilbur that, although he had the right to fire him and replace him with a Catholic, the archbishop recognized Wilbur's past hard work—Wilbur had first started working with the Tohono O'odham as an attending physician in 1871—and sought only to ensure that he continue to look after the Tohono O'odham's continued "Spiritual Welfare." In other words, as long as Wilbur did not try to convert the archbishop's "Catholic Indians," he could continue working with them.[29]

Franciscan Father Bonaventure, who was responsible for putting in place a system of day schools for the Tohono O'odham, further demonstrated this willingness to accommodate other political actors (even after the Presbyterians had made major inroads among the Tohono O'odham) when he wrote to a variety of Catholic Church and mission officials: "Since we have matured our plans without any antagonistic intentions toward the Government, and since by far the greater majority of the people are Catholics, I would kindly request you not to thwart our plans. At the same time we guarantee that these plans shall be brought to execution as stated, as long as the Federal Government shall not make it impossible."[30] And indeed, there were many examples of one group or the other negotiating and placing schools in such a way as to serve as many students as possible without engaging in competition.[31]

Nonetheless, the struggle over schools sometimes was truly a battle, as various factions claimed they spoke for Tohono O'odham wishes. When the Land League sent a letter to the OIA commissioner claiming that "*All the People in Every Village Do Not Wish Sectarian Schools,*" Bonaventure responded,

> I hope that this is a lie. If possible I would be pleased if you would get us a petition containing the signatures by thumb mark and two witnesses declaring this to be false. Get as many men as you can to sign this after explaining well to them what this all means. See to it that only grown up *men* sign this document. We must act fast if we do not wish to make fools out of ourselves. Now is the time for Catholics to show themselves. . . . Now is the time for everyone who calls himself a Catholic to profess his faith.[32]

The issue of which schools children attended was nothing less than a battle over life's most important issues—family, religion, and culture. Father Bonaventure, who spent many years among the Tohono O'odham, is worth quoting at length because he wrote with passion about the complex nature of the issues at hand. When he was appointed, he thought that the first thing that needed to be done was to provide schools. In part this was an issue of defense—fending off Presbyterian encroachment was key for Catholic missionaries. Father Bonaventure stated his intention: "We're going to beat those others [the Presbyterians] to the schools." He identified this as a constant struggle: "Our biggest trouble we had was keeping our own in religious schools. Schools that taught religion."

One of his greatest concerns about government boarding schools was that

> after third grade, no child over the third grade could be with his parents. Just taken away. Oh, what I saw up here in the country. The misery! The people yelling! And papa and mama screaming about the kids. Oh! This is the matter. This is no way to run a free country! But they were just taking them. It was like a slave. . . . What right have they got to take a child from the father and mother? I don't know but it was a terrible violation of parental rights. And so, I say "They belong to you and nobody in the world has got a right to take your kids away. . . . Your Government wants you to go to school. That's a law."

His response to this perceived affront to family, and religion, was for the Catholic Church to build more schools to serve the local students. He gave as his reasons:

> So the Government can't come and take 'em away from you. Because they're not doin' the right thing. If you grow up without religion . . . without believen' in God and doin' what He wants . . . you're gonna have bad luck. You're just gonna die out. Nobody's gonna care. But if you stick with God . . . you're gonna have all kinds of luck. And you're gonna be where nobody can do anything against you. Now, if you work, and do mighty good work, God will help you to get out. . . . That's what we need, in order to help.[33]

On whole then, family, religion, and community cohesion mixed in interesting ways—and Father Bonaventure believed that all three were at stake when children were forced to go off to boarding schools, at least in the case of government—and thus broadly speaking Protestant—boarding schools. However, it is worth pointing out that the Presbyterian school in Tucson, for some time a government contract school but in much of the twentieth century a private, mission-funded school, generally reported more applications than spots for students. Regular reports suggested that were funding to allow it, the student body could easily have grown significantly.[34] This may not, however, suggest that the Tohono O'odham were increasingly supporting Presbyterianism or Presbyterian schooling. It could simply be an indication that more and more Tohono O'odham were taking up residence in Tucson.

Often priests advocated on a case-by-case basis to keep Tohono O'odham youth at their local schools. In 1924, for example, Father Bonaventure wrote to the commissioner of Indian affairs about five individual children who had been sent to the government schools at Fort Mohave and Fort Yuma without parental consent or against their will. In each case he asked that the children be returned to St. John's, stating, "we do not object against any school, but that we most emphatically request that the right of a parent to chose a school for their child be respected."[35] Of particular concern were the actions of Tohono O'odham Chief of Police Hugh Norris, who though a professed Catholic was responsible for forcing children into government schools off-reservation. Father Bonaventure suggested that Norris defamed the day schools to try and persuade parents to send children off-reservation and also that he went after children already enrolled in Catholic schools rather than trying to identify children who were not yet in school.[36] By the end of that year, Father Bonaventure believed that more than fifty children had been removed against parental wishes from day schools. He expressed similar concerns in future years. Most specifically he laid blame for this on school employees and overzealous policemen: "All are anxious to get their quota as quickly as possible. The Indian policemen are anxious to satisfy these men, and do their share to discredit the day schools."[37]

In response, offering an interesting insight into the conflict, Rev. William Hughes, who worked for the Bureau of Catholic Indian Missions, wrote candidly to Father Bonaventure to suggest that pressure to increase numbers in schools often subverted the goal of the system in general. In commenting on the pressure that nonreservation government schools put on field supervisors to provide them with students, Hughes wrote, "While these schools are of value for the Indian children, there is a tendency on the part of some whose jobs depend on the schools to think that the Indian children were created for the benefit of the schools instead of the schools being created for the benefit of the children."[38] The number of stories that appear in the records of school officials and policemen rounding up children and taking them to schools indicates that a major factor in Indian education was the desire of institutions—and their staff—to continue to exist. Whether this was motivated by a belief in the righteousness of their cause, or by a desire to continue their employment (or a combination of the two), it is difficult to say. But it is clear that, once created, schools and their staffs, whether Catholic or government, made significant efforts to perpetuate their existence, often with little regard for—or even awareness of—the interests and desires of the children themselves and their families.

Native children were impacted by the fighting and were, at least in some cases, clearly aware of the friction, even as they were unsure of their own place in the conflict. In his autobiography *Papagos and Politics*, Peter Blaine recalls: "There was a little trouble between the Catholics and Presbyterians. I didn't know what religion I belonged to. My people were Sonora Catholics, but Escuela was a Presbyterian school. Us Indian Catholic boys in Tucson didn't know the difference. When the San Xavier mission priests found out that some of the boys were going to school there, they didn't like it. That's when Father Bonaventure Oblasser pulled us out of Escuela."[39] Expressing little sense of agency or even opinion in the matter, Blaine and his friends were virtual pawns in the battle over schools. In other cases, as will be discussed later, the existence of multiple and often competing schools provided opportunities for choice and negotiation.

Finally, on the issue of belief, it is worth noting that OIA documents suggest a high-level awareness of the problems on the ground. The battles between Catholics and Protestants for control of native children and assumably for the salvation of their souls became so contentious that eventually "General Regulations for Religious Worship and Instruction of Pupils in Government Indian Schools" were issued in 1910. These contained elaborate rules for determining which denomination a particular student belonged to, and the many restrictions suggest the commissioner who wrote them, R. G. Valentine, was trying to limit "poaching" by one faith or another—that is, the proselytizing and eventual switching of a student from one denomination to another.[40] Certainly the Presbyterians believed that Christianity—and they most certainly meant Protestant Christianity—was the cornerstone of any educational effort. Superintendent Herndon wrote in his 1926 speech: "The school has succeeded best in the fact that it has been a real character builder. The Bible instruction and the Christian training given in the school have been the greatest factors in lifting the Papagoes out of superstition and ignorance and placing it on the road to Christian civilization."[41]

But the Catholic Church and supporters of Sonoran Catholicism were also able to influence the Tohono O'odham, maintaining religious and cultural practices that many Protestants were sure to see as based on "superstition and ignorance." For example, Antonia Garcia, a Tohono O'odham student at Topawa, remarked at length about her visit to Cowlic for Holy Week. Although this trip was not a part of the standard curriculum in Catholic-run day schools, the fact that she was encouraged to attend and that her reflections were published in the *Indian Sentinel*, a Bureau of Catholic Indian Missions newspaper, suggests that the encouragement had its intended effect:

> The thing that we Indians enjoy best of all is to watch the Holy Week Devils. The people of the little village of Cowlic have the custom of dressing some boys as devils. These devils are supposed to tempt people, by trying their patience. They go around the houses by day and by night and steal as many things as they can. The only way of protecting the houses against them is by marking the doors with crosses and also painting crosses on every object that must remain outside of the house. Whenever the cross is found, the devils keep away, for the devils are afraid of the cross. Whatever things the devils are able to carry away because the owners neglected to have the cross on are placed in a hole and on Holy Saturday all the people gather together there and pay the devils a certain amount of money if they want their things. If there is anything that remains unclaimed it must be burned. When they have disposed of all these things, all the people form in front of the church, the women to one side and the men to the other leaving the devils in the middle. Some little boys stand near with sticks in their hands and as the devils walk to the church they hit them with all their might. Next to the boys are the girls who throw flowers upon them. Then they stop before the door of the church and take off their costumes. The little boys now come forth and lead them into the church and make the sign of the cross upon them. This puts an end to their devilish powers and leaves the village free from them until the next year.[42]

The OIA had more general educational goals. H. B. Peairs, the chief supervisor of education for the OIA, addressed them in a circular produced for *Education Week*. Notably, the goals focused heavily on attendance rather than on the quality of schools or even the nature of the education offered:

> Goals:
> 1. Every eligible Indian child in school
> 2. As nearly perfect attendance as possible

3. all available school capacity utilized; no overcrowding
4. more pupils and better schools

Means of accomplishing goals:

1. Make education the main thought through the week
2. have every Indian home visited and every parent or guardian interviewed
3. bring every resource of the reservation to bear
   a. secure cooperation of the missionaries
   b. enlist the influence of traders
   c. use every government employee, every auto, every horse, everything
   d. enlist the efforts of the leading Indians
4. Encourage Indian youth to seek more education than the government schools offer
5. Utilize Church services and neighborhood school rallies
6. Enroll children to:
   a. Attend public schools if possible
   b. Attend Government schools only if they require Federal aid[43]

Getting Tohono O'odham children to attend schools (preferably locally funded public schools) was only a first step in the educational process. Once the children were there, the curriculum itself was crucial, as it strongly shaped the experiences of the children in attendance and in many cases their overall success in the schools, and reflected the beliefs and goals of those who ran the schools. One theme running clearly throughout the curriculum was a strong belief in the importance of gender-specific vocational training. Parallel educational efforts aimed at other minority or non-American communities, such as those focused on the African-American community and those for recent immigrants, were vocational rather than purely academic. Such training was seen as the key to the advancement of the race. The author of a 1916 annual report compared the curriculum for the Tohono O'odham with the normal "State Course of Study" in Arizona:

> The State Course of Study is followed as far as possible, a few changes having been made to fit the needs of the Indian children. Special training is given to industrial work. For instance some manual training, gardening, etc., for the boys at the San Xavier School were sent over to the demonstration farm where the farmer instructed them in irrigation, gardening, etc., Cooking and sewing are the things most needed by the girls, therefore I would ask for more supplies and equipment for the

> kitchen and sewing room. The girls are quick to learn sewing, and make all the school uniforms besides sewing for themselves, and families at home.[44]

Presbyterians reported much the same. The curriculum at La Escuela comprised half a day of the "normal public school course of study" plus Bible study, and half a day of vocational training.[45] We can infer a similar focus in Catholic day schools from a Tohono O'odham student's thank-you note: "We want to thank you for giving us that new sewing machine. Every day we pray for you. I made a new dress for myself on the sewing machine. (I had my picture taken wearing the new dress I made.) It is a blue dress with figures on it . . . now some of us are making quilts with the cloth that people send us."[46]

The reason for making vocational training the centerpiece of Tohono O'odham education is suggested by a report from 1925 written by Malcolm McDowell of the Phoenix Indian Vocational School. The school was attended by students from a variety of tribes, with 167 of the 877 students being Tohono O'odham. In reviewing his various students, McDowell explains,

> I was much interested in noting the difference between his full-blood student body at Phoenix and the mixed-blood students of some of the other nonreservation schools I have visited. The large proportion of white blood in the latter group made the schools[,] in so far as the progress and conduct of the children were concerned[,] but little different from the schools of white children. At Phoenix the real Indian characteristics were so evident that the contrast between the Phoenix children and those of the mixed-blood schools is strongly marked.[47]

Eugenics clearly influenced McDowell's understanding of Indian education; in his mind Indian children were quite different from white children or even mixed-race children, and needed education appropriate for their abilities. His thinking also fits within the general bias of government school curriculum toward vocational training, described in Frederick Hoxie's work on native education.

In the Phoenix school curriculum:

> Girls have sewing, including dress-making and the finer branches of needlecraft, millinery, cooking, laundering, and general housekeeping. . . . Boys are required to do a prescribed number of weeks' work in each

> shop and in each branch of agriculture during the pre-vocational years. This includes harness-making and shoe repairs, plumbing and sheet metal work, steam and gasoline engineering, electric wiring and care of motors, carpentry, painting, farm, garden and dairy with separate instructors, black-smithing and wheelwrighting.[48]

As a government boarding school, the Phoenix institution had a curriculum that mirrored that of the larger civilization plan of the OIA. Like with broader acculturation efforts, originally school curriculum focused on proper vocations for both boys and girls. As described in the previous chapter, boys would become land-owning farmers (or ranchers), and thus proper citizens, and girls housekeepers, and thus proper wives.[49] As Robert Trennert has emphasized, "One of the more notable aspects of this program was the removal of young Indian women from their tribal homes to government schools in an effort to transform them into a government version of the ideal American woman by training them in the skills necessary to meet the American ideal of femininity including sewing, cooking, baking and housekeeping."[50] Historian Katherine M. B. Osburn elaborates on this "gendering" of curriculum when she points out that subtle but strict "Euro-American gender roles also underlay the vocational training offered in OIA schools," pointing to the ways in which girls' work at the school, like laundry and cooking, remained unpaid, but boys produced goods that were sold. As such, over time the schools focused more on a standard for boys working for "wages," while girls completed work that was considered subsistence.[51] It is worth pointing out, however, that the outing system, which placed Tohono O'odham girls in the homes of white middle-class families, often subverted this aim, as Tohono O'odham families often responded by having their sons engage in subsistence farming while their daughters worked for cash wages.

School Inspector J. O. Barnd provided the Tohono O'odham day schools with an ideal "Daily Program" of instruction that was less vocational than what would be found at an industrial school. Still, beyond basic academic subjects, it too featured elements of health and hygiene, manners and conduct, "appropriate" handicrafts and an industrial period:

> Daily Program
> 9 to 9:10 Wash and comb
> 9:10 to 9:30 Morning exercise
> 9:30 to 10:20 Arithmetic
> 10:20 to 10:40 Recess

Figure 4.3 Papago boy gathering wood. (Courtesy of Department of Special Collections and University Archives, Marquette University Libraries, *Indian Sentinel*, 5, no. 45 (1925): 163.)

10:40 to 11:05 prepare spelling for afternoon recitation
11:05 to 11:10 manners and right conduct
11:10 to 11:30 prepare reading, geography, and history for afternoon recitation
11:30 to 12 lunch

12 to 12:50 recreation
12:50 to 1 girls comb and boys fill wash pans
1 to 1:15 all wash hands, faces, and teeth
1:15 to 1:30 writing
1:30 to 1:50 language for all classes
1:50 to 2:05 Physiology, history, or geography
2:05 to 2:20 spelling; writing words prepared in morning
2:20 to 2:40 recess
2:40 to 3:30 reading recitation; drawing and paper folding; sewing and other hand work
3:30 to 4 Industrial period[52]

In 1922 the OIA completed a survey of all government schools for Native Americans including those within the Sells agency. At that point information was provided about four day schools for the Tohono O'odham, including one at San Xavier that employed two teachers and an Indian assistant; and schools at Sells, Santa Rosa, and Vomari, each staffed with a teacher

Figure 4.4 Toothbrush drill, US government Indian day school, San Xavier, 1922. (Courtesy of University of Arizona Libraries, Special Collections, University of Arizona, Cooperative Extension Service, Photographic Album of Activities in Pima Co., 1922–1930, AZ-520.)

and housekeeper. According to a report by Superintendent McCormick, the teachers were all male: "Our Day Schools on the Reservation proper are taught by men, in fact the isolated districts are not proper places for a woman teacher, as there are absolutely no white neighbors."[53] While officials deemed the reservation unsuitable for female teachers, female housekeepers, who taught female Tohono O'odham proper gender roles by example, were acceptable. Several times in the report McCormick notes that the teachers and housekeepers did more than teach; they provided occasional handouts to the community, visited and cared for the sick, helped with farm tool repair, and of course prepared lunch for the students.

The curriculum in these primary and grammar schools had a significant focus on gender-based life skills, even for very young children. McCormick reported that "the girls are taught to sew and wash and many things that are helpful to them in after life. The boys are taught gardening, carpentering etc. to a limited extent, owing to the fact that none of them are old enough to do much and to the fact that day schools are not equipped for industrial classes."[54] While individual teachers wrote of games, music, football, and fishing parties, they also reported girls doing laundry on Mondays and learning to prepare lunch, set the table, and serve. Boys worked with gardens and poultry. As teacher William Wells described this work, it was as much about training as it was about utilizing student labor. "We require this not only because the work needs to be done but for the reason we believe all children should have duties of their own, and as everyone knows, Indian children have no duties at home."[55]

This last comment, while meant to reassure his superiors about why the work was assigned, also reveals the cultural biases and lack of cultural understanding that often shaped the actions of local OIA workers. While Wells perceived Tohono O'odham children as having no duties in the home—and thus needing instruction in responsibility—anthropologist Ruth Underhill was gathering a very different view of Tohono O'odham child-rearing practices. In her work *Papago Woman*, based on interviews with tribal members at roughly the same time, she offers the following Tohono O'odham child-rearing rules: "Draw the children into your own life. Give them from birth love, companionship, and responsibility."[56] American teachers were, it seems, trying to inculcate values like personal responsibility that tribal members not only supported but worked hard to instill in their children. A disconnect between the goals of the majority culture and the shared values already present in the tribal culture led to missed opportunities for the school officials.

Minutes from a meeting of teachers in 1919 also suggest that underlying cultural assumptions were potentially undercutting the effectiveness of teaching. A lecture at the meeting by School Inspector Barnd, while urging sensitivity and professional behavior, reveals what was and was not occurring. Barnd urged teachers to follow five guidelines:

1. Spirit of sympathy and kindness is essential
2. Treat children as human beings and not like wild animals
3. To see things from the Indian child's point of view (e.g., a new language is learned one word at a time)
4. Interest is essential (don't go to sleep with your feet on the desk; the children may go to sleep also)
5. Interest, a chief factor in successful teaching (Humor, fun, and games promote interest; pictures of animals, fruit, and vegetables, also promote interest; stories are difficult to intelligently communicate for beginners).[57]

Urging teachers not to view their pupils as "wild animals" and not to sleep during class seem modest aims at best and suggests the existence of significant problems in Indian schools. But they also hint at a view of the pupils that was not academically ambitious or rigorous.

Beyond basic reading, writing, and math—and the emphasis on industrial or domestic training—a concern for "American" values like discipline and hard work was pervasive in the school curriculum. Once again this mirrors the national trend of native education that focused more and more on the creation of wage-based industrial workers.[58] As J. O. Barnd wrote about his work with the Maricopa Day School, "It is good to consider ourselves a part in the movement to make America truly American, by helping everyone to get at least a common school education. . . . Our teaching must reach beyond reading, writing and arithmetic; it must serve to develop proper character."[59] In another report he recommended a teacher should take a more authoritative approach to teaching, suggesting that, "In other schools and in their work they will be directed to do whatever is their work. For example, in dismissing your class, instead of saying, 'Those who wish to go out and play please stand. You may please go out.' I would suggest, 'It is time for recess, you may pass out quietly.'"[60] At a time, nationally, when mandatory public education was seen as the key to building a stronger nation, acculturating recent immigrants and avoiding class struggle, it was hardly surprising that Indian schools were also expected to assist in the movement from Indian culture to majority culture.

Instruction in patriotism was certainly a strong component of the effort to educate Tohono O'odham. A 1917 program for closing exercises at the San Xavier Day School included standards of childhood culture such as "Hickory, Dickory, Dock"[61] but also recitations on citizenship and the flag, the pledge, and songs about the nation. A report on the event stated, "The combination of the sylvan with the patriotic imparted a picturesque effect to the decoration." The author went on to say:

> The recitations were patriotic in character, and evinced the spirit of the day. Working for the Red Cross, by the girls, exhibited the manner in which children can assist this laudable movement so universally loved and revered. The brave soldiers and their Red Cross nurses in Patriotic Americans, were realistic in the extreme, bringing home to all the horrors of [what] was endured by our soldiers in foreign lands. The boys' recitation, Our Flag, awakened in all hearts every feeling of loyalty to our beloved country.[62]

The goal of inculcating proper patriotic values in the children, and the audience, is unmistakable. Ironically, the Tohono O'odham themselves, though some served in the armed services during the war, were not even eligible for citizenship until 1924; so this was at best "pre-citizenship" training.[63]

Closely related to the instruction in patriotism, the Presbyterians especially focused on training students for leadership—both ecclesiastical and civic. One list of goals for the schools, based on existing problems in the area, mentioned five items: need for adequate Christian leadership, development of better economic conditions, development of home life, improvement of health, and development of social consciousness, like democratic ideas. Notably the first and last mixed citizenship, religion, and leadership.[64] Records of the school also frequently point out that all the native elders, deacons, and church leaders in the area were former La Escuela pupils, as were tribal leaders, BIA workers, and other civic leaders.[65] Because the Presbyterians established a lasting school in the Tucson area prior to the Catholics (and as we will discuss below, because they demanded that their students learn English), they really had the advantage in cultivating future tribal leaders in the United States. While the majority of their students were and remained Catholic, efforts to reform the tribe politically such as through the Papago Good Government League were strongly led by Protestant graduates of Presbyterian schools.[66]

Perhaps the largest battle in schools was fought over language. Almost without exception educators believed that the speaking of English—and only English—in schools was crucial to the future success of their students. As one teacher wrote, "Forbidding native language in school is not cruel. It is infinitely more cruel to allow a child to grow up ignorant of English; and then be later obliged to compete with an English speaking community in gaining a livelihood."[67] If students were being prepared for assimilation into the national workforce, then English language skills were a component of both cultural and economic success. The use of English, and conversely the abandoning of native language, was a key goal of most schools. The situation that educators encountered on the Tohono O'odham and San Xavier reservations was more complicated than that elsewhere. Not only did many Tohono O'odham speak one of five native dialects, many also spoke Spanish as their second tongue. As noted earlier in the chapter, Catholic educators in the region were still teaching school in Spanish in the 1860s and 1870s (and probably later) and often taught in Papago as well. Furthermore, because of the two-village system, many Tohono O'odham migrated seasonally, spending part of their year in Mexico, where they were likely to be exposed to (if not use) Spanish. Not surprisingly, some Tohono O'odham attended school in Mexico, where the not dissimilar goal was to get them to lose their native language and adopt Spanish as their primary tongue.

Tohono O'odham student resistance to speaking in English was notable. One report about the Santa Rosa day school in 1920 notes that a ruling was put in place that students "must talk English at the dinner table, when asking for things, or not talk at all." Assumedly the desire for food would overcome resistance to English, but this report continues, "They (the children) have chosen the latter and have held out several weeks, but Mr. Benton hopes to win out in the long run and have them use English they are learning."[68] Similarly, a visitor to La Escuela reported, "English textbooks only are used, the children being required to learn that language, and does a child forget and speak in his own tongue, bread and water only, for so many days, reminding him that he has broken a rule."[69]

The adoption of English, however, proved not only difficult but a barrier to achieving other goals. For example, the insistence on English was viewed by some officials as an issue that drove students away and caused attendance problems. One day school inspector commented, for example: "At Santa Rose the problem of attendance must be overcome before too much stress can be placed upon talking English."[70] Speaking the English language was viewed as key to becoming truly "American," but teachers struggled continually to teach basic English literacy to Tohono O'odham children.

Thus schools mixed academic basics, especially in English, with lessons in patriotism, the values of the majority culture, and gendered vocational training. Ideally the curriculum prepared native children to assimilate into the majority culture, bringing the tribe along with them. Boys would become the ideal American male—yeoman farmers, ranchers, or (increasingly) wageworkers. Girls would move into their proper sphere, embracing domesticity as dictated by the ideals of the majority culture. However, the imposition of the majority culture through schooling was uneven at best. Often individual experiences varied greatly from the ideals, with unintended consequences. One striking example is found in the autobiography of Tohono O'odham leader Peter Blaine Sr. As historian Frederick Hoxie has shown, "Indian schools were 'racist' and 'class biased' in the sense that their explicit goal was the overthrow of traditional cultures and the imposition of 'civilized' lifeways. [Yet] neither Indian nor white children were to be exposed to haphazard, personalized learning. Rather they were to be introduced systematically to a common version of life in modern America." But this was not always the result. On a personal level Blaine found that school reinforced his native identity in a surprising way.[71] While as a child he spoke only Spanish at home, getting some exposure to Tohono O'odham at San Xavier, when he switched from St. Johns School to a local Catholic mission school he found "the fathers and sisters spoke Papago" and he began to learn this language.[72] Thus individual schools, and their faculty, greatly shaped the learning experience, as did student choice.

Student choices, as well as parental choices, shaped the impact of schools on native children in many ways. Written records are replete with concerns about poor school attendance among the Tohono O'odham and discussions of strategies for increasing enrollment. However, the reasons for nonattendance were complex and often not completely understood by those running the schools. Native records suggest a wide variety of reasons for children staying out of school. Distance and issues of travel, financial problems, the need for children's labor at home, and many other issues shaped family choices.

Those who were in charge of schools reported on the reasons children did not attend schools, but often dismissed those reasons out of hand rather than seriously exploring the issues. In 1921 the superintendent on the reservation reported on opposition to the Yuma school by parents: "they all object to sending their children there on the grounds that the children have insufficient clothing, no shoes and that the food is poor." His response to these concerns suggests an unwillingness to take the children's reports seriously: "Of course the children must have some excuse for running away and that is what they all tell their people. I do not know whether there is any truth in these reports or not as I have never been at the Yuma school."[73]

Another account relates to Chief Konerone, who did not support the attendance of his tribe's children at government schools. Konerone had two sons die while away at a Pima school and showed an unwillingness to send other children off-reservation to schools. The government's reaction to this was strong: the district supervisor for Indian Education hoped the chief could be persuaded to understand the deaths were no fault of the government. However, if persuasion failed, he urged legal action to bring the chief under the power of the law. Even the death of one's children was viewed as an unacceptable reason for resistance to modernization. In writing to Superintendent McCormick, the district supervisor stated:

> The Office understands Chief Konerone's attitude, but feels we ought to be able to explain to him that his sons' death was not due to lack of care on the part of the Government, and wants us to do so. I know you have tried to convince the Chief of his error, but I ask you to try again to overcome his prejudice against the schools. It would be well to give him a list of all the children that have died in one year on the reservation to convince him that his sons' being in school was not the cause of their deaths. . . . If he proves obdurate, do not hesitate to bring him to trial before the Indian Court on the charge of opposing the admission of children to schools contrary to the provisions of Section 1 and Section 2 of the Regulations concerning the enrollment of Indian Children in School, pursuant to Act of February 14, 1920. This should of course be done as a last resort—but the Office suggests that it should be done in case of obduracy. If the Chief is already at Florence, the effect on him would be more lasting if you secured the co-operation of the Florence school authorities to try him before the justice of the peace. A suspended sentence could be secured. This would make the Chief understand that compulsory attendance was the law of the land, and not merely a whim of the superintendent.[74]

One man, and his personal experiences or losses, was not to stand in the way of progress.

A more common reason for nonattendance was the seasonal migration of the Tohono O'odham and the need for children's labor at points during the agricultural cycle. A teacher commented on irregular attendance being tied to migration made necessary by poor weather conditions in 1920. Migration related to cotton picking in the Salt River Valley, which the OIA actively supported,[75] and copper mining also kept children out of school.[76]

Officials often took a strong stand on school attendance, utilizing a variety of legal options to compel parents to send their children to school. A 1903 report to the OIA provides one example of the struggle between community and authorities over school attendance and the harsh legal tactics used to bring tribal members under government control. J. M. Berger reported:

> An employee of the Phoenix Indian School called upon me for assistance to return about twenty pupils belonging to the school. Some of these children were runaways and others did not return after vacation and most of them were living among these faith healers [i.e., the least assimilated sections of the reservation], they being their parents or relatives. The Indians fully under control and influence of their female Chief healer, stubbornly and in a very independent manner refused to return the children to school and no arguing or reasoning with them was of any avail; I therefore put five of their leaders under arrest for refusing to return pupils to school and for resisting Indian Police and School employes [*sic*] in the discharge of their official duties, in accordance with Sec. 21, rules Indian School, 1900 and I sentenced each of them to thirty days imprisonment and manual labor on the Reservation. . . . As events have since shown, it was also a good lesson for them and it has undoubtedly broken, to a great extent, their rebellious spirit.[77]

Additional sources reported similar actions—mostly against parents who did not send their children to school and thus violated the state's compulsory education law. But a few reports talk about holding children who ran away in jail until they could be returned to their schools and made an example of.[78] While the prevailing view was to force children into schools—through the use of police and courts—as a way of both promoting attendance and bringing tribal members under control, there was at least one mention of using a carrot rather than a stick. OIA Commissioner Cato Sells suggested in 1915 that it might be more efficacious to avoid legal action by trying instead to sell parents on the idea that school is a privilege, so as to encourage them to embrace schooling in its own right.[79] But reports from later years suggest that Sells did not settle this issue in favor of his approach.[80]

Official reports aside, individual pupils told more complex stories—suggesting that while some strategies, like sending policemen into homes, had some efficacy, school attendance issues were far more complex than officials understood. Peter Blaine, for example, relates the end of his schooling to other life decisions rather than to educational progress or even desires. He explains: "I decided in the spring of 1919 that I wanted to go back to school at Phoenix Indian. I told my uncle that I wanted to go back in the fall. He said that my marriage was arranged and I couldn't go back to school."[81]

The records provide details on a few cases of successful negotiation between parents and OIA officials regarding school attendance, suggesting common sense and humanity sometimes made inroads on official policy. For example, in describing the case of Georgia in 1923, A. M. Philipson pointed out that she was a widow and kept her son at home because he was her only source of support, cutting and hauling wood for money. Philipson stated that he found this reasonable and suggested that her other son who was at school should be kept home next year so this boy could go instead. In another case a nineteen-year-old boy was not sent back to school as he was needed at home because of sickness in the family.[82]

For other children the path in and out of school was less clear; individual stories suggest that complex social and cultural factors, and perhaps fate, determined which schools many children attended and for how long. Here we can return to the case of James McCarthy, the Tohono O'odham featured at the beginning of this chapter. His literal and figurative wanderings into and out of school help us uncover realities that policies and records from officials barely hint at. In his autobiography McCarthy relates more than a decade spent at various schools. In the beginning his story resembles those sketched above—attendance at school brought about by police intervention. But subsequently he describes a mixture of agency, negotiation, and domination that colored many school experiences.

Native agency can also be observed in a rare petition filed by the Good Government League. In 1912 the league petitioned the federal government for a reservation day school, something they believed had been promised and was long overdue. Clearly recognizing the governmental preference at this time for boarding schools, these Presbyterian school-trained tribal leaders argued for a local school in a way that seemed calculated to appeal to the government. They began with a focus on patriotism by suggesting, "We want to become good and useful citizens of our great country, but how are we to become so if means for securing an education are not provided?" They then went on to find fault with boarding schools, suggesting that children who go away to school "are ashamed of our simple ways of living and very often they go to some distant American city never to return," and that children often become ill at boarding schools and cannot advance. The league instead put its hopes on local schools that would, they argued, best allow the tribes to embrace progress: "If our children are educated in our own villages they will help us to improve our ways of living and help us to live like our white brothers."[83] While willing to embrace the larger culture's emphasis on education for youth, the league worked hard to shape at least the location of that education.

Regardless of student or tribal agency, change in school policy would ultimately come not from within but without. In 1928 the Merriam Report offered an almost complete condemnation of the work of Indian schools, for reasons implied in this chapter. The report expressed grave concerns over the qualifications—or lack thereof—of educational personnel.[84] Perhaps even more importantly it asserted that

> the Indian Service has not appreciated the fundamental importance of family life and community activities in the social and economic development of a people. The tendency has been rather toward weakening Indian family life and community activities than toward strengthening them. The long continued policy of removing Indian children from the home and placing them for years in boarding school largely disintegrates the family and interferes with developing normal family life.[85]

Certainly this suggested a move away from boarding schools and toward community schools, an approach advocated by Catholic missionaries all along, and a shift of emphasis from "Americanization" to support of native community identity.

Future generations would find the plan for Indian schooling vastly altered, but through the early 1930s the complex negotiation over attendance, efficacy, and outcomes continued. Native education stands out as a contentious and highly contested issue. In large part the struggle was among three parties who wanted to shape the acculturation and education of the natives—Catholic leaders, Protestant leaders, and government officials. However, the Tohono O'odham themselves—parents, children, tribal leaders, and law enforcement—also had a great deal at stake in this struggle. As such, through petition, resistance, and co-option, tribal members did what they could to negotiate the nature, location, and outcomes of their participation in the growing educational system.

CHAPTER FIVE

Vocation

Of Men and Women, Farmers and Housewives

All worked for each other, but no money passed.

—PETER BLAINE, TOHONO O'ODHAM

Unlike many other Indians of the United States, the Papagoes are independent and self-supporting. They are making their own way and have done so for hundreds of years. However, they are pursuing such laborious methods of agriculture that it is distressing to see the men, women and children toil and sweat in the fields when we consider the very small returns which they get.

—JEWELL MARTIN, SUPERINTENDENT, 1917

The Tohono O'odham calendar reflected their traditional, often transnational, two-village subsistence system.[1] They had two homes, one for summer and one for winter, and a temporary camp for gathering the fruit of the saguaro cactus. The year began in the cactus-gathering camps in late June, where the Tohono O'odham collected saguaro fruit—as much as 450,000 pounds per year in the 1920s and 1930s—made syrup, and celebrated the Wine Feast.[2] They then moved to their summer field home, which was located in a valley where they awaited the arrival of the summer monsoon rains in July and August. There they practiced *ak chin* (arroyo mouth), or flash-flood farming.[3] Men would communally build brush dams at the mouths of arroyos to spread water onto their fields and construct dikes and *charcos* (earthen basins) with fire-hardened ironwood sticks to store excess water for use in the home.[4] Tribal elders would sing the necessary songs as women planted the wide variety of corn, beans, and squash seeds (as well as cotton, tobacco, sweet potatoes, tomatoes, green chilies, and devil's claw) saved from the previous year.

In general, men were responsible for tending to fields, a task that Underhill called "hard work for the men" because it consisted not only of weeding by hand, but also keeping a vigilant watch in the scorching sun to prevent predation by birds, coyotes, and other animals.[5] Meanwhile, women were responsible for harvesting and preparing food, though men did help with the harvest when necessary. Fontana estimates that the average family could provide for a fifth of their sustenance through this method.[6] While waiting for their crops to mature, men communally hunted a wide range of game, including feral cattle, "deer, mountain sheep, mountain lions, doves, rabbits, and other rodents."[7] Women, responsible for "the largest part of the family diet," went into the desert in groups of ten to fifteen to gather the "wild fruits, roots, seeds, and greens" of the desert.[8] They brought along the young boys and girls to assist, and so they could provide child care on the move. A couple of men followed with bows and arrows to make sure that the women were safe.[9] After the harvest in October, the Tohono O'odham would move to their winter well (or spring) village, where they had better access to water. They continued to hunt and also engaged in the domestic production of goods, like rope, pottery, baskets, and rawhide goods, which they often exchanged with the nearby Pima for products that they could not produce themselves.[10] They lived on stored foods and the gathering of plants that bloomed in early spring, such as mesquite pods, until it was time again to return to their cactus-gathering camps.

But change was coming. As in so many areas of native life, non-native peoples—reformers, government workers, and others—applied pressure on the Tohono O'odham to change the ways in which they did their work and engaged in their vocations. Yet as was the case with other reform efforts, whites would not achieve cultural hegemony in the area of vocation. Rather, the Tohono O'odham engaged in negotiation and adaptation, modifying the training and advice offered by the OIA to suit their needs and values. For example, as Peter Blaine notes in one of the epigraphs to this chapter, farming often maintained its communal (or reciprocal) nature: "At San Xavier three or four farmers worked together, plowing up a field, then moving on to another. They helped each other, no money was passed. The only thing provided was the food at noon. The wives of the working men helped. In harvesting the same way. All worked for each other, but no money passed."[11] In the end, however, the power of a market economy accounted for the greatest changes. Its appeal to many Tohono O'odham led to significant changes in vocation as the Tohono O'odham entered strategically into the cash economy.[12] As Peter Blaine suggests in his personal narrative:

> The people quit eating wild plants when the trading posts opened. The young don't want to harvest and gather what grandma used to get from the desert. Gathering seeds and buds is nourishment but nobody wants that anymore. When old people died the gathering and harvesting died with them. It's easier for the young to run to the store or the trading post. They buy a load of bread, while grandma used to grind her corn, her wheat for bread. Cook a pot of beans all day long. Who wants to do that now.[13]

Women were also drawn into the cash economy. The making of pottery had always been an integral part of the Tohono O'odham calendar year. Women made pottery in April and May, prior to going to their temporary saguaro fruit harvesting camps and just after the harvesting of cholla buds. As early as the 1880s, women (with their children)[14] started adding trips to eastern Arizona mining camps, mainly Tombstone and Bisbee, to peddle their ollas, pottery specifically designed to hold liquids, for as much as $1.50 each. They could make as many as fifteen ollas per day.[15] The story of this highly gendered transition—from traditional agriculture and domestic roles to ones closer to those of mainstream society—is the focus of this chapter.

In 1917 Superintendent Jewell D. Martin wrote a report about agricultural practices on the Tohono O'odham reservation. His observations are worth quoting at length:

> The Papago Indians thresh their grain by means of treading with ponies. They raise several thousand bushels of grain, reaping it by hand with small reap-hooks and threshing it in this way, winnowing it in the wind. . . . Unquestionably it would be wise to provide small threshing machines at each of the two large centers of Indian population [Topawa and Santa Rosa] which could be belted to these machines. . . . Later some progressive Indian in each of these communities will be found who will purchase for himself a gasoline engine and will operate this threshing machine as a portable outfit, but it is now contemplated only to use it at the pumping station for the first year, until the Indians become accustomed to its use.
>
> The Papago Indian women grind their flour and meal by sliding one rock upon another by hand. They have done this from time immemorial

> and they produce a good quality of flour and meal, but they do so at an infinite expense of time and labor. It is unbelievable that any people would contribute the amount of effort necessary to produce good, wholesome food by so crude a means and it can be explained only by saying that the most adverse natural circumstances have absolutely driven them to it.[16]

This description provides much insight into the views of the OIA in regard to Tohono O'odham farming and domestic practices. First of all, it describes what were viewed as the very labor intensive practices, by both men and women, to produce high-quality foodstuffs. It also makes clear that the OIA viewed these practices as gender specific, even prior to modernizing efforts. Beyond description, it also offers an evaluation of these methods shaped by the value and opinions of the majority culture. For example, "progressive" Indians were those who adopted technology, who embraced modern ways, who worked with the OIA. Anything else was a poor use of time and labor—wasteful and lacking. Thus "progressive" in this case was synonymous with good, traditional with flawed.

Later in the report, in the second passage quoted at the beginning of the chapter, the author notes something else equally crucial about the Tohono O'odham in 1917—they were self-supporting.[17] Why then, if the Tohono O'odham were self-sufficient and happy with their traditional ways, did the majority culture force agricultural modernization upon them even when it made them, at times, burdens on the state? The answer seems to lie, as it did with the question of monogamous, civil marriage, in the values of the majority culture—values that favored technology over physical labor; large economic returns over self-sufficiency; employers over laborers; and modern techniques over traditions. To become assimilated Americans the Tohono O'odham needed to embrace mainstream culture and values (as well as their proper place), regardless of the often unexpected costs associated with that transition.

At the time of the Dawes Act, tied to the implementation of allotment, the OIA set forth on a major campaign to assimilate Native Americans. Along with marriage, the eradication of vice, and education, changing vocations was a key element. The OIA aimed to shape native men into very specific types of farmers and ranchers and native women into idealized "American" housewives and domestic workers. The very concept of allotment was tied to a vision of the connections between property ownership, manliness, and citizenship. As Frederick Hoxie has suggested, "This statute assumed that landownership, citizenship, and education would alter traditional cultures, bringing them to 'civilization.'"[18] As Katherine Osburn has described in her study of the Ute, implicit in these ideas were highly gendered and patriarchal notions of male wage-earning heads of household and dependent female homemakers.[19]

Other historians, such as Susan Sleeper-Smith, have also highlighted the ways in which "the popular nineteenth-century perception that Indians were agriculturally unskilled was promoted by the desire to appropriate Indian lands."[20] Native Americans, perceived as landowners who failed to cultivate their lands, would best forfeit that land to others who could put it to good use. The case of the Tohono O'odham, though slightly different, followed these same patterns. Although Commissioner Cato Sells noted that the Tohono O'odham were industrious and self-reliant (and, wrongly, that they had never "shed the blood of a white man"), opponents of the Tohono O'odham Reservation argued that the federal government had set aside too much land for them. Alan B. Jaynes, head of the Tucson Chamber of Commerce, claimed in the *Tucson Citizen* that

> those interested are desirous of respecting the rights of the Papagos and are willing that the Indians should be allotted lands sufficient to insure them a good living but they rightfully object to this absurd action in tying up a domain greater in extent than several of the eastern states for the exclusive use of 5,600 Indians, belonging to a tribe whose population is not increasing and who will never make any beneficial use of more than one tenth of the land reserved to them.

The *Arizona Republican* also objected to the appropriation of some of the choicest acres for a tribe already well endowed with lands.

Then Democratic congressman of Arizona Carl Hayden complained that not only did Mexican Tohono O'odham send their children to Arizona to have them educated at taxpayer expense, but the creation of the reservation would undermine white mining and ranching in the region, thus destroying the region's tax base. He managed to get the secretary of the interior to send an inspector to the region, who suggested that the reservation be abolished. In the end, opposition to the reservation resulted in the elimination of a 475,000-acre strip as well as leaving it open to non-Indian mineral prospecting.[21] In the mainstream cultural view, resources were meant to be utilized. Leaving "excess" lands to Native Americans wasted them. Thus the motivations behind the promotion of modern agriculture were complex and mixed; but the policy itself simply focused on fundamentally changing Native vocations in both patriarchal and capitalist ways.

Reformers, if not tribal members, viewed a movement toward gendered vocations that matched those of the larger society as progress for tribal members. As George Hunt, governor of Arizona and reservation backer, wrote in 1914 in reference to the Tohono O'odham,

> I remember, when I came thirty-three years ago with a pack train down the Gila and up the San Carlos, the Apaches were then wearing only a G-string and moccasins, and seemed truly a barbarous race; and even though their advancement in all these years seems slow, still, as I look back and remember what they were even within my own memory and realize their transformation from warlike savages into quiet, peaceful farmers, I feel proud of our Government that has, within this comparatively short period, brought about such a change in its wards.[22]

This harks back to Thomas Jefferson's view of the nation—good Americans were quiet, peaceful farmers. The transformation of the Tohono O'odham into "American" farmers was the way of progress.

The "American value" of hard work was believed to be lacking in traditional native vocational pursuits, and was noted as a character flaw or perhaps even a moral deficiency of native people. As one OIA superintendent wrote: "I believe the underlying principle involved in the problem is the fact that so many of our Indians, especially those of this reservation, do not feel the necessity for work such as the average white man feels." He pointed out that this "failure" to embrace a most basic American value was both cultural and biological: "The centuries and centuries of heredity back of the Indians are, were and will continue to be for sometime antagonistic to regularity in industry—no race or people can escape that biologic and fundamental fact or law. We must not expect too much until we have at least balanced the past. For his own sake we should demand the best of each individual, but we should not be too disappointed if he is not able to escape his limitations."[23] Natives needed to be saved from themselves and from their traditional ways. Billman, a Presbyterian superintendent of La Escuela, made a similar point when he said, "We propose to civilize the Indian by teaching him the beauty of the blistered hands. Among my own people I used to exhort, Remember the Sabbath day and keep it Holy. Now, I bear down on the Indian boys and girls, 'Six days shalt thou labor.'"[24]

Looking at this issue from another angle, historian Nancy Cott, in her work on marriage in the United States, writes: "To Christian settlers, missionaries, and government officials, Indian practices amounted to promiscuity. Since first contact, they had derided Indian men for laziness and lack of manliness because they went out hunting and did not exert authority over wives and children, as heads of households, and did not own property or cultivate land."[25] As was discussed in chapter 3, legal, monogamous marriage was a key to Americanization. However, it was not enough to ensure assimilation into mainstream society. To properly assimilate, Indians required not just the existence of legal families but mainstream gender roles within those families as they related to economic activity. Traditional ways seen as flawed, like hunting (feral cattle and other prey) for subsistence, would have to be changed to ways and roles, like raising and breeding cattle and hunting only for leisure, that matched those of the larger society.[26]

From early in the nation's history, American leaders had embraced a theoretical model that equated subsistence agriculture with a "lack" of social development. As David Rich Lewis writes in his book on agrarian change and American Indians, "From the 1830s on, government officials, missionaries, and reformers emphasized the possibility of Indian development and assimilation—'through the states of the hunter, the herdsman, the agriculturalist, and finally reaching those of commerce, mechanics, and the higher arts.'"[27] An evolutionary development of vocation—for both men and women—with the ultimate goal of inclusion into a capitalist market-driven culture, was crucial to the acculturation of tribal members. Because almost all Native Americans lived in rural areas and three quarters of them were engaged in agriculture in 1910, assigned gender roles corresponded closely with rural life.[28] Thus the adoption of "modern" vocations—farming and ranching for men, housework and domestic production for women—was the logical goal of assimilation efforts, crucial to changing the very nature of Native Americans.[29] It is important to recognize that this view challenged Native notions of gender. Traditional native ways that featured men as hunters and women as cultivators, for example, were viewed as a means to idleness for men and slavery for women.[30] Thus reformers looked, among other things, to improve men and save women through instruction in proper vocation.

The Tohono O'odham, though in some ways unusual in their farming methods and climate, were not immune from this policy, a policy based on assumptions about the nature of agriculture, modernization, the importance of a cash economy, and perhaps most importantly gender. By considering the writings of agency workers, we can begin to understand the motivations and goals of these vocational efforts, and to see the ways in which they were contested, altered, and sometimes accepted by the Tohono O'odham.

In a 1917 report, Samuel Eliot of the Board of Indian Commissioners wrote: "The Indians at San Xavier should be encouraged to farm their allotments with closer application and more persistent industry. Many of them continue to earn their living primarily by wood cutting and then hauling the loads of wood into Tucson where the driver and wood cutters are inevitably exposed to temptation."[31] Tribal members needed to be instructed and encouraged to become better, hardworking farmers rather than being distracted by a quick buck and the big city. Other vocations that showed a lack of industry—and perhaps character—could easily lead to trouble. Reinforcing this idea, the commissioner went on to write about the cotton industry in the Salt River Valley where eight thousand acres were picked by workers, including Native Americans and especially Tohono O'odham: "What our Indians need most is to be taught to work. There are nearly 50,000 Indians in Arizona, and a very small percentage of them do any useful work."[32] This was a mischaracterization. The Tohono O'odham did respond to the perceived need for massive, low-paid seasonal labor in the Salt River Valley, adopting, according to Fontana, "a new kind of migratory pattern." This type of cotton—which Goodyear, Firestone, and Dunlop needed to make tires—was grown domestically only in the US Southwest; World War I had cut off American producers from their overseas suppliers. The fact that natives responded in such large numbers as they did—Fontana notes that "the total numbers of Papagos living on or off the reservation at any given moment afforded a reliable indicator of what was happening in Arizona cotton farming"—is rather surprising, given the working conditions.[33] As historian Thomas E. Sheridan explains, they were abysmal:

> Most pickers lived in camps unfit for animals. They slept in tents or overcrowded shacks. They drank from canals. There were no showers, no laundry facilities, and no electricity. Some camps did not even have running water or outhouses. The pickers were paid 1 1/2 to 2 cents a pound, and an entire family was lucky to make $18 a week, half of which . . . evaporated as repayments for the debts the workers accumulated in company commissaries that charged exorbitant prices.[34]

Arizona's historical attempts to limit the influx of Mexican laborers (which was especially supported by pro-union progressives like Governor Hunt), inability to recruit seasonal laborers from outside the state, and the 1917 passage of the Immigration Act, which placed a head tax on and required a literacy test for foreign workers, put corporate planters in a bind. They could either improve working conditions and wages or actively recruit Native Americans and Mexicans (in spite of the Immigration Act) to work in substandard conditions. They chose the latter.[35]

Three groups of OIA officials were on the front lines of vocational reform—the agency farmer, the field matron, and the agency stockman. The OIA expected each to train natives of a particular gender for occupational roles in mainstream society. The male half of the equation was to be shaped and improved under the close guidance of agency farmers and agency stockmen. Across the nation Indian agencies reported hiring farmers in large numbers in the last decades of the nineteenth century. David Rich Lewis has documented that in the last decades of the nineteenth century and the first of the twentieth, about 80 percent of agencies hired farmers.[36] The Sells agency was not an exception.[37] While the Tohono O'odham had not traditionally approached agricultural labor in the way ascribed to most tribes, they were still viewed as needing vocational reform to bring them into the modern world. Agency stockmen played a less central role overall, particularly in the case of the Tohono O'odham. Perhaps the best indicator of this was the fact that the OIA named José X. Pablo, a progressive Tohono O'odham graduate of the Presbyterian La Escuela, as the tribal stockman in 1917.[38]

To "create" the male half of the equation, the modern farmer and rancher, the OIA fashioned policies focused on land use, agriculture, and ranching. However, changing the agricultural structure of the tribe was a nearly impossible task given desert conditions that were not well suited for agricultural techniques developed elsewhere and independent tribal villages with often very different connections to the local economy, resulting in stark class differences.[39] Ranching also faced severe environmental obstacles. Though much time and energy was spent trying to "modernize" farming and ranching practices, these efforts were not entirely successful. In fact, in spite of the drilling of twenty-nine wells, access to 17,500 acres of arable land, and farming instruction, by the end of the 1920s only 850 of approximately 5,000 Tohono O'odham living in the region were engaged in OIA-directed agriculture, the main occupation that the OIA wanted to promote; those outside of the "Presbyterian, cattle-rich sections [of the reservation] in the southeast" supplemented their non-OIA-directed subsistence farming with occasional migrant labor, mining, and wood collecting.[40] The OIA's failure might be explained in many ways—some having to do with policy and personnel decisions made by the OIA, others having to do with Tohono O'odham resistance and agency. Meanwhile, the majority of Tohono O'odham who engaged in raising cattle did so "for subsistence rather than for commercial reasons."[41] Furthermore, most Tohono O'odham refused to cull their herds in the manner promoted by the BIA because doing so "meant a reduction in generosity, in status."[42] In other words, it undermined tradition. In fact, the Tohono O'odham reluctance to manage their herds, and OIA insistence on it, nearly undermined the OIA's efforts at establishing a reservation-wide tribal government in the mid-1930s.[43]

There was some recognition that the native agricultural situation was unique. In fact, some OIA officials—counter to the national trend—argued that sending Tohono O'odham children away to boarding schools to learn farming techniques was sure to backfire, as the conditions in the Papaguería were unique and the farming methods needed to overcome those conditions would have to match the conditions. OIA Superintendent Jewell D. Martin told his superiors that "it would be better if their young could be trained under the same peculiar environment where they are to battle Nature for a living."[44]

In 1914 the superintendent of the Tohono O'odham wrote a report clarifying all the issues at hand. For their part the Tohono O'odham, he believed, were "well versed" in the methods of dry farming best suited for the region. He even admitted that white settlers in the area would never be able to make a profit. However, this was not to suggest that OIA efforts were in vain:

> I do not wish the Office to receive the impression that they cannot be assisted in this important industry of work along this line among the semi-nomadic Papagos. For instance, in many places they use small plows and even crooked sticks with small degenerated Indian ponies hitched to do their plowing; and their harrowing is performed by dragging mesquite logs and brush over the fields. This is manifestly a waste of time and effort and they should be furnished with good plows and all labor saving implements and equipment suited to their needs of dry farming.[45]

One assumes that the OIA then intended to teach the Tohono O'odham how to use their newly earned spare time to engage in domestic production for market. In fact, they already did this, but received little credit for it.

OIA officials, though they recognized that the Tohono O'odham had agricultural practices uniquely adapted to the desert climate of their ancestral homelands, nonetheless pointed to the much greater efficiencies that could be had if tribal members would introduce modern methods.

Tohono O'odham were seen as needing direction by superior whites, mostly because of their lazy cultural ways. "These Indians all know how to farm in general but they need to be incited and impelled and told when to plant, as they are prone to defer their plowing, planting, etc. till the last minute; they procrastinate and have the climatic 'Manana' habit too much. This urging and hurrying up, with the furnishing of more suitable tools and implements with which to cultivate their land, is the principle [*sic*] work of an additional farmer."[46] The issue, the superintendent suggested (conflating them with Mexican migrant workers), was more one of character than ability. With the right work-related values in place, the Tohono O'odham would thrive economically. Presbyterian missionaries offered similar views of their efforts to train boys to be farmers. One described the work on the farm lands of La Escuela: "sixty acres of cultivated farm land at the school have much to offer the Indian boys not only in agricultural lessons but in new hope of being able to make a living from their un-reclaimed grant of land down in 'the Papago country.'"[47] Clearly the Presbyterians had a different definition of making a living than the Tohono O'odham, who, as noted earlier, had been self-sustaining for countless years.

To accomplish the change in agricultural practices, the OIA brought in an agency farmer to provide a "demonstration farm" as a means of showing what could be accomplished with irrigation and the application of modern farming methods. Yet, for reasons that will be discussed shortly, the demonstration farm was often an utter failure. The OIA also kept track of and promoted the example of "full-blooded" Tohono O'odham farmers such as Hugh Norris, Toribio Aragon, Lucas Moreno, José Manuel, and Federico Rios, who successfully grew staple crops such as hay and wheat for sale in Tucson.[48] In addition, they promoted the modern methods of twenty-eight "progressive" Tohono O'odham cattle ranchers located in Coyote Village, San Pedro, Little Tucson, Indian Oasis, Topawa, Komalick, San Miguel, Vamori, and Cowlic.[49]

Accordingly, an OIA agency farmer trained the majority of men on how to "modernize" their agricultural production, transforming their seasonal "two-village" system into one that focused on the intensive cultivation of monocrops for the market.[50] If successful, this would have transformed the Tohono O'odham from transnational people into modern US yeoman farmers. The OIA officially tasked agency farmer A. M. Philipson with convincing the Tohono O'odham to adopt modern farming techniques.

To do so, Philipson held an annual Papago Indian Farmer's Institute at the San Xavier Day School. The institute featured specialists on horticulture, forage crops, and livestock from the University of Arizona in addition to local county government officials. The program was aimed at "the general improvement of farms, farm products and live stock on the reservation . . . the marketing of any products they may have to sell and the purchasing of anything that may be needed in large quantities."[51] Those engaged in ranching worked with stockman José X. Pablo. Lewis notes that there was less resistance among the Tohono O'odham to the adoption of livestock raising than there was to monocrop agriculture.[52] Likely this was because the Tohono O'odham had "considerable experience in working with cattle" by the twentieth century, along with the fact that Pablo worked most closely with the Tohono O'odham from the reservation's southeast, who had the largest herds and were predisposed to adopting modern methods.[53] It was Pablo's duty to pick men from each village to take part in the annual roundup and branding, to oversee the sale of tribal cattle, to introduce new breeds and modern breeding to the herd, and to work with Anglo ranchers whose cattle might (and often did) get onto the Tohono O'odham Reservation.[54] We can gain a sense of what the annual roundup was like, as well as the gendering of cattle raising, from an essay that Sonny Chico wrote at St. Anthony's day school in Topawa:

> Mostly all Papago boys are cowboys, at some time. The spring or calf round-up is a time of hard work and fun for us. A four horse wagon carries the food, dishes and blankets to the round-up. The cook drives the wagon. The wagon moves wherever the men go. The cook tried to stop near water. He makes a fire. The cooks gets breakfast, dinner and supper for the cowboys. The food we get is meat, bread, beans, and coffee. The cooks gets up early to get breakfast perhaps 3 o'clock. When breakfast is ready the cowboys are soon out of their blankets. They pull on their boots, roll up their blankets and wash and then they are ready. Each man gets a tin plate and helps himself. The men sit on the ground to eat. There is much work to do at the round-up. Each man knows what he is to do. In the spring the calves are branded. Each day some of the men drive in the cattle from the desert and mountain sides. They drive the cattle to a corral. Then two men work together. They ride into the herd and drive out a cow and her calf. The calves are roped and branded. Then they are turned loose. They find their mother again. Every mother cow knows her calf. Each cowboy has his own brand. Then he can tell which cows are his. Our brand looks like this [drawing of brand]. . . . After supper the cowboys sit around and smoke. They talk about the horses and cows.[55]

However, the expansion of livestock raising, along with the introduction of "new plant species and livestock breeds" and the maintenance of traditional values of generosity and reciprocity, would overburden the "fragile ecosystem" of the Papaguería.[56]

In addition to providing positive examples, the OIA also promoted technology as a solution for age-old problems. For example, Superintendent Martin pointed out in 1917 that the Tohono O'odham's entire process of harvesting and processing grains could be improved. At the time of his report, the Tohono O'odham reaped their harvest by hand and threshed it using ponies and the wind. Women then took the grain and ground it by means of a metate. Jewell suggested instead that the government provide the Tohono O'odham with gasoline-powered pumps for their wells that could also be hooked up to threshing and grinding apparatuses. He estimated that running them even just two days a week would provide the Tohono O'odham in the area easy access to water and eliminate the need for horses to thresh grain and women to grind it.[57] Thus he hinted here at vocational changes brought about by modernization that impacted not only men as farmers but women as housewives. We will return to this last point in a bit.

These changes were accepted, but not without modification by the Tohono O'odham. Such was the case when it came to vocational training for youth.[58] The majority of the Tohono O'odham who were in regular contact with the OIA were open to sending their children to school for vocational training and the introduction of modern technology and farming methods as long as they worked to tribal members' advantage. When they did not, the Tohono O'odham pushed back. For example, the superintendent of the Phoenix Indian School, John B. Brown, ran into serious parental resistance when he refused to let children leave the school early to attend to their families' agricultural needs. It is obvious from the record that Brown did not believe most parents when they said that their children would be "actually and continuously engaged in farming." Brown demanded that the Tohono O'odham provide him with signed affidavits from the superintendent or OIA farmer before he would release children into the custody of their parents.[59] The archival records are rife with such requests, suggesting that many parents learned how to leverage local powerbrokers—such as the superintendent, field matrons, and farmers—to balance both their desire that their children be educated and their need for the children's agricultural labor. In addition, and perhaps more importantly, many parents pulled their children from school after only a couple of years, taking advantage of educational opportunities at an age when their children were of little use on the farm (and would require looking after).

The Tohono O'odham also pushed to transform agricultural modernization programs more to their liking, especially when OIA personnel failed to respond properly to local needs. The case of OIA farmer Wilbert O. Hodgson provides an excellent example. When he arrived in Arizona, he set up his demonstration farm—as well as a separate personal farm—in Tucson, about sixty-five miles from the Indian agency's headquarters and a good distance from most of the Tohono O'odham engaged in agriculture. In addition, he filed several mineral claims on the reservation.[60] His devotion to the assessment of his mineral claims (located north of Indian Oasis, later renamed Sells), his personal farm in Tucson, and his family (also in Tucson) left him with little time for the Tohono O'odham. These initial actions no doubt convinced the Tohono O'odham that Hodgson did not have their best interests in mind. They pushed successfully to have the demonstration farms transferred to the Indian agency headquarters in Indian Oasis. When this did not bring about Hodgson's renewed dedication to the Tohono O'odham, twenty-seven tribal leaders wrote a letter directly to the commissioner of the OIA, Cato Sells. The letter is remarkable for a number of reasons, not the least of which is the clear expectations they had of the agency farmer's duties and priorities. These ranged from keeping the local roads and bridges in functioning order to overseeing the disbursement of water to providing the Tohono O'odham with agricultural advice to noninterference in tribal matters.

In regard to the roads and bridges, tribal leaders not only expected Hodgson to maintain existing infrastructure, they expected him to work alongside the Tohono O'odham that he employed. Two of their major complaints related to his failure to do so. First, after assigning Indian workers to infrastructure upkeep, Hodgson would return to his home in Tucson. Second, he would tell them to leave the government-owned tools that they were using at the worksite when they finished, promising to pick them up later. When he failed to make his way back in a timely manner and the tools disappeared, he blamed the Tohono O'odham for stealing them.

Tohono O'odham tribal leaders also wanted to install a dam on the East Santa Cruz River so that they could capture and disburse the water before it was used up by the inhabitants of Tucson. Their complaints regarding water management were more pointed. In the first place, they questioned whether Hodgson should have control over the running of the irrigation pumps; they thought the OIA engineers could do better. In addition, they argued that Hodgson had replaced the experienced water overseers, who had historically worked communally, with inexperienced tribal members who did not know how to best cooperate to maximize efficiency.

The disagreements about the new water overseers also imply that water was not being disbursed to the liking of tribal members. It highlighted the fact that the Tohono O'odham did not take lightly changes to their tribal structure that did not provide benefits.

Not surprisingly, given his investment in a farmstead in Tucson, Hodgson was against this. But the Indians had two damning accusations: "That he don't [*sic*] show us much about farming," and that "he can talk all about farming, but by looking at the fields where he is located we think he don't [*sic*] know any more than we do." Not only did they expect the OIA to send them an expert who could help them to modernize their agricultural methods and practices, they expected Hodgson to come to their fields and work alongside them.

Finally, the Tohono O'odham expected the OIA farmer to refrain from interfering with tribal business. On a number of occasions, Hodgson intervened in cases that had already been settled by tribal judges. The Tohono O'odham were not against some interference by the OIA; they agreed that the superintendent had the authority both to appoint tribal judges, with their approval, and to assist in settling tribal disputes. The farmer, however, was put there to look after tribal agriculture—nothing more and nothing less. They noted ironically that this was one occasion where Hodgson could actually be found out in the countryside instead of in Tucson. In the end, the Tohono O'odham asked the OIA to replace Hodgson and send them someone "that will help us."[61]

Although Hodgson was able to hold on for another year, Tohono O'odham resistance to him demonstrates the ways in which they embraced certain aspects of the OIA's modernization program—especially those that helped to improve their lives—and tried to gain control over other aspects all while working to limit its impact on tribal culture and ways of life. Many Tohono O'odham did not doubt that they had much to learn from the OIA and its employees. Nonetheless, they also wanted to have an active voice in exactly how the OIA delivered its modernization program and what its priorities were. They expected the OIA to respond to their needs, be it letting their children out of school prior to the end of the school year or building dams and wells in locations that maximized their access to irrigation water.

More importantly, they expected OIA employees to respect them enough to be willing to work alongside them. Perhaps this was why there were few complaints about stockman Pablo's OIA work;[62] he not only worked alongside them and advocated on behalf of the tribe, he was one of them and was already a successful rancher prior to being named to his post. The fact that Hodgson was more interested in advancing his personal economic agenda than in promoting the well-being of the Tohono O'odham was not lost on them. The fact that he was only willing to talk to them, not work with them, was unacceptable. When later farmers, such as A. M. Philipson, placed the needs of the Tohono O'odham ahead of those of non-Indians in Tucson, the Tohono O'odham responded by creating civic, social, and fraternal organizations such as the Tohono O'odham Farm Improvement Society and attending the annual Papago Indian Farmer Institute in large numbers. Although Philipson was later accused of diverting OIA resources to the local school district that his children attended and although he continued to force Tohono O'odham parents to send their children to school for the entire school year, a practice frowned on by many Tohono O'odham members, tribal members increasingly collaborated with him and even approached him for help with personal matters.[63] Indeed, although the agency farmer's job was to increase agricultural and ranching productivity, the written record suggests that, as mentioned in a previous chapter, OIA farmers spent time on many issues other than agriculture, such as combating vice and enforcing mandatory schooling for children. These moral issues were seen as the necessary underpinnings to create effective, modern farmers and ranchers. As has been discussed, these ancillary roles were the most controversial.

In the end it was the environment that forced both sides to compromise and adopt methods other than those the OIA was pushing nationally. By 1918 McCormick was admitting:

> The Papagoes have a system of farming of their own in which they are very successful if they get the proper amount of rain. To discourage them in their method of farming and have them adopt the improved methods would result in a total failure; about the only thing that is lacking under their system is that they do not cultivate their crop a sufficient number of times. Last year under their own method of farming they raised the finest pink beans in the State and took first prize at the Arizona State Fair. The total amount of land under cultivation on the Reservation at the present time is about sixteen thousand acres. In a normal season this land is all in crops, but the past year has been very dry and but very little farming has been carried on in the lower country.[64]

In the cultural negotiation over agricultural practice, neither the OIA nor the Tohono O'odham won; rather the reality of the environment modified the intentions of both.

Moving from farmer to housekeeper, we see similar efforts by the OIA to shape vocation along gendered lines. We also find contestation of those ideas, modifications, and even in some cases acceptance as reformers pushed women to adopt "traditional" domestic roles in their homes and in the homes of others. The workers most specifically responsible for working with native women were undoubtedly the field matrons of the OIA. The field matron program was established by the Bureau of Indian Affairs in 1890.[65] The commissioner of Indian affairs at the time wrote, "If intelligent, earnest, practical women could be sent among the Indians to instruct women . . . substantial progress in Indian civilization would be thus effected."[66] While the training of men had long been undertaken by the government, and reservation and nonreservation schools had focused on children, women—except as school students—had received little attention. With this in mind, the initial goal of this new program was for women from the dominant US culture to live and work among the natives, teaching them American cultural values and domesticity. Ideally, matrons would prepare native women to live like their "civilized" white counterparts, by providing them with the training and sensibilities necessary to run a happy and healthy home.[67]

Like the archetypal Progressive institutions of the day—settlement houses—which offered educated, middle-class women the option of professional, paid work, the field matron program offered women a paid, full-time job with the government. Women who chose to become field matrons worked for the Indian Office and were stationed on or near reservations throughout the West. Some stayed on the job only briefly, but many viewed the position as a career. The number of matrons in the field varied greatly. In the early years fewer than a dozen women were employed, but that number grew in the twentieth century, peaking twice—in 1912 and again in 1918—at around ninety. By the late 1920s, the program was gone, but for more than thirty years it aimed to change the lives of native women.[68]

For several decades, field matrons, and their homes, served as important points of contact for white women and Tohono O'odham women. Matrons working with the tribe included Lydia Gibbs (1911–1914), Minnie Estabrook (1914–1916), Janette Woodruff (1915–1929), Mary Doyle (1916–1930+), and Libbie Light (1929–1930). Based on the national norm, these women were most likely Protestant and single, though occasionally wives of Indian Bureau officials and other married women took jobs as field matrons. Many viewed their work as a field matron as a career choice. Janette Woodruff, for example, spent almost thirty years in government service, working with three separate tribes.[69] One matron considered here, Mary Doyle, was a rare exception to the norm in that she was actually Sister Alfrida, a sister of the San Xavier Mission; another, Libbie Light, a former public school teacher from Ohio and mother of three boys, was married to William A. Light, a longtime Indian Service employee.[70]

To get beyond official bureau statements about the field matron program and its goals, and really understand what was happening on the ground, we need to look at the writings of these women. They left behind a series of reports, often addressed to their higher-ups, describing their activities, the problems faced by the women they worked with, and their demands for resources to serve the population.

These reports give historians a fairly clear picture of the matrons' job. The reports make it obvious that matrons had to complete paperwork as part of their job, but there is little indication that the matrons spent much time at their desks or that they worked anything like regular business hours. In fact, their tasks seem to have been hands-on, were quite varied,

Figure 5.1 "Living poster" for health teaching. 1 Thin Girl + Milk = 1 Fat Girl. (Courtesy of University of Arizona Libraries, Special Collections, University of Arizona, Cooperative Extension Service, Photographic Album of Activities in Pima Co., 1922–1930, AZ-520.)

and required service to many segments of tribal society. For example, field matrons were responsible for dealing with tribal health. This included offering classes on baby care, instruction on common health concerns, and a major campaign to eradicate the house fly from reservation homes. In addition to public health, matrons were also involved in wider domestic education campaigns focused on topics like needlework and sewing and food preparation.

Matron Mary Doyle reported progress in 1920, giving us some insight on the "skills" viewed as necessary for good housewifery. "The progress of the class in domestic science is very satisfactory. They are becoming quite proficient in the making of light bread, biscuits, and fruit pastry, as well as their laundry work."[71] Her 1919 annual report shed even more light on both her views of the natives she worked with, and of the "proper" roles they should be assimilated into. Once again it is worth quoting at length. She begins with an evaluation of their backwardness: "It is indeed gratifying to note some changes, which are indicative of progress not a few of them being departures of customs from time immemorial. The Papagos are as you know, a conservative people, and cling tenaciously to all the traditions and usages of their tribe." She then continued to note her particular version of progress:

> The cleanliness of the homes and premises, which I noticed on the occasion of these visits is certainly worthy of remark as is also, the tasteful adornment of their interior. There is no doubt in my mind but that this new regime is the fruit of the Mother's Meetings. Neatly made curtains of pleasing pattern hang at the windows and pretty cards on the wall. Dish cupboards made of fruit boxes one over another provided with the screen or netting to protect the contents from flies, while the mosquito bar placed over the babies' cradles serves the same purpose. The tables are covered in a similar manner. Several new sewing machines have been added to the number already in use, and the work done on them is highly creditable. Not the least deserving mention are the layettes of excellent make and design.

Issues of taste and design and adornment seem key here, perhaps even more than health concerns, which did receive some comment. She continued:

> The young women and girls, often frequent the sewing room to do fancy work and crocheting, and have turned out many articles both useful and

> ornamental. It is at such times, that they especially enjoy unexpected treats I serve them. . . . The children's cleanliness of person and neatness of dress receive due need of attention, and are often the subject of comment. Greatly to my satisfaction, many of them are so neat and clean when they come to school, that it is unnecessary to change them, though it not infrequently happens, that it becomes my duty to see that they regularly attend.[72]

Wives and mothers were trained in both the useful and the ornamental. Cleanliness was praised above all things—as a sign of civilization and sophistication.

Another OIA report made similar assertions: intelligence was equated with embracing the modern, progressive and civilized with material goods.

> In the southern part of the reservation, adjacent to the Mexican line, the Indians are more advanced, more progressive, more alert and quicker to take hold of new things than the Indians in other parts of the reserve. There are more houses with corrugated iron or shingle roofs, with two or three rooms, with wood floors, with windows and porches, in the southern part. There are seen more stoves, beds, sewing machines, scrubbing boards, better stock and more road improvements.[73]

This report reflects two facts: First, the OIA had, from the beginning, paid little attention to the Tohono O'odham living away from San Xavier/Tucson or the southern (and more accessible) parts of the reservation.[74] Second, the southern portion of the reservation was the center of the Catholic and Presbyterian missionaries' struggles for Tohono O'odham souls, and thus represented the location of greatest investment.

Matrons were also educators in a broader sense, offering counsel on a variety of topics—topics that suggested the matrons' views on gender ideals. As Janette Woodruff reported, "My work as field and outing matron involved much more than the two words seemed to imply. It made me mother, physician, nurse, financial manager, spiritual adviser, chaperon, and arbiter in domestic disputes."[75] As was discussed more fully in the previous chapter, the types of behavior that were considered appropriate were consistently discussed in field matron reports where matrons worried about protecting women from "influences." Those included women of bad reputation, men, and drink.[76]

The need to provide advice and counsel was seen as particularly acute when dealing with individuals who had left the reservation and gone to work in the cities. Though the matrons to the Tohono O'odham were field matrons, they also ended up serving as outing matrons—helping individuals to find jobs in the city of Tucson and elsewhere and serving as intermediaries when employment and social problems arose. While women were trained to be good housewives, some, especially young unmarried women, were recruited to work as domestics and washerwomen in Tucson. Woodruff wrote: "I actually conducted an employment bureau, finding work for the red unemployed, and providing suitable help for the whites who were in need of it."[77]

Here we find one of the anomalies of the OIA policy. Ideally native women were to be trained to be good housewives, properly dependent on wage-earning husbands. However, employment opportunities available in Tucson were most often domestic jobs—jobs that involved laundry or cleaning—and were thus considered women's work. Young, unmarried Tohono O'odham women found wage-earning opportunities that ran counter to ideas of dependency. Often these positions were temporary, held in the years prior to marriage and child-rearing. However, there is

Figure 5.2 Woman cleaning laundry, Little Tucson, Arizona, 1941. (Courtesy of Department of Special Collections and University Archives, Marquette University Libraries, #11012.)

substantial evidence that women continued to work as laundresses, and sometimes housekeepers, once they were married. Often the most available connection between families and the cash economy came through the mother rather than the father.[78]

Thus many Tohono O'odham women sought paid work in the city as domestic workers and washerwomen throughout their lives. In 1917 Woodruff reported: "There has been many more Indians move in from the country, every home is full, and some homes have two families in. The ones that came in from the country tell me there has not been enough rain to make their wheat grow, and it is drying up. . . . The first part of the week every woman that has to help earn the living is working in town, leaving at home one of the larger children to take care of the smaller ones, and to clean up the house."[79] When new agricultural methods failed to produce prosperity—especially during dry years—women moved in greater numbers out of their homes and into those of white families. As a result, both young women and married women often took jobs for cash as part of their family's overall economic strategy. Though this meant moving into the paid workforce, it was in very gender-specific, and thus acceptable, lines of work.[80]

Perhaps it was because of this tension that when the matrons wrote about this part of their job, they seldom discussed a desire to create good workers or satisfy the needs of employers. Instead, there seems to have been an overwhelming concern for the moral well-being of the native girls they worked with and a focus on providing the girls with protection and a safe place for recreation and leisure. As was discussed in chapter 3, a Victorian sense of the need to protect women from corruption pervaded the matrons' records. In some cases, the concern was to protect girls from the wrong sort, generally referring to Mexicans and railroad workers. Woodruff reported: "There were delinquencies among the Indians as a matter of course. . . . White teachers tried to build up ideals, but the proximity to low standards sometimes created a situation that was destructive to the general morality of the community."[81]

There is some evidence that the wives of Presbyterian missionaries in the region also worked as pseudo-outing matrons from their homes in Tucson. A historical account of the Presbyterian work noted about Superintendent Herndon's wife: "Since the government had no field matron to supervise the Indian girls who were working in Tucson, Mrs. Herndon supervised in that capacity for many years. She placed those girls who desired to work as maids in homes and acted as counselor in difficulties which arose between the girls and their employers. She also planned social occasions for them in their free time."[82] While Presbyterian records also are clear that their schools were raising wives not maids, they made an effort to support and protect girls engaging in paid work in the city.

Though reformers expressly said that they were not trying to produce maids, they nonetheless did advise girls on how to become good workers and bargain for a job in the cash economy. This was something the OIA increasingly focused on during the first decades of the twentieth century. Woodruff recalled: "When I put them in homes I teach them to talk with the lady first, to find out what there is to do, and how many in the family, and whether they want her to cook, or to be a helper, and tell them what wages they want. If the girl chooses to work for less that is up to her, but if she wants to wait until we can get another place, she can do so."[83] Native girls were receiving specific instruction on labor and wage negotiation. This, coupled with the skills of a "proper" housewife, made them effective workers in the market economy.

Thrift was a value commonly encouraged by matrons, another sign of training for life in a cash economy. Matrons provided advice on thrifty spending habits and the starting of saving accounts. As a mark of success in this area, Mary Doyle reported in 1920: "You will doubtless be both surprised and pleased to learn of the progressive attitude manifested by several of our women. Desiring to purchase certain articles of clothing, they consulted me as to the advisability of sending away for them, since they could procure them at a more reasonable price."[84]

Matrons also encouraged the Tohono O'odham to save money and to spend wisely. They got women under their guidance to set up accounts at local banks and, during World War I, to purchase war bonds. After a number of tribal members sold land for a profit, Woodruff reported:

> I took charge of the little sums as they came in to make the weekly payments, and reminded the forgetful ones not to spend their money for something foolish until the property was in complete possession. Truly, before I realized that this was to be one of my spheres of action, I had become unofficial financial adviser for most of the Indians in the village. I helped my people start bank accounts, and taught them how to make deposits and write out checks. It required long practice before even the most self-confident would trust themselves to write out a check without the supervision and moral support of some trusted white person.[85]

In another case she reported working with a woman who had debts, no source of income, and real needs.[86] To become Americanized, Tohono

O'odham women needed to ascribe to a specific view of domesticity and they needed to embrace the cash economy.

Thus, although agency farmers and matrons envisioned very different gender roles for the natives under their guidance, they ended up supporting a shared goal for both men and women: movement into the larger capitalist, cash economy. While men were tasked with producing agricultural products for sale, women were to be educated as domestic workers, consumers, and savers.

In some ways the work of the farmers and matrons can be viewed as a success. As David Rich Lewis has noted, this process of modernizing Native Americans was more or less complete by 1940. At that time "most groups had been fully incorporated on the periphery of American society and market economy."[87] As Tohono O'odham tribal member Peter Blaine suggests in a passage quoted early in this chapter, the opportunities and appeal of capitalism dealt a serious blow to tribal traditions. Not the least of these challenges was the paradoxical situation caused by the training of women as modern housekeepers. While the intention may have been to create wives similar to those in the middle class of white America, the training actually opened the world of the cash economy to female Tohono O'odham. In fact, the long-term impact of the outing system seems to have resulted in the exact opposite of what the OIA wanted. Eric Meeks notes that by the late 1960s, a large percentage of Tohono O'odham women lived in Tucson, engaged in the cash economy, and were putting off starting a family. Perhaps more startling, the Tohono O'odham nation elected Vivian Juan-Saunders in 2003 as the first female chair of the Tohono O'odham nation with 59 percent of the vote.[88]

Providing a bit of irony, records tell us of at least one case where a Tohono O'odham became perhaps too much of a capitalist. A newspaper account tells of a Tohono O'odham named Blaine who was charged with changing the numbers written on a check he had received as payment for firewood: "'I raised the checks because I did not think I got enough for my wood, and I wrote the amount that I thought I ought to get,' is what Lawrence Blaine, clever young Papago who is charged with raising two checks from $2.50 to $5.50, given him in payment for wood, and passing them on Hymen Gold, a Meyer street merchant, said yesterday to officers." Blaine cheerfully admits that he did the neat job of check raising, but his novel defense is that he only raised the amount to what he believed to be a just price for the wood.[89] An unintended consequence of capitalism was crime!

As a final side note, it is worth considering that the choice of moving into the cash economy would not serve the tribe well, especially those from the more conservative areas of the reservation that relied on cash wages, as the Great Depression hit. Superintendent J. W. Elliot reported in 1931:

> There is a group of Papagos, under this jurisdiction, who live at Tucson, and who depend largely upon such work as they are able to secure among the white population for a livelihood. These people, due to the great amount of unemployment which prevails, are in very poor circumstances this year, and we fear the coming Christmas will be a dismal, cheerless event for many of them. In fact, the Indian people generally are seriously affected by the existing depression.[90]

James McCarthy recounts the need for government intervention, especially the Indian Division of the Civilian Conservation Corps (CCC-ID), throughout the 1930s when jobs were scarce.[91] Having made the shift from self-sufficiency to engagement in a larger economy, the Tohono O'odham, like many minorities, found themselves in a particularly precarious position during national economic downturns. It is ironic perhaps that as self-sufficiency was shed in favor of inclusion into the larger society, it was the problems of American society—rather than its benefits—that the Tohono O'odham often experienced.

CHAPTER SIX

Mexico

A Counterexample

The tribe has been notably stable in racial qualities during centuries of contact with whites. Intermixture to-day rarely takes place except in Sonora, where the Mexicans have taught the Indians new customs.

—CARL LUMHOLTZ, EXPLORER, 1910–11

I was born right here in Pozo Verde on February 13, 1917. I have always lived here. My daughter, Julia, was born on Tohono O'odham lands about one mile south of the boundary on May 22, 1951. My husband was born on my Nation's lands to the north and worked on both sides. I remember when there was no boundary. We O'odham just came and went as we pleased.

—RITA BUSTAMANTE, 2001

What might the Tohono O'odham Reservation and San Xavier Reservation have looked like if the OIA, the Bureau of Catholic Indian Missions, and the Presbyterian Homes Mission Board had not—for better or worse—taken an interest in the Tohono O'odham and their welfare?[1] What if there had been no reservations? No attempt to "detribalize" and then assimilate the Tohono O'odham through the transformation of their gender roles? Perhaps some answers can be provided by the history of the Tohono O'odham in Sonora, and the Mexican government's similar efforts at "liberating" indigenous people of their "language, customs, and culture" through *mestizaje*—an ideology of race and cultural mixing—and *indigenismo*—an elite-led attempt to redeem indigenous people by transforming and modernizing them—in order to assimilate them into mainstream society.[2] As Mary Kay Vaughan has made clear, the postrevolutionary Mexican government used gender as a focal point of its assimilation efforts.[3] It is also becoming increasingly clear that these uses of gender as prescriptions for assimilation (as well as the ideology and practice of indigenismo) predated the Mexican Revolution.[4]

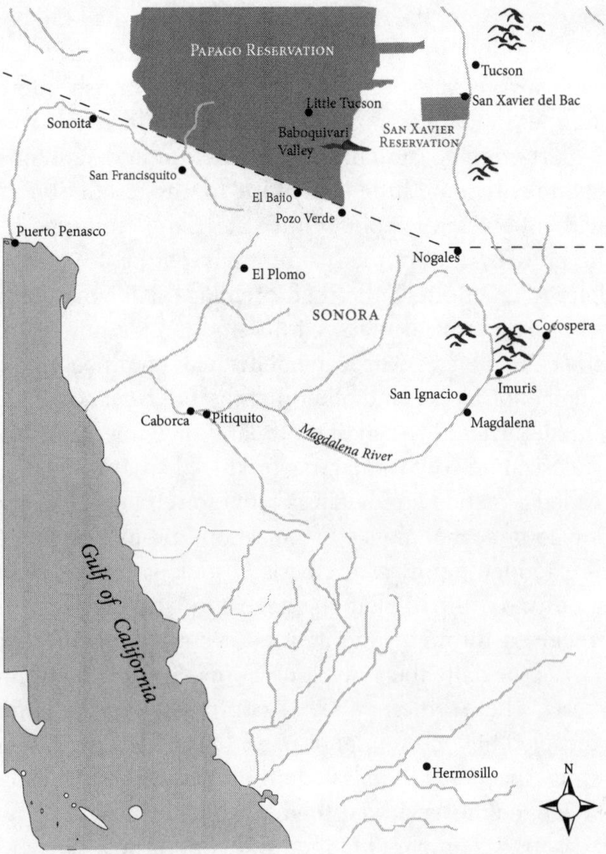

Figure 6.1 Tohono O'odham villages in Mexico. (Map by Tracy Smith.)

Previously we have argued that the Tohono O'odham Reservation in the United States was located at the edge of two empires, a place where local officials like Father Bonaventure, Reverend Herndon, Matron Woodruff, and Stockman Pablo had much more power in shaping the terms and application of policies that had been made at some distance from the region. We have also noted that although the region was located at the edge of an empire, Arizona was economically linked, especially after 1880 and the arrival of the Southern Pacific Railroad, to the industrialized East Coast and its powerful mining and ranching concerns and West Coast commercial centers.[5] Likewise, Sonora had long been on the periphery of Mexico. Sonoran elites transformed the state from an isolated frontier outpost in the 1850s to a cattle, agricultural, and mineral exporter that was more closely connected with the US economy than with the rest of Mexico by the turn of the century. In fact, Sonora had rail connections with Arizona but only limited access to internal Mexican markets. As a result, foreign investors, especially American and British interests, came to dominate the Sonoran mining and rail sectors, largely leaving the less lucrative export-oriented agricultural production and ranching to traditional Hispanic elites, and little if anything for the rest of Sonorans.[6]

Along with an economic policy aimed at maximizing exports, Mexican federal land policies undermined communal (corporate) rights and identity and thereby sanctioned "the theft of village lands by wealthy hacendados" and proletarianized many campesinos.[7] Like how allotment was viewed in the United States, Mexican intellectuals saw this as a positive good, preparing indigenous folks (and other members of rural corporate communities) for modernization. In addition to land divestment, state authorities pushed secularization. Both programs produced what historian Elizabeth Dore has called a "gendered liberalism" that served to undermine the state and its ability to protect corporate organizations, promoting in its place the male-ruled extended family as the basis of society. Land divestment and secularization undermined women's access to land—both the commons and land received through inheritance—even as they bolstered patriarchy.[8] This was especially the case along Sonora's northern frontier and in the Papaguería, where settlements were composed mainly of military colonists who received title to their lands in exchange for their military service against raiding Apaches, which lasted until around 1880.[9] Because of their military service, colonists viewed themselves as civilized (*gente de razón*, people of reason) as compared to their indigenous neighbors, whom they considered uncivilized and backward.

By the 1890s, given the official replacement of communalism with individualism, the "'Indian social problem' that remained to be solved," argued famed Mexican intellectual Justo Sierra, "was largely a matter of reforming individuals, with better schools, a better diet, and . . . through mestizaje."[10] This complete assimilation would eradicate individual indigenous identities, creating a single unified Mexican people composed of men and women with their own spheres of influence and their own specific duties. Of course, the social construction of gender is locally and regionally constructed, and conceptions of proper gender roles along Sonora's northern frontier were no different.[11] Northern frontier women belonged in the home where they were to practice selflessness, self-sacrifice, and the willingness to give up their public existence for the benefit of others. Nonetheless, they were expected to hold "a measure of moral authority over men," preventing them from engaging in excessive drinking, gambling, and other unsavory activities that might undermine their ability to work and support their families.[12] Northern frontier men's gender identities were based on the ideals of warriorhood and hard work. Properly socialized men were honest, generous, and dedicated to protecting their families and local communities; in the process they gained control over their household, and the women and the children in it, as well as the right to "patrimonial leader[ship] in the political sphere."[13] Perhaps historian Debra Cohen said it best: "In brief, proper manhood required being a head of a household that included a wife, children, extended family, and often unrelated members. This kind of man worked hard, provided for his family, and monitored and controlled the labor and sexuality of his wife and children without abusing the privilege of control."[14] But if indigenous people settled at the outskirts of the colonies were unwilling to either adopt these norms by assimilating into mainstream culture or to open up their ancestral lands to "civilized" outside developers, the federal government engaged in a war of extermination. In Sonora, the power of the state was especially brought to bear against the Yaqui and the Seri, but the Tohono O'odham were not left unscathed.[15] Federal officials tried not only to assimilate campesinos and indigenous people into mainstream norms, but also sought to transform them by promoting the influx of European, and then later, Chinese immigrants into the region.[16] Historian José Angel Hernández notes that even these new immigrants were required to Mexicanize themselves and serve as role models for the "backward" campesinos and indigenous people already settled there.[17] Mexico's efforts, at both attracting migrants and having migrants serve as a transformative force in the regional community, were not very successful, leading Porfirian officials to promote expansion of primary schooling as a means of training Mexico's homegrown population of supposedly backward mestizos and indigenous people. The federal government, however, lacked the resources to do more than promote the idea of expanded education, resulting in a focus on expenditures in central Mexico and an under-institutionalized federal, and state, government in the rest of the country.[18] This remained the case long after the Mexican Revolution; even when the federal government was able to fund expanded primary education, the federal government's presence and power to transform people's everyday lives remained ephemeral.[19] Even at its peak of strength under Cárdenas (1934–1940), the federal government was, in the words of noted historian Alan Knight, more of a "jalopy" than a "juggernaut." In other words, Mexico's northwest borderlands fit the criteria for a weak state with little capacity to redirect a strong, and often mobilized, society.[20] Most importantly, the federal government lacked the ability to tame capital and, in many cases, its own mobilized citizenry.[21]

Here it is worth recalling the background offered in chapter 1, because it sets the context within which the Tohono O'odham lived even as the OIA and Catholic and Presbyterian missionaries reached out to them in the United States (and occasionally in Mexico when, for example, Father Oblasser and Reverend Herndon followed their charges and attended the annual Tohono O'odham festivities in Magdalena). This background is also worth revisiting because it was the absence of the state as an actor on the behalf of the Tohono O'odham as Tohono O'odham, and sometimes the state as an actor against the Tohono O'odham as Tohono O'odham, from the time of the collapse of the missions in the 1830s until the creation of the National Indigenous Institute (INI) in 1938 under President Lázaro Cárdenas, that resulted in the very different outcome in Mexico.[22]

Federal protection, or lack thereof, of Tohono O'odham ancestral lands was the key, though not only, difference between the disparate outcomes on each side of the border. As Eric Meeks argues, a land base sufficient for subsistence farming and herding allowed the Tohono O'odham in the United States to enter the cash labor market on their own terms in the United States. In addition, it was the loss of a land base in Mexico that forced the vast majority of Tohono O'odham to move to cities, where they were more likely to assimilate into mainstream culture.[23] And it was the cotton industry, in alliance with government and religious officials in Arizona, that made ample use of Tohono O'odham seasonal labor, and pushed back against the Tucson Chamber of Commerce's attempts to gut the Tohono O'odham Reservation in 1917. They had reason to, because it was from the most "isolated" and "traditional" communities, deep within the reservation, that major employers drew most of their laborers. This arrangement, though not as good as the restitution of all of the ancestral lands, also benefitted the Tohono O'odham. The end result was that "migration in and out of the developing industrial economy permitted families to incorporate wages into their subsistence strategies while maintaining a relatively high degree of control over the direction of cultural adaptation within their communities."[24]

This contrasted sharply with the situation in Mexico where the Tohono O'odham entry into the cash economy proletarianized and assimilated them as they lost control over their ancestral lands. In the words of environmental historian Donald Worster, the proletarianization of workers turned them into an "anonymous human army" and in the process destroyed their sense of community.[25] We turn to that story now.

In Mexico, the Tohono O'odham did successfully defend militarily their ancestral lands against the eighteenth-century Apache threat. They proved no match, however, against the steady flow of internal Mexican migrants in search of gold, silver, and ranching lands. The Tohono O'odham did not face a state-led war of extermination like the Yaqui and the Seri, but that is because, other than the El Plomo incident in 1898, they had on the whole, by the 1840s, adopted nonmilitary methods of defense.[26] Had they continued to militarily defend their ancestral lands like the Yaqui and Seri, there is little doubt that the federal and state government would have mobilized to violently force them off.[27] In fact, the government did so in Caborca, Pitiquito, and Altar between 1905 and 1908, compulsorily conscripting many of the newly landless Tohono O'odham into the military to use against the Yaqui.[28]

One option was defending their lands through Mexico's legal system. The Tohono O'odham embraced this option but saw few successes given a government that refused to recognize them as a corporate (i.e., tribal) entity prior to 1938.[29] Landownership claims based on the Tohono O'odham being there since time immemorial fared poorly in Porfirio Díaz's legal-rational "Order and Progress" modernization program. In fact, Díaz's regime hired foreign land-surveying companies in the 1880s to identify "vacant" lands—that is, lands without legal title—so that the lands could be auctioned off to the highest bidder.[30] In addition, the surveying companies were paid with title to a third of the "vacant" lands that they identified, incentivizing them to overestimate unused lands and commodify land at the same time. Not surprisingly, this led to a concentration in landownership among elites, both foreign and domestic, such that the richest 1 percent of landowners owned as much as 85 percent of all land. Famed historian Friedrich Katz calls this assault on indigenous and rural corporate landholdings "the greatest catastrophe in the history of the Mexican peasantry since the massive Indian mortality of the sixteenth and seventeenth century."[31]

In spite of this assault, the Tohono O'odham continued to use the available legal tools to protect their land, and reclaim lost land, in the 1920s and 1930s when the federal and state government, in response to the massive mobilization of rural people during the Mexican Revolution (1910-1920), began to take a greater interest in both campesinos and indigenous people and their well-being. For example, Tohono O'odham leaders in Sonoyta and Pozo Verde petitioned state and federal officials to win back their ancestral lands and, equally important, regain access to water. As Andrae Marak has argued, these early attempts generally resulted in inaction, the status quo, or the Tohono O'odham's expulsion.[32] State and federal officials were trying to balance the political need to assuage the wants of their rural constituents and their desire to promote increased foreign investment.[33] In the case of Pozo Verde, federal officials spent several years defending the rights of the San Carlos Cattle Company and its US representatives, Jesus M. Zepeda and Mose Drachman, against Tohono O'odham claims. The company, based in Tucson, had received title to Tohono O'odham lands as a result of the land surveys of the 1880s. There was no doubt that the land deeds and titles were legal. In fact, the federal government had given the Tohono O'odham legal ownership of three square miles of nearby land at the same time. But since the lands surrounding the Tohono O'odham's officially deeded lands "clearly . . . belonged to their ancestors" since "time immemorial" and since no one had tried to occupy them, they had seen no reason to attempt to claim them in the 1880s, especially given the Porfirian political climate favoring foreign investors.[34]

A major break occurred for the Tohono O'odham in 1924 when the federal government classified Pozo Verde as a *congregación* so that it would qualify for consideration under the postrevolutionary agrarian laws. Qualifying did not mean, however, that it was a done deal. For example, the Calles regime denied Tohono O'odham claims in Sonoyta in 1927. Nonetheless, just as he was about to leave office in 1928, President Calles created the Pozo Verde ejido, setting aside 7,675 acres of communal property for the Tohono O'odham.[35] This minor victory should not be overstated. The further loss of land in the 1930s led to the majority of the remaining Tohono O'odham crossing the border to settle in the United States.[36]

Those that refused to permanently migrate to the United States had few options other than partial assimilation and intermarrying with non-Tohono O'odham, as they did in Sonoyta, or settling on the fringes of non-Tohono O'odham settlements as a distinct minority. An example of the latter was the barrio in Caborca called "la Papaguería."[37] The observation at the beginning of the chapter by noted explorer Carl Lumholtz during his 1910–11 journey through the ancestral lands of the Tohono O'odham is evidence that they had already adopted these strategies in the early twentieth century, even if he was wrong to claim that Mexicans "taught" them these new customs. Fontana corroborates Lumholtz's statement, noting that

> after the 1850s such former Papago settlements as Cocospera, Imuris, San Ignacio, and Magdalena were basically non-Indian in their makeup.

> Farther to the west along the Río Altar and at the Pitiquito and Caborca, Papagos continued to live. But as the nineteenth century wore on, they found themselves living as members of a minority population surrounded by more powerful and affluent Mexicans.[38]

Nonetheless, just as the assumption that more "traditional" Tohono O'odham were less likely to engage in the cash economy was wrong, so too was it incorrect for contemporaries to view racial purity as the standard for cultural integrity. In fact, the reverse was probably true. Those Tohono O'odham who most held on to their traditional culture were viewed by outsiders as being racially pure. This assumption was based, at least in part, on the nineteenth-century ideal of mestizaje, or racial mixing, which asserted that there was a direct connection between biological race and culture (i.e., advancements in culture were positively correlated with increased whiteness) and, more importantly, that the fusion of whites and Indians—biologically and culturally—was both inevitable and, for the most part, beneficial. By reverse logic, remaining racially pure, at least in the case of Indians, was positively correlated with backwardness and the inability to change.[39] As Alan J. McIntyre has pointed out, the Tohono O'odham had a long record of adapting "remarkably well to succeeding incursions of dominant Spanish, Mexican, and American cultures, interferences, and influences."[40] Although Tohono O'odham intermarriage with non-Tohono O'odham was an open secret among tribal members, contemporary observers often failed to notice Tohono O'odham adaptability or denied people of mixed ancestry their indigeneity. Instead, they assumed that those who maintained their tribal culture were "full-blooded" and those who did not were mixed race.[41]

Anthropologist Jack D. Forbes, for example, has touted the pliability of the Pima in noting that "by the early 1900's the Pimas were also [like the Opata] being absorbed rapidly into the Mexican population," but contrasted them with the Tohono O'odham, claiming that "the Papago were continuing to live in almost aboriginal fashion."[42] Mexican officials drew similar conclusions, insisting that tribal members were naturally lazy and did only enough to satisfy their most basic needs.[43] They attributed these supposed characteristics to their race. Officials were often blinded by their own assumptions. For example, after the head of federal education in Sonora, Elpidio López, sought out Francisco Domínguez, a Tohono O'odham who had attended an Indian boarding school in Mexico City aimed at assimilating indigenous children, to ask him to help in the federal efforts to assimilate other Tohono O'odham into mainstream Mexican society, he reported that Domínquez's boarding school education had failed. Instead, López asserted, Domínguez had reverted to the "savage" customs of his ancestors.

In fact, López happened upon Domínguez as he was gathering firewood to sell in Tucson. Although Domínguez was neither interested in becoming a teacher for the Education Ministry nor in settling down to become a yeoman farmer—a difficult prospect at best in a desert with only seasonal rains, measured by the ideal used as a standard by government officials for assimilation/civilization—he had adapted quite well to the regional cash economy. López was simply incapable of seeing through his own ideological blinders; Domínguez could both be Tohono O'odham and adapt to the regional economy, even if it was not on the terms that the Education Ministry had hoped.[44] What the Education Ministry hoped for was that the Tohono O'odham would act more like their fellow Sonoran indigenous neighbors, the Seri Indians. Between 1926 and 1928 the desert-dwelling Seri negotiated increased governmental involvement in their community. In exchange for expanded access to government funds and resources, the Seri agreed to give up their migratory lifestyle of fishing, hunting, gathering, and petty trading for the sedentary life of yeomen farmers. They constructed a pueblo in Pozo Peña (near Kino Bay) around a 115-by-115-meter plaza, including a new schoolhouse, modern houses and outhouses, and perhaps most importantly for the Education Ministry, a road that would connect them with "civilization" and make it easier for them to sell both their excess farm production and the craft goods that the women and children would be trained to produce. The men would be allowed to continue hunting and fishing to supplement their agricultural production, but women and children would no longer be allowed to go along or engage in gathering. Instead, women would remain in their homes carrying out craft production and reproductive labor, while children would attend school. Not surprisingly, the Seri were unable to eke a living out of their local environment as yeoman farmers, and the experiment failed miserably.[45]

Domínquez provides us with just one example of how the Tohono O'odham confronted economic and social changes in Mexico without the support of a government willing or able to create a large reservation. Geographer Kenneth Dean Madsen notes that the US–Mexico border, coupled with historical Tohono O'odham two-village connections, also played a major role. Mexican Tohono O'odham villages that had strong ties across the border with sister villages, especially those on the eastern end of the Papaguería such as Pozo Verde, continued to maintain those connections.[46] Hence, Domínguez took advantage of Education Ministry resources in Mexico but also tapped into the market economy of Tucson as well as (presumably) US government resources on the Papago and San Xavier Reservations. But for members of Mexican Tohono O'odham villages that had historical ties with sister villages on the Mexican side of the border, the options were much more limited. Many of these Tohono O'odham migrated from their ancestral desert villages to nearby cities as a result of federal and state land and water policies. Guillermo Castillo Ramírez has traced these migrations for Tohono O'odham who, after leaving the desert and their two-village way of life, ended up in Caborca and Sonoyta. In fact, Castillo Ramírez argues that the 1930s were the last decade in which the Sonoran Tohono O'odham were firmly rooted, both physically and socially, in the desert. The Tohono O'odham suffered "severe transformations" during the two following decades, leaving their desert villages "practically vacant" and separating them from their symbolic and practical connection to the desert. By the 1960s they were more or less fully incorporated into urban centers. In spite of these geographical changes, and the changing social practices that accompanied them, the children and grandchildren of these desert-dwelling O'odham still identified themselves as O'odham.[47]

Lest we overstate our argument, we acknowledge that the federal and state governments did not simply and consistently act against the Tohono O'odham and their interests. As was true in the United States, the different levels of government and different government entities in Mexico were not unified actors and often worked at cross purposes. In addition to the many governmental institutions working against the Tohono O'odham, those that might have been predisposed to work in their favor—namely, the Education Ministry—were mostly absent. As previously noted, prior to the Mexican Revolution the federal government was more or less nonexistent in the Sonoran countryside, and state elites were tied closely to US economic interests. The 1920s saw the first concerted effort to expand the federal government's reach. Noted intellectual José Vasconcelos, who advocated a "cosmic" mestizo race as the outcome of modernization, tried to kick-start rural development by promoting an "each-one-teach-one" literacy campaign, sending out "cultural missions" to teach rural dwellers new, more productive habits, and encouraging the incorporation of indigenous people into mainstream Mexican society.[48]

As part of this campaign, the Education Ministry established a primary school for twenty Tohono O'odham children in Pozo Verde in 1923; the goal—like that in the case of the Seri referred to earlier in this chapter—was to Mexicanize the Tohono O'odham: turning the men into yeoman farmers and the women into proper housewives who also produced petty goods for market. Although there is no direct evidence, later events suggest that the Mexican government's decision to place a school in Pozo Verde resulted from the very strong connections (and resources) that residents of Pozo Verde had with their brethren in the United States. In fact, as a result of Pozo Verde's strong transnational connections, the school had more resonance in the United States than it did in Mexico. Thomas F. McCormick, the superintendent of Indian affairs in Sells, was surprised by the Mexican government's intervention on behalf of the Tohono O'odham; indeed, we found no records of this school in state or federal archives in Mexico. And although McCormick was wrong about the Mexican government setting aside land for the Tohono O'odham in Pozo Verde in 1923 and about the teacher's salary, his response is worth relating in full:

> A rather surprising arrangement has taken place at the Poso [*sic*] Verde Indian village which is just across the line in Mexico. This village is inhabited by Papago Indians and the Mexican Government has set aside a track of land consisting of a league each way from the center of the village. They have started a school and have an enrollment of twenty Papago children. No Mexicans live inside of this land grant. The Government pays the teacher seventy five dollars per month and furnishes her with living quarters. The Indian children are taught the Spanish language. This village has been occupied by Papagoes for generations but have never before got such recognition from the Mexican Government. Practically all the Indians living in Poso [*sic*] Verde have relatives living on this side of the line. I mean in the United States, and at one time or another reside in the United States with some of their relatives. The location of this village is very desirable, there being a spring there with sufficient amount of water to do a little irrigating. I understand that we have nothing to do in this matter. I only make this report to let the Office know about the attitude of the Mexican Government towards the Indians. It is such a marked change as to the treatment the Indians in Mexico have received in the past.[49]

The ties that residents of Pozo Verde had with Tohono O'odham on the US side of the border would be reflected later when the US government counted residents of Tohono O'odham villages with strong traditional connections to the United States as official members of the tribe in the 1930s. But the Mexican government's focus on Pozo Verde also highlights the fact that outside of this one school, there is no evidence that any of their educational programs had a meaningful impact on the Tohono O'odham in Sonora.

It was not until 1928 that the Tohono O'odham and the Education Ministry again made contact, with the contact being initiated by the Tohono O'odham, not the Education Ministry. José X. Pablo, a "progressive" Tohono O'odham, member of the Good Government League, an employee of the OIA, and a resident of the southeast portion of the Papago Reservation with strong ties to Pozo Verde, approached the Education Ministry to ask for a major investment of resources immediately after the Calles administration set aside Tohono O'odham lands in Pozo Verde.[50] Pablo, with the help of Reverend Herndon, Father Bonaventure, and other local notables, had effectively done the same thing a decade earlier after the establishment of the Tohono O'odham Reservation in Arizona. The 1930 census highlights Pablo's connections to Pozo Verde and its Tohono O'odham governor, Antonio L. Bustamante. Pozo Verde was the only Sonoran settlement where Tohono O'odham self-identified as Protestant. Additionally, a large number of Tohono O'odham there spoke only Tohono O'odham and English, suggesting their strong connections to the United States and the likelihood that they had attended the Presbyterian school there. Bustamante, for example, often sent letters and petitions on behalf of his constituents in Pozo Verde from Arizona. Finally, a number of inhabitants went so far as to indicate that their primary residence was in the United States.[51] Pozo Verde is located right across the US–Mexico border from the Presbyterian's main stronghold in the Baboquivari Valley, also facilitating these connections. No doubt, Pozo Verde continued to be part of their two-village migratory pattern.

Education Ministry officials seemed amenable to Pablo's overture, hoping that they could assimilate the Sonoran Tohono O'odham into Mexican society as well as, it appeared, Pablo had assimilated into US society. The head of federal education in Sonora, Fernando F. Dworak, went so far as to share his surprise with his superiors about the "elevated concepts of this indigenous Papago [Pablo]."[52] They recognized, however, that they could not meet Pablo's demands of matching the investments that the OIA had made in Arizona.[53] The Education Ministry sent David Torres Orozco, a federal education inspector, on a fact-finding mission, where he reported that the majority of Tohono O'odham were scattered across the desert or located on the fringes of towns, making investing in them difficult. He also worried that the Tohono O'odham's strong brand of Catholicism would make them difficult to modernize.[54] This is particularly ironic given that the Tohono O'odham who had reached out to him were Protestants. Notably, Mexico's postrevolutionary anticlericalism was against organized Catholicism, not religion in general.

When a year had passed and the Education Ministry still had not responded to Pablo's request for additional resources, Bustamante renewed the Tohono O'odham's appeal. In response, the local education inspector, Gustavo A. Serrano, told his superiors that given the Tohono O'odham's lack of access to water resources, the SEP would have to invest at least ten thousand pesos for wells, agricultural equipment, and training to incorporate the Tohono O'odham into mainstream society. Serrano did not think the investment worthwhile, arguing that the Tohono O'odham were already incorporating themselves into US society and culture and that the SEP had little chance of overcoming that obstacle.[55] Of course, he was basing his report on the community that arguably had the strongest connections to the United States and was most strongly influenced by the Presbyterian Church and Reverend Herndon. Interestingly, Castillo Ramírez has argued that it was Tohono O'odham connections in both Mexican cities and the United States that displaced them from their ancestral lands. Castillo Ramírez focuses on the escape valve that migration offered the Tohono O'odham.[56] We would add two factors to his assessment. First, Mexican officials' knowledge of this escape valve made them less likely to advocate on behalf of the Tohono O'odham.[57] Second, Tohono O'odham displaced from their ancestral lands who came from villages without transnational connections to the United States would likely not have registered as indigenous people to educational inspectors since their living in urban areas would reconstitute them as mestizos. In any case, when the Education Ministry did send personnel out to the Tohono O'odham, it tended to be either in response to Tohono O'odham inquiries, to recruit more Tohono O'odham for the indigenous boarding school in Mexico City, or at the behest of other local officials. In the third case, which also occurred in Pozo Verde, we cannot be sure that these local officials were not pressured locally by Pablo and Bustamante.[58]

In this sense, the attempts by Pablo and Bustamante to leverage US investment in the Tohono O'odham Reservation to gain similar investment in Pozo Verde backfired. One problem was that in the United States the OIA paid the Tohono O'odham for infrastructure improvements such as road and school building, providing some tribal members temporary jobs in the cash economy, while in Mexico the SEP demanded that the Tohono O'odham donate the labor and materials.[59] Another problem, at least from the point of view of the Education Ministry, was that the Tohono

O'odham would only accept SEP support and investments on their own terms. For example, Tohono O'odham officials in Sonoyta would agree to send their children to school only if the Education Ministry would create a Tohono O'odham-only school on the model of Indian day schools in the United States. Unlike in Caborca, in Sonoyta the Tohono O'odham lacked their own barrio and worried about wholesale assimilation into mestizo culture.

In San Fransiquito the Tohono O'odham demanded that the Education Ministry assign them a female teacher who spoke English and Tohono O'odham, again demonstrating their connections with the United States; when the SEP assigned a teacher who did not fit this profile, they pulled their children from the school. The Education Ministry did manage to set up one Tohono O'odham school in Pozo Verde in exchange for naming Bustamante the Vocal del Comité de Educación, thus placing the school under the authority of the local Tohono O'odham leader with strong ties to the United States.[60] Overall, the number of Tohono O'odham children attending Mexican schools remained negligible, and it was not until 1939, when President Cárdenas granted the Tohono O'odham land in Puerto Peñasco, that the federal government again reached out to them.[61]

In the end, in the absence of a robust governmental effort on their behalf, Tohono O'odham adaptation strategies provided them with a viable future, but a future with fewer and fewer possibilities in Mexico. The example of the former boarding school graduate Francisco Domínguez collecting firewood for sale in Tucson demonstrates that the Tohono O'odham had readily adapted to new economic realities. But the Tohono O'odham loss of both land and access to water in Mexico left many of them unable to engage in either agriculture or ranching. The ancient Tohono O'odham practice of *niári* dictated that, given the harsh and unpredictable nature of the desert, all must share the bounty of their harvests with others in need. McGee noted that by the 1910s more and more Tohono O'odham families residing in Arizona were turning away from the practice as their Sonoran brethren were increasingly unable to reciprocate. This was only one of the negative impacts of mestizo depredation of Tohono O'odham resources. Additionally, as already noted, the Tohono O'odham used the contacts they had made through their two-village lifestyle to migrate to Mexican cities and to the United States. Finally, Mexican officials, noting the Tohono O'odham propensity to make use of these avenues to escape oppression, viewed their out-migration as inevitable and failed to intervene on their behalf in a consistent and meaningful way. The US–Mexico border would, in the future, further separate the remaining Sonoran Tohono

O'odham from their relatives in the United States in both language and culture[62] and turn them into "illegal aliens."[63]

Today, the Tohono O'odham based in Sonora "no longer live in their desert communities nor do they live by cultivating their own lands and very few speak the language [O'odham]." As of 2002, there were only between 363 and 1,400 Tohono O'odham in Mexico, clustered mainly in Caborca, Sonoyta, and Puerto Peñasco, with smaller populations in Luis Río Colorado and Pitiquito; of these only 119 still spoke "Papago."[64] This represents up to a 90 percent drop in population from the estimated 3,000 to 4,000 that lived in the region in the nineteenth century.[65] Without an active OIA, reservations, a major educational effort, and massive investment in infrastructure, the vast majority of tribal members in Mexico assimilated, intermarried, or moved on. This outcome is ironic because by doing nearly nothing prior to the creation of the INI in 1938, the Mexican government achieved the final outcome that many in the United States, prior to John Collier's reign as head of the OIA, might have wanted—the assimilation of the majority of the Tohono O'odham into mainstream culture and the adoption of mainstream gender norms. This is not to say that life for the Tohono O'odham on the US side of the border has been easy or that the United States has consistently tried to assimilate the Tohono O'odham. Tohono O'odham self-governance has been uneven and the Tohono O'odham Nation is currently struggling to counter the drastic rise in diabetes among tribal members, dealing with continued lack of water resources, and is caught in the middle of the binational debates (and enforcement actions) regarding immigration and the war on drugs.[66] Nonetheless, the reservation, their tribal government, and casino revenues have given them the opportunity to invest in the continuation of their own culture. Perhaps even more ironic than the weak postrevolutionary Mexican government achieving what the much stronger US government could not is the fact that the Tohono O'odham Nation today fights not only for its own continued political and cultural survival, but also that of the Sonoran Tohono O'odham. The Tohono O'odham Nation views itself as binational and has pushed for restitution of its Mexican lands and its Sonoran members as well as the right for all members to cross the US–Mexico border freely.[67]

Conclusion

As we began this book, we noted that as reformers went West expanding America's empire at the turn of the last century, they carried with them a desire to assimilate and acculturate the Native American tribes they encountered. There were many "vehicles" for assimilation—from the use of law and the judicial system to bring vice, and thus Native Americans and many of their cultural practices, under control to a focus on educational and vocational training, which served as means of eliminating the illicit. Notions of gender heavily shaped the construction and application of these vehicles, as did the thoughts and actions of the "subjects" of their policies and efforts, the Tohono O'odham. Indeed, the inculcation of "proper" gender roles infused all reform efforts examined here. Reformers often embraced the views of their larger society, for their clients if not always for themselves. As they did so, they negotiated with tribal members who brought their own views and ideals and practices to the discussion. Negotiation—defined to include everything from exchange and borrowing to circumvention and passive resistance—resulted in efforts at assimilation that were incomplete, complicated, and sometimes unexpected in their application and outcomes.

Tohono O'odham commonly resisted reformers' ideas about marriage and sexual impropriety. In fact, those who embraced civil marriage during the period of our study seem to have been a distinct minority, albeit a minority held out by reformers as an example for others. The majority of Tohono O'odham continued to live in the "Indian way."

Reformers' notions about vice, especially as this intersected with gender and race, also show the negotiated nature of outcomes as well as the incompleteness and complications that resulted. The Presbyterians, among others, associated the use of alcohol with broader social problems and poverty. To combat the ill effects of alcohol, reformers believed they needed to harness the naturally superior morality of Tohono O'odham women to restrain the men. However, these women were not trusted to avoid placing themselves in compromising positions, which were especially plentiful in Tucson and other urban environments.

Of course, reformers were not able to root out the use of alcohol among the Tohono O'odham, just as they were not able to do so in mainstream society. The prohibition against drinking was complicated by many factors. For example, the wine-drinking ceremony was, and continues to be, central to Tohono O'odham culture, and even "respectable" Tohono O'odham like Peter Blaine enjoyed drinking alcohol in moderation. This resulted in his unwillingness as a tribal law enforcement officer to enforce anti-alcohol laws lest, as he noted, he be forced to arrest himself. Nonetheless, Tohono O'odham such as Chona also recognized the problems that alcohol could bring and decried the rise in drunkenness that accompanied the introduction of non-Tohono O'odham drink such as whiskey and tequila. At times, then, the Tohono O'odham and reformers were at odds, but at other times they were of like mind.

The battle over schooling, too, suggests incompleteness, complexity, and negotiation. As we noted in chapter 4, James McCarthy's twisting story of agency, negotiation, and domination epitomizes the ways in which sheer chance and fate often determined outcomes. Tohono O'odham—adults and children—weighed in on their educational choices with both words and actions.

What should not be lost in this narrative is that there were competing visions even among reformers. The eventual shift away from boarding schools and "Americanization" in favor of community schooling and native identity had long been advocated by Father Oblasser and his Tohono O'odham constituents. Government leaders and Protestant reformers, on the other hand, long held firm in their support of both. A variety of factors—from location to leadership—often determined which vision impacted any given individual.

Perhaps the most unexpected outcomes were those involving gender and work. The work of the agency farmers, matrons, and stockmen was arguably more successful than efforts focused on vice, sexuality, marriage, and schooling; capitalism dealt a serious, though not lethal, blow to tribal traditions; this was especially the case in Mexico. One negative result of Tohono O'odham entry into the capitalist economy—and away from two-village subsistence—was that the tribe faced unexpected obstacles during the Great Depression when more exposed to national and international markets. Another unexpected outcome was the entry of Tohono O'odham women into the cash economy, and their often becoming the family breadwinner. The training of native women as modern housekeepers, which was intended to encourage them to embrace behavior modeled on middle-class white women, actually provided them with the tools to undermine this very notion, providing them entry into the world of paid work. It is somewhat ironic, then, that by the late 1960s a large percentage of Tohono O'odham women lived in Tucson, engaged in the cash economy, and delayed starting a family. In 2003 the Tohono O'odham Nation elected its first female chair, an action that would have been unthinkable when the Presbyterians, Catholics, and OIA arrived.

Finally we must return to our consideration of the periphery. Being at the edges of empires meant local forces had the most impact on the implementation of national policies. We have utilized both the United States and the Mexican case to consider not only what the leaders and policy-makers wanted to happen, but also how events played out in the lives of individuals in two national settings. Individual reformers in both nations targeted not only the illegal but the illicit, with strong views of the proper in mind. In the United States the federal government, mostly through the actions of the OIA, were joined by scores of secular and sacred institutions and a myriad of reform-minded individuals, including new types of federal employees and teachers, farmers, field matrons, and other professionals. These individuals and organizations, representing divergent slices of the majority culture, worked together, negotiated with each other, and sometimes fought among themselves, as they pushed toward the end goal of changing Native American life forever. In Mexico, where the government, both state and federal, aimed to undermine corporate groups and assimilate indigenous people into mainstream society as mestizos, the Education Ministry had only minimal contact with the Tohono O'odham, and then mostly in communities with strong ties to Tohono O'odham villages in the United States.

Jacob Torfing suggests that we know the majority culture has extended its hegemony over the minority culture when the minority culture adopts a "discourse of norms, values, views, and perceptions" to describe the world that on the whole matches the discourse of the majority culture. Philip Corrigan and Derek Sayer further note that the adoption of mainstream cultural routines and rituals by the minority culture is an indication of new identity formation. The reformers we have researched dreamed of boys who, as adults, would take on the role of yeoman farmer or rancher, breadwinner, and citizen, and girls who would become homemakers and morally persuasive wives and mothers. In this they were surprisingly successful, to a point. By the mid-1930s, the majority of Tohono O'odham men were engaged in agriculture and ranching, even as they seasonally tapped into the broader cash economy at local mines, on railroads, in the cotton fields, and in Tucson, Phoenix, and elsewhere. Most Tohono O'odham women were quick to learn new domestic techniques, eager to hire on as domestic help in Tucson and Phoenix prior to marriage, and willing to return to the domestic sphere after they married. What reformers were unable to accomplish was to convince the Tohono O'odham to give up their culture and lifeways even as they assimilated some aspects of mainstream culture. In fact, OIA officials quickly learned to adapt to the Tohono O'odham. For example, there was little purpose in trying to prevent the Tohono O'odham from attending their annual festivals in San Xavier del Bac and Magdalena. At best, reformers could join them to make sure that they engaged in these activities with the proper propriety and decorum. Perhaps most telling is, as Eric Meeks has noted, that it was the "most traditional" communities that sent the most people into the seasonal cash economy, demonstrating that the Tohono O'odham did not have to give up their culture to embrace change. Perhaps those Tohono O'odham communities who were viewed at the time as making the fewest changes were most attuned to the off-reservation cash economy, or most in need of it.

Even in Mexico, where a weakly instituted federal government was more interested in industrial development and export-led growth (during both the Porfiriato and the postrevolutionary periods) than in protecting indigenous peoples and their patrimonies, and where there was a massive assault on the Tohono O'odham's ancestral landholdings, cultural assimilation or destruction was incomplete. While few Tohono O'odham could continue their two-village system of agriculture and ranching and associated cultural and ceremonial practices, they were able to adopt a range of strategies to counter this assault. They tapped into the regional (and binational) cash economy, sued for land and water restitution, migrated from their arid ancestral lands to nearby urban centers and the United States, and married into non-O'odham families. In spite of the many difficulties and obstacles that they faced, many Tohono O'odham successfully fought to maintain their O'odham culture and identity, even if it is a culture and identity different from that of Tohono O'odham living north of the border. Once again we found that reformers were unable to convince the Tohono

O'odham to give up their culture and lifeways even as they assimilated some aspects of mainstream culture.

Ironically, it may have been the connections the Sonoran-based Tohono O'odham made with their brethren in Mexican cities and the United States that weakened the willingness of Mexican officials predisposed to assist them to actually do so in a consistent and meaningful way. The thought process may have gone like this: The Tohono O'odham are already assimilating into US culture, and since there is no way that we can match the resources that the United States provides, they are bound to migrate to the United States eventually. There is no point in wasting our precious resources on them. Alas, their approach made this a self-fulfilling prophecy for some Tohono O'odham. But other Tohono O'odham stayed and today continue to work with, and sometimes against, the INI in hopes of salvaging their culture.

The Tohono O'odham lived at the extreme edges of two empires, but their experience has much to tell us about cultural negotiations. Though often peripheral to our historical understanding, their experiences provide a lens for gaining an understanding of assimilation—the complex process of imperialism and colonialism in the day-to-day lives of real men, women, and children. Their social and cultural struggles would forever change Tohono O'odham life, but the results fell far short of what the optimistic US reformers imagined. This book thus has provided both a glimpse of an uncompleted quest for full assimilation and an exploration of broader societal ideas about culture, femininity and masculinity, and empire at the turn of the last century.

Notes

Introduction

1. See Alexander S. Dawson, *Indian and Nation in Revolutionary Mexico* (Tucson: University of Arizona Press, 2004), xix–xx, and Claudio Lomnitz, *Deep Mexico, Silent Mexico: An Anthropology of Nationalism* (Minneapolis: University of Minnesota Press, 2001), 73–78.

2. For an excellent discussion of changing views of Native American citizenship, see Frederick Hoxie, *A Final Promise: The Campaign to Assimilate the Indians, 1880–1920* (Lincoln: University of Nebraska Pres, 2001), chap. 7. For more on the ways in which gender was used as a means of nation-building, see Amy Dru Stanley, *From Bondage to Contract: Wage Labor, Marriage, and the Market in the Age of Slave Emancipation* (Cambridge: Cambridge University Press, 1998); Alice Kessler-Harris, *In Pursuit of Equity: Women, Men, and the Quest for Economic Citizenship in Twentieth-Century America* (New York: Oxford University Press, 2001); and Margot Canaday, *The Straight State: Sexuality and Citizenship in Twentieth-Century America* (Princeton, NJ: Princeton University Press, 2009).

3. Gilbert Joseph, "Close Encounters: Toward a New Cultural History of U.S.–Latin American Relations," in *Close Encounters of Empire: Writing the Cultural History of U.S.–Latin American Relations,* edited by Gilbert Joseph, Catherine Legrand, et al. (Durham, NC: Duke University Press, 1998), 5. For another useful description of this "in-between" frontier space, see also Margaret Jacobs, "Working on the Domestic Frontier: American Indian Domestic Servants in White Women's Households in the San Francisco Bay Area, 1920–1940," *Frontiers: A Journal of Women's Studies* 28, nos. 1 and 2 (2007): 172–173.

4. Irene Silverblatt, *Modern Inquisitions: Peru and the Colonial Origins of the Civilized World* (Durham, NC: Duke University Press, 2004). A study in the reverse remains undone and would raise a completely different set of questions about the impact of assimilationist policies and cultural imperialism on the metropole itself.

For such a study in English culture, see Catherine Hall and Sonya Rose, eds., *At Home with the Empire: Metropolitan Culture and the Imperial World* (Cambridge: Cambridge University Press, 2006). See also Catherine Hall, *Civilizing Subjects: Colony and Metropole in the English Imagination, 1830–1867* (Chicago: University of Chicago Press, 2002).

5. Jeremy Adelman and Stephen Aron, "From Borderlands to Borders: Empires, Nation-States, and the Peoples in Between in North American History," *American Historical Review* 104, no. 3 (June 1999): 814–841; Robert Chao Romero, "Chinese Immigrant Smuggling to the United States via Mexico and Cuba, 1882–1916," in *Smugglers, Brothels, and Twine: Historical Perspectives on Contraband and Vice in North America's Borderlands*, ed. Elaine Carey and Andrae Marak (Tucson: University of Arizona Press, 2011), 13–23; Grace Peña Delgado, "At Exclusion's Southern Gate: Changing Categories of Race and Class among Chinese *Fronterizos*, 1882–1904," in *Continental Crossroads: Remapping U.S.–Mexico Borderlands History*, ed. Samuel Truett and Elliott Young (Durham, NC: Duke University Press, 2004), 183–207; and Andrae Marak, *From Many, One: Indians, Peasants, Borders, and Education in Callista Mexico, 1924–1935* (Calgary: University of Calgary Press, 2009), chap. 6.

6. Benjamin H. Johnson and Andrew R. Graybill, "Borders and Their Historians in North America," in *Bridging National Borders in North America: Transnational and Comparative Histories*, ed. Johnson and Graybill (Durham, NC: Duke University Press, 2010), 23. See also Elaine Carey and Andrae Marak, introduction to *Smugglers, Brothels, and Twine: Historical Perspectives on Contraband and Vice in North America's Borderlands*, ed. Carey and Marak (Tucson: University of Arizona Press, 2011), 4–5.

7. Rachel St. John, "Divided Ranges: Trans-border Ranches and the Creation of National Space along the Western Mexico–U.S. Border," in *Bridging National Borders in North America*, 116–140, and S. Deborah Kang, "Crossing the Line: The INS and the Federal Regulation of the Mexican Border," in *Bridging National Borders in North America*, 167–198.

8. Samuel Truett, "Neighbors by Nature: Rethinking Region, Nation, and Environmental History in the U.S.–Mexico Borderlands," *Environmental History* 2, no. 2 (April 1997): 160–178.

9. Jacob Torfing, *New Theories of Discourse: Laclau, Mouffe, and Zizek* (London: Blackwell, 1999), 302.

10. William J. Novak rightly argues in regards to the United States that even in the most remote places of American empire, the state has been able to penetrate people's daily lives through a combination of public (though often local) governmental officials and private interests that carried out the state's aims. See William J. Novak, "The Myth of the 'Weak' American State," *American Historical Review* 113, no. 3 (June 2008): 752–772. Gary Gerstle, however, is right to critique Novak in noting that both public and, perhaps especially, private interests could also serve as counterhegemonic forces. See Gary Gerstle, "A State Both Strong and Weak," *American Historical Review* 115, no. 3 (June 2010): 779–785.

11. Alan L. Karras correctly argues that the mere act of breaking state laws, even if they are supported by those who break them, is a means of negotiating with the state and "a test of the boundaries that exist between citizens (or subjects) and the state over what the role of government in people's lives should be." See Karras, *Smuggling:*

Contraband and Corruption in World History (Lanham, MD: Rowman and Littlefield, 2010), 137.

12. Attempts to assimilate indigenous people occurred much earlier in Mexico's northwest under the tutelage of the Jesuits and then the Franciscans. On the Jesuits, see Edward Spicer, *Cycles of Conquest: The Impact of Spain, Mexico, and the United States on the Indians of the Southwest, 1533–1960* (Tucson: University of Arizona Press, 1962), and Susan Deeds, *Defiance and Deference in Mexico's Colonial North: Indians under Spanish Rule in Nueva Vizcaya* (Austin: University of Texas Press, 2003). On the Franciscans, see Cynthia Radding de Murrieta, "The Function of the Market in Changing Economic Structures in Mission Communities of Pimería Alta, 1768–1821," *The Americas* 34, no. 2 (October 1977): 155–170; Cynthia Radding, *Wandering Peoples: Colonialism, Ethnic Spaces, and Ecological Frontiers in Northwestern Mexico, 1700–1850* (Durham, NC: Duke University Press, 1997); and Stuart F. Voss, *On the Periphery of Nineteenth-Century Mexico: Sonora and Sinaloa, 1810–1877* (Tucson: University of Arizona Press, 1982), 19–22. This assimilation policy was replaced by a policy to strip them of their rights and remove them from their lands during the Porfiriato. See Leticia Reina, "Local Elections and Regime Crises: The Political Culture of Indigenous Peoples," in *Cycles of Conflict, Centuries of Chaos: Crisis, Reform, and Revolution in Mexico,* ed. Elisa Servín, Leticia Reina, and John Tutino (Durham, NC: Duke University Press, 2007), 91–125; John Kenneth Turner, *Barbarous Mexico* (Austin: University of Texas Press, 1969); Miguel Tinker Salas, *In the Shadow of the Eagles: Sonora and the Transformation of the Border during the Porfiriato* (Berkeley and Los Angeles: University of California Press, 1997), especially chaps. 1 and 2; and Friedrich Katz, "The Liberal Republic and the Porfiriato, 1867–1910," in *Mexico since Independence,* ed. Leslie Bethell, 49–124 (Cambridge: Cambridge University Press, 1991).

13. For a compact summary of the work on settlement houses, the archetypal Progressive institution focused on acculturation and Americanization of immigrants, see Walter Trattner, *From Poor Law to Welfare State: A History of Social Welfare in America,* 4th ed. (New York: Free Press, 1989), chap. 8. See also Allen Davis, *Spearheads for Reform: The Social Settlements and the Progressive Movement, 1890–1914* (New York: Oxford University Press, 1967); Roy Lubove, *The Progressive and the Slums* (Pittsburgh: University of Pittsburgh Press, 1962); and Clarke Chambers, *Seedtime of Reform: American Social Service and Social Action, 1918–1933* (Minneapolis: University of Minnesota Press, 1963). For an interesting colonial comparison, see Eileen Findlay, "Love in the Tropics: Marriage, Divorce, and the Construction of Benevolent Colonialism in Puerto Rico, 1898–1910," in *Close Encounters of Empire: Writing the Cultural History of U.S.–Latin American Relations,* ed. Gilbert Joseph, Catherine Legrand, et al. (Durham, NC: Duke University Press, 1998), 139–172.

14. Kenneth Kusmer, *A Ghetto Takes Shape: Black Cleveland, 1870–1930* (Urbana: University of Illinois Press, 1976); Elizabeth Lasch Quinn, *Black Neighbors: Race at the Limits of Reform in the American Settlement House Movement, 1890–1945* (Chapel Hill: University of North Carolina Press, 1993); and Margaret Spratt, "To Be Separate or One: The Issue of Race in the History of the Pittsburgh and Cleveland YWCAs, 1920–1946," in *Men and Women Adrift: The YMCA and YWCA in the City,* ed. Nina Mjagkij and Margaret Spratt (New York: New York University Press 1997), 188–205.

15. The growth in the number of students perversely led to tracking in schools along with the increasingly lower value of a high school diploma. See David F. Labaree,

The Making of an American High School: The Credentials Market and the Central High School of Philadelphia, 1838–1939 (New Haven, CT: Yale University Press, 1988), 168–170.

16. They would need to be assimilated, however, as members of the working class, not as white-collar workers. See Matthew B. Crawford, *Shop Class as Soulcraft: An Inquiry into the Value of Work* (New York: Penguin Books, 2009), 31.

17. Robert Wiebe, *The Search for Order, 1877–1920: The Making of America* (New York: Hill and Wang, 1967), 57–58, 119. The OIA probably had the most success with the Cherokee:

> the affluent councilmen and their wives subscribed to the value system of the upper class in the antebellum South, including the belief that women should be educated in order to lead the "social salvation" of their community and to lend stability and solidarity to the population by instructing the young. In this regard, education would serve to reform or mold Cherokee society into a copy of white society, a goal that many Cherokees shared. Educated females would become pious homemakers and companions to their prominent husbands.

See Devon Mihesuah, *Cultivating the Rosebuds: The Education of Women at the Cherokee Female Seminary, 1851–1909* (Urbana: University of Illinois Press, 1993), 21.

18. For a brief summary of the developments in the social sciences, see Hoxie, *A Final Promise*, 116–123.

19. Jeffrey Ostler, *The Plains Sioux and U.S. Colonialism from Lewis and Clark to Wounded Knee* (Cambridge: Cambridge University Press, 2004), 150. Others have also noted the attempts to solidify white supremacy over Native Americans. See, especially, Ned Blackhawk, *Violence over the Land: Indians and Empires in the Early American West* (Cambridge: Harvard University Press, 2006); and Benjamin Madley, "California's Yuki Indians: Defining Genocide in Native American History," *Western Historical Quarterly* 39, no. 3 (Autumn 2008): 303–332.

20. James C. Scott reminds us that many centrally planned social engineering projects have utterly failed. See James C. Scott, *Seeing Like a State: How Certain Schemes to Improve the Human Condition Have Failed* (New Haven, CT: Yale University Press, 1998).

21. Philip Corrigan and Derek Sayer, *The Great Arch: English State Formation as Cultural Revolution* (Oxford, England: Basil Blackwell, 1985), introduction.

22. Katherine Osburn, *Southern Ute Women: Autonomy and Assimilation on the Reservation, 1887–1934* (Lincoln: University of Nebraska Press, 2008), 3.

23. Mihesuah, *Cultivating the Rosebuds*, xii.

24. Gail Bederman, *Manliness and Civilization: A Cultural History of Gender and Race in the United States, 1880–1917* (Chicago: University of Chicago Press, 1995), 10.

25. Pekka Hämäläinen argues that we need to move beyond even this history that sees "European powers as the principal driving force of history" and Native Americans as actively resisting it. See Pekka Hämäläinen, *The Comanche Empire* (New Haven, CT: Yale University Press, 2008), 6–7.

26. Marsha L. Weisiger, *Dreaming of Sheep in Navajo Country* (Seattle: University of Washington Press, 2009). Another study that examines cultural "interaction" in this

region but does not focus on Native Americans is Sarah Deutsch, *No Separate Refuge: Culture, Class, and Gender on an Anglo-Hispanic Frontier in the American Southwest, 1880–1940* (New York: Oxford University Press, 1987). See her introduction for further discussion of the historiography of studies of interaction between cultures.

27. Richard White, *The Middle Ground: Indians, Empires, and Republics in the Great Lakes Region, 1650–1815* (Cambridge: Cambridge University Press, 1991); James Axtel, *Beyond 1492: Encounters in Colonial North America* (New York: Oxford University Press, 1992); and Matthew Restall, *Seven Myths of the Spanish Conquest* (New York: Oxford University Press, 2003), 64–76.

28. For an excellent theoretical consideration of this issue, see Joseph, "Close Encounters," 3–46.

29. Ostler, *Plains Sioux*, 4.

30. Here we are fortunate that a number of recent studies of the Tohono O'odham have explored issues of power and agency, though with focuses complementary to ours. See, for example, Eric V. Meeks, *Border Citizens: The Making of Indians, Mexicans, and Anglos in Arizona* (Austin: University of Texas Press, 2007); Peter Macmillan Booth, "Creation of a Nation: The Tohono O'odham Political Culture, 1900–1937," PhD diss., Purdue University, 2000; and Kenneth Dean Madsen, "A Nation across Nations: The Tohono O'odham and the United States–Mexico Border," PhD diss., Arizona State University, 2005.

31. Ann Laura Stoler, *Carnal Knowledge and Imperial Power: Race and the Intimate in Colonial Rule* (Berkeley and Los Angeles: University of California Press, 2002), 12.

32. A wave of new scholarship has begun to reimagine the borderlands region from the point of view of the borderlands itself. See Samuel Truett and Elliott Young, eds. *Continental Crossroads: Remapping U.S.–Mexico Borderlands History* (Durham, NC: Duke University Press, 2004); Andrés Reséndez, *Changing National Identities at the Frontier: Texas and New Mexico, 1800–1850* (New York: Cambridge University Press, 2005); Jeremy Adelman and Stephen Aron, "From Borderlands to Borders: Empires, Nation-States, and the Peoples in Between in North American History," *American Historical Review* 104, no. 3 (June 1999): 814–841; Raúl Ramos, *Beyond the Alamo: Forging Mexican Ethnicity in San Antonio, 1821–1861* (Chapel Hill: University of North Carolina Press, 2008); Alexis McCrossen, ed. *Land of Necessity: Consumer Culture in the United States–Mexico Borderlands* (Durham, NC: Duke University Press, 2009); Alejandro Lugo, *Fragmented Lives, Assembled Parts: Culture, Capitalism, and Conquest at the U.S.–Mexico Border* (Austin: University of Texas Press, 2008).

33. Bernard Fontana, *Of Earth and Little Rain* (Tucson: University of Arizona Press, 1986), 120. Booth notes that when the Tohono O'odham tribal council first began to meet in 1937 it was plagued by "non-activity and apathy," often failing to make quorum. In fact, the council's greatest success was to stymie the implementation of the OIA's range management program. See Booth, "Creation of a Nation," 410–416.

34. Benedict Anderson, *Imagined Communities* (London: Verso, 1991), 6.

35. For details, see Will Fowler, *Santa Anna of Mexico* (Lincoln: University of Nebraska Press, 2007), 304–308. The survey itself was not completed until 1855; see Amy S. Greenberg, "Domesticating the Border: Manifest Destiny and the 'Comforts of Life' in the U.S.–Mexico Boundary Commission and Gadsden Purchase, 1848–1854," in *Land of Necessity: Consumer Culture in the United States–Mexico Borderlands*,

ed. Alexis McCrossen (Durham, NC: Duke University Press, 2009), 83–112; and Ramón Eduardo Ruiz, *On the Rim of Mexico: Encounters of the Rich and Poor* (Boulder, CO: Westview Press, 1998), 22.

36. For example, William Walker and a number of filibusters invaded Baja California in 1853 and declared it an independent country before being overwhelmed by Mexican forces and surrendering. In 1857, Henry Crabb and a hundred men attacked Sonora in hopes that the state would later be annexed by US officials as Texas was. Other less well known, and less successful, filibusters continued throughout the Porfiriato (1876–1911). See Oscar J. Martínez, *Troublesome Border* (Tucson: University of Arizona Press, 1988), 38–47.

37. As Daniel D. Arreola shows, in many places along the border there was little that separated one side from the other. See Arreola, "The Fence and Gates of Ambos Nogales: A Postcard Landscape Exploration," in *On the Border: Society and Culture between the United States and Mexico*, ed. Andrew Grant Wood (Lanham, MD: SR Books, 2001), 43–79.

38. Jewell D. Martin to Commissioner of Indian Affairs, August 1, 1916, Advance Estimate for 1918, Files of the Superintendent, Jewell D. Martin, Sells Indian Agency, Record Group 75, National Archives and Records Administration, Pacific Region, Laguna Niguel (hereafter SIA-RG75-NARA/PR/LN).

39. Superintendent to Mr. Dwight B. Heard, May 7, 1917; Dwight B. Heard, Chairman, Arizona Council of Defense, to Mr. Jewell D. Martin, May 14, 1917; Dwight B. Heard to Superintendent Martin, April 23, 1917, Mexican Conflicts with Papagos, 1916–17, Subject Files of the Superintendent, Jewell D. Martin, SIA-RG75-NARA/PR/LN. The 10th Cavalry and the 35th Infantry worked with the Tohono O'odham riders to guard the border against Villista raids. See E. B. Meritt, Assistant Commissioner of Indian Affairs, to Mr. Jewell D. Martin, March 20, 1917, and Commanding Officer, Colonel, 35th Infantry to the Indian Agent, Papago Indian Reservation, May 22, 1917, Mexican Conflict with Papagos, 1916–17, Subject Files of the Superintendent, Jewell D. Martin, SIA-RG75-NARA/PR/LN. For a depiction of Villista raids into the United States, see Friedrich Katz, *The Life and Times of Pancho Villa* (Stanford, CA: Stanford University Press, 1998), 545–614. The Arizona Council of Defense was created at the onset of World War I to "arouse and stimulate the spirit of patriotic service on the part of all citizens" of Arizona. Interestingly, it worked closely with the Tohono O'odham, who had yet to be granted citizenship rights. The Pima County council included an "Americanization Committee." See *A Record of the Activities of the Arizona State Council of Defense from April 18, 1917 to Dissolution, June 1919* (Phoenix: Republican Print Shop, 1919), 6 and 29.

40. Edward Farmer, "Un Nacionalismo Pragmático: El Gobierno Callista en Sonora y el Capital Extranhero," *Boletín* 31 (May–August 1999): 1–23; Miguel Salas Tinker, *In the Shadow of the Eagles: Sonora and the Transformation of the Border during the Porfiriato* (Berkeley and Los Angeles: University of California Press, 1997), 173.

41. Alan Knight, "The United States and the Mexican Peasantry, circa 1880–1940," *Rural Revolt in Mexico: U.S. Intervention and the Domain of Subaltern Politics*, ed. Daniel Nugent (Durham, NC: Duke University Press, 1998), 40.

42. John Mason Hart, *Revolutionary Mexico: The Coming and Process of the Mexican Revolution* (Berkeley and Los Angeles: University of California Press, 1987), 9.

43. Oscar J. Martínez notes that not only were the majority of owners of these establishments from the United States, but also the majority of customers. See Oscar J. Martínez, *Border Boom Town: Ciudad Juárez since 1848* (Austin: University of Texas Press, 1975), 30–31.

44. See Marak, *From Many, One*, 135–157, and Andrae M. Marak, "Forging Identity: Mexican Federal Frontier Schools, 1924–1935," *New Mexico Historical Review* 80, no. 2 (Spring 2005), 163–188. It is possible that these schools (and other similar policies) were effective, as historians and anthropologists have noted that borderlanders often display a stronger sense of *mexicanidad* than Mexicans from the interior. See Howard Campbell and Josiah McCheyman, "The Study of Borderlands Consumption: Potentials and Precautions," in *Land of Necessity: Consumer Culture in the United States–Mexico Borderlands*, ed. Alexis McCrossen (Durham, NC: Duke University Press, 2009), 325–332.

45. William T. Hagan, "Kiowas, Comanches, and Cattlemen, 1867–1906: A Case Study of the Failure of U.S. Reservation Policy," *Pacific Historical Review* 40, no. 3 (August 1971): 333. This mirrored the arguments put forth by the Jesuits and Franciscans in favor of missions; they claimed that "if Spaniards or *castas* (individuals of mixed race) were allowed to settle among the Indians, the Native Americans would be exploited, corrupted, and destroyed." See Thomas E. Sheridan, *Where the Dove Calls: The Political Ecology of a Peasant Corporate Community in Northwestern Mexico* (Tucson: University of Arizona Press, 1988), 8. SEP officials, on the other hand, viewed the isolation of indigenous people as the root cause of their oppression.

46. Minutes of Council with Papago Indians at Indian Oasis, September 21, 1916, Minutes of Council with Papago, 1916, Subject Files of the Superintendent, Jewell D. Martin, SIA-RG75-NARA/PR/LN.

47. Karyn Galland and Guillermo Castillo Ramírez have already begun this work. See Karyn Galland, "La etnicidad O'otham como estrategia politica: Ensayo antropológico sobre la otredad étnica," MA thesis, Universidad Nacional Autónoma de México, 2006, and Guillermo Castillo Ramírez, "Las veredas entre el desierto y la ciudad: Reconfiguración de la identidad en el proceso histórico de cambio de los Tohono O'odham," PhD diss., Universidad Nacional Autónoma de México, 2010.

48. Guadalupe Castillo and Margo Cowan, *It Is Not Our Fault: The Case for Amending Current Nationality Law to Make All Members of the Tohono O'odham Nation United States Citizens, Now and Forever* (Sells, AZ: Tohono O'odham Nation, Executive Branch, 2001).

Chapter 1

1. Fontana is alluding to the creation of the Good Government League (1911) and the League of Papago Chiefs (1928). Fontana, *Of Earth and Little Rain*, 120.

2. Ruth Underhill, *Social Organization of the Papago Indians* (New York: AMS Press, 1969), 70.

3. Spicer, *Cycles of Conquest*, 134.

4. Booth, *Creation of a Nation*, 6.

5. Henry F. Dobyns, *The Papago People* (Phoenix: Indian Tribal Series, 1972), 10.

6. Underhill, *Social Organization*, 70–83.

7. Quote from Sheridan, *Where the Dove Calls*, 7; David Rich Lewis, *Neither Wolf nor Dog: American Indians, Environment, and Agrarian Change* (New York: Oxford University Press, 1994), 134; Thomas Sheridan and Gary Nabhan, "Living with a River: Traditional Farmers of the Río San Miguel," *Journal of Arizona History* 19, no. 1 (Spring 1978): 1–16.

8. The Tohono O'odham also quickly adopted horses and cattle into their culture, though the majority did not adopt "modern" forms of raising stock until after the time period covered in this book. See Peter Iverson, *When Indians Became Cowboys: Native Peoples and Cattle Ranching in the American West* (Norman: University of Oklahoma Press, 1994).

9. Sheridan, *Where the Dove Calls*, 7.

10. Father Bonaventure Oblasser would later claim that, in regard to fighting the Apaches, "one Papago is worth seven Mexicans." Transcript of an interview with Bernard Fontana, 1959, AZ 397, Bonaventure Oblasser, University of Arizona, Special Collections (hereafter SC/UA).

11. James S. Griffith, *A Shared Space: Folklife in the Arizona-Sonora Borderlands* (Logan: University State of Utah Press, 1995), 36.

12. Underhill, *Social Organization*, 83–84.

13. Dobyns, *The Papago People*, 33–34.

14. Bernard Fontana, "History of the Papago," in *Handbook of North American Indians*, vol. 10, ed. William C. Sturtevant (gen. ed.) and Alfonso Ortiz (vol. ed.) (Washington DC: Smithsonian Institution, 1983), 139–141. See also Thomas E. Sheridan, *Landscapes of Fraud: Mission Tumacácori, the Baca Float, and the Betrayal of the O'odham* (Tucson: University of Arizona Press, 2006), 74–76; and Donald Bahr, "Pima-Papago Christianity," *Journal of the Southwest* 3, no. 2 (1988): 133.

15. In the United States, citizenship was equated with the internalization of "white, male Protestant norms." See Douglas Firth Anderson, "'More Conscience Than Force': U.S. Indian Inspector William Vandever, Grant's Peace Policy, and Protestant Whiteness," *Journal of the Gilded Age and the Progressive Era* 9, no. 2 (April 2010): 171.

16. Lewis, *Neither Wolf nor Dog*, 135. John Russell Bartlett, the first American commissioner of the US–Mexico Boundary Commission (which directly preceded the Gadsden Purchase), viewed the region as desolate and unfit for Anglo "settlement and development." See Greenberg, "Domesticating the Border," 83–112 (citation on 85).

17. Fontana, "History of the Papago," 140.

18. Spicer, *Cycles of Conquest*, 134–136.

19. It was around this time, 1859, that the Catholic Church also reestablished official contact with the Tohono O'odham. See Fontana, "History of the Papago," 142.

20. Anderson, "More Conscience Than Force," 173.

21. Brevet Colonel Geo. L. Andrews, US Army, Superintendent Indian Affairs, Arizona Territory, to US Indian Agency Gila River Reservation, December 3, 1869, box 2, PI 163, entry 570, Records Concerning Papago Land Case, RG 75, NARA/PR/LN.

22. Special Agent to Superintendent, December 20, 1871, AZ 344, SC/UA.

23. Fontana notes that prior to the establishment of the Tohono O'odham Reservation in 1916, it was primarily access to cash and the things that cash could buy that drew the Tohono O'odham to settle around San Xavier del Bac. Fontana, *Of Earth and Little Rain*, 75–76. See also Eric V. Meeks, "The Tohono O'odham, Wage Labor,

and Resistant Adaptation, 1900–1930," *Western Historical Quarterly* 34, no. 4 (Winter 2003): 468–489.

24. Booth, "Creation of a Nation," 3–4. Booth notes that there were six different cooperative complexes, one of which connected the Tohono O'odham of current-day northern Sonora with their relatives along the Santa Cruz River near Tucson.

25. Wilbur and the sisters spoke and wrote Spanish. The sisters were paid $600 yearly to teach. Special Agent to Superintendent, March 9, 1873, Special Agent to Commissioner of Indian Affairs, March 31, 1873, AZ 344, SC/AU.

26. Charles Ewing, Commissioner of Catholic Indian Missions, to Columbus Delano, Secretary of the Interior, November 3, 1873; Rt. Rev. J. B. Salpointe, Vicar Apostolic of Arizona, to Charles Ewing, November 1, 1873; Charles Ewing to J. B. Salpointe, November 13, 1873, folder 2, series 1, box 1, Bureau of Catholic Indian Mission Records, Department of Special Collections and University Archives, Marquette University (hereafter BCIM/SC/Marquette). Bishop Salpointe moved quickly to relieve Wilbur of his position, purportedly for his anti-Catholic disposition. Salpointe's first nominee to replace him was rejected because he spoke only Spanish. See Charles Ewing to Columbus Delano, Secretary of the Interior, June 27, 1874; Charles Ewing to J. B. Salpointe, July 15, 1874; Edward Palmer, Commissioner of Indian Affairs, to General C. Ewing, August 10, 1874; Charles Ewing to Maj. John M. Corrigan, October 16, 1874; and Charles Ewing to Columbus Delano, December 12, 1874, folder 2, series 1, box 1, BCIM/SC/Marquette. The Catholic Church originally appointed Salpointe as the parish priest of Tucson in 1866. See J. B. Salpointe, *Soldiers of the Cross: Notes on the Ecclesiastical Period of New Mexico, Arizona, and Colorado* (Whitefish, MT: Kessinger Publishing, 2006), 250.

27. Fontana, "The Papago Indians," part 2, Arizona State Museum Library, 129.

28. See Charles Ewing to Columbus Delano, Secretary of the Interior, June 27, 1874; Charles Ewing to J. B. Salpointe, July 15, 1874; Edward Palmer, Commissioner of Indian Affairs, to General C. Ewing, August 10, 1874; Charles Ewing to Maj. John M. Corrigan, October 16, 1874; and Charles Ewing to Columbus Delano, December 12, 1874, folder 2, series 1, box 1, BCIM/SC/Marquette.

29. Coryn to Edward P. Smith, Commissioner of Indian Affairs, September 14, 1875, folder 2, series 1, box 3, BCIM/SC/Marquette.

30. The OIA also worried that not enough Tohono O'odham were permanently settled on the reservation. See Charles Ewing to the Department of the Interior, March 30, 1876, folder 2, series 1, box 3, BCIM/SC/Marquette.

31. Charles Ewing to Edward P. Smith, August 18, 1876; Father J. B. Brouillet, Director of the Bureau of Catholic Indian Missions, to the Acting Commissioner of Indian Affairs, October 7, 1876, folder 2, series 1, box 3; and Father J. B. Brouillet to R. E. Trowbridge, Commissioner of Indian Affairs, June 2, 1880, folder 2, series 1, box 14, BCIM/SC/Marquette.

32. Fontana, "The Papago Indians," part 2, 128, and William L. Bowie, Special Supervisor, to Hon. John F. Truesdell, Asst. to the US Attorney General in Denver, CO, June 5, 1918, box 2, PI 163, entry 570, Records Concerning Papago Land Case, RG 75, National Archives and Records Administration, District of Columbia (hereafter NARA/NA/DC). Special Agent to Commissioner of Indian Affairs, June 24, 1874, AZ 344, Salpointe to Wilbur, November 11, 1873, folder 11, box 1, AZ 565, R. A. Wilbur Papers, 1840–1882, SP/UA.

33. Ana María Alonso, *Thread of Blood: Colonialism, Revolution, and Gender on Mexico's Northern Frontier* (Tucson: University of Arizona Press, 1995), 119–147, and William E. French, A *Peaceful and Working People: Manners, Morals, and Class Formation in Northern Mexico* (Albuquerque: University of New Mexico, 1996).

34. Lewis, *Neither Wolf nor Dog,* 137.

35. Migratory resistant adaptation is the use of migration as a strategy to avoid outright assimilation. The Tohono O'odham selectively tapped into the "modern" economy to earn wages, but used those wages (and their contact with mainstream society) to perpetuate their two-village system of subsistence and their ancestral culture. For further discussion, see Meeks, "The Tohono O'odham."

36. Randall H. McGuire, *Archaeology as Political Action* (Berkeley and Los Angeles: University of California Press, 2008), 166. McGuire notes that non-Tohono O'odham Mexicans claim that the El Plomo incident drove all the remaining Tohono O'odham from Mexico, essentially rendering them US Indians with no claims to their ancestral lands on the Mexican side of the border. Fontana has a good description of the results of the incident, which displaced many Tohono O'odham from El Plomo to the future Chukut Kuk (Owl Hoot) District of the Tohono O'odham Reservation. See Fontana, *Of Earth and Little Rain,* 89–90. On Díaz and the rurales, see Michael C. Meyer, William L. Sherman, and Susan M. Deeds, *The Course of Mexican History,* 7th ed. (New York: Oxford University Press, 2003), 435–439, and Paul Vanderwood, *Disorder and Progress: Bandits, Police, and Mexican Development* (Wilmington, DE: Scholarly Resources, 1992).

37. Fontana, *Of Earth and Little Rain,* 90–91. See also Carl Lumholtz, *New Trails in Mexico: An Account of One Year's Exploration in North-Western Sonora, Mexico, and South-Western Arizona, 1909–1910* (Tucson: University of Arizona Press, 1990).

38. William L. Bowie, Special Supervisor, to Hon. John F. Truesdell, Asst. to the US Attorney General in Denver, CO, June 5, 1918, box 2, PI 163, entry 570, Records Concerning Papago Land Case, RG 75, NARA/NA/DC.

39. On the flexibility of the statute, see Hoxie, A *Final Promise,* 70–71. On the dispossession of Indian lands, see Stuart Banner, *How the Indians Lost Their Land: Law and Power on the Frontier* (Cambridge: Harvard University Press, 2005), and Janet A. McDonnell, *The Dispossession of the American Indian, 1887–1934* (Bloomington: Indiana University Press, 1991).

40. In 1908, lawmakers undermined the twenty-five-year waiting period, allowing the secretary of the interior to waive it for "competent" Native Americans. See Fergus M. Bordewich, *Killing the White Man's Indian: Reinventing Native Americans at the End of the Twentieth Century* (New York: Anchor Books, 1996), 121–125.

41. If the principles behind the Dawes Act were overly idealistic, their implementation was often corrupt. Some OIA officials opened up land not eligible for allotment, allowed for the leasing of allotted lands to non-Indians, and forced Native Americans not desirous of being deemed competent (and therefore eligible to sell their allotments) to be declared competent. See McDowell, *The Dispossession of the American Indian.*

42. Railroad speculators saw the extension of railroads through Tohono O'odham lands as a means of controlling future pasture lands and, most importantly, their water rights. See Sheridan, *Landscapes of Fraud,* 129.

43. OIA officials set aside 27,566 acres of "worthless mesa land" for the Tohono O'odham as communal property. Citation from Lewis, *Neither Wolf nor Dog,* 139.

Acreage number from Meeks, *Border Citizens,* 46. See also Bordewich, *Killing the White Man's Indian,* 122.

44. Father Bonaventure Oblasser argued that the real problem with allotment was that it was undertaken by a bunch of easterners who "got things mixed up." Transcript of an interview with Bernard Fontana, 1959, AZ 397, Bonaventure Oblasser, SC/UA.

45. Fontana, "The Papago Indians," part 2, 130–133.

46. Personal correspondence with Bernard Fontana, June 26, 2010. Catholic leaders were well aware of the Presbyterian advantage and tried to counter it. For example, Monsignor William Henry Ketcham told Henry Granjon, Bishop of Tucson (1900–1922): "It is very important that we make a serious effort to get as many Catholics into the Indian Service as possible," but noted that there were very few who were qualified. In fact, there were seven total Catholics working for the Indian Service in Arizona, only two of whom were Native American and two of whom were "fallen off" Catholics. See Ketcham to Granjon, November 22, 1909; Director to Henry Granjon, November 26, 1909; and William Ketcham, "Report on Catholics in Government Indian Service," n.d., folder 13, series 1, box 62, BCIM/SC/Marquette.

47. Anonymous, "High School Girls' Home," typewritten report, 1939, RG 103, box 1, folder 31, Presbyterian Historical Society (hereafter PHS); and John M. Hamilton, "A History of the Presbyterian Work among the Pima and Papago Indians of Arizona," MA thesis, University of Arizona, 1948.

48. Fontana, "The Papago Indians," part 2, 131. Father Bonaventure Oblasser also had a hard time getting non-Tohono O'odham to teach in isolated locations. Transcript of an interview with Bernard Fontana, 1959, AZ 397, Bonaventure Oblasser, SC/UA.

49. Hamilton, "History of the Presbyterian Work," chap. 5.

50. Ibid., 105.

51. Father Bonaventure Oblasser claims that there were only four Tohono O'odham families settled in Indian Oasis when the Herndons had their school there. Transcript of an interview with Bernard Fontana, 1959, AZ 397, Bonaventure Oblasser, SC/UA.

52. Transnational Tohono O'odham family connections tied Sells, San Miguel, and Pozo Verde together. For example, George Ignacio's father, José Ignacio, was the first chairman of the Tohono O'odham, while his grandfather Vicente Bustamante was the governor of Pozo Verde. See Castillo and Cowan, *It Is Not Our Fault,* 59.

53. Hamilton, "History of the Presbyterian Work," 123; Booth, "Creation of a Nation," 94.

54. Hamilton, "History of the Presbyterian Work," 125.

55. Fontana, "The Papago People," part 2, 132.

56. Henry Granjon, Bishop of Tucson, to Rev. Dear Father, November 10, 1900, and Secretary to Henry Granjon, November 17, 1900, folder 33, series 1, box 38; Director to R. G. Valentine, Commissioner of Indian Affairs, February 7, 1910, and Director to Sister Aquinas, February 7, 1910, folder 22, series 1, box 66, BCIM/SC/Marquette.

57. Bishop Granjon did agree with the federal government's decision to open a day school for the Tohono O'odham and the Yaqui near Tucson, if only to counter the effects of La Escuela. See Ketcham to Rev. Justin Deutsch, O.F.M., March 1, 1902, folder 35, series 1, box 42; Henry Granjon to Father Ketchum, June 14, 1906, Charles Lusk, Secretary, to Henry Granjon, June 23, 1906, and Henry Granjon to Charles Lusk, June 27, 1906, folder 30, series 1, box 50, BCIM/SC/Marquette.

58. Department of the Interior to Ketcham, February 15, 1910, folder 22, series 1, box 66, BCIM/SC/Marquette.

59. It was around this time that an international consensus emerged in favor of universal elementary education for children coupled with declining support for child labor. These new "modern" conceptions of a "child-centered view of the family" conflicted with the long-held beliefs and practices about children's social and economic roles. Ann S. Blum, "Speaking of Work and Family: Reciprocity, Child Labor, and Social Reproduction, Mexico City, 1920–1940," *Hispanic American Historical Review* 91, no. 1 (February 2011): 63–66. See also Viviana A. Zelizer, *Pricing the Priceless Child: The Changing Social Value of Children* (Princeton, NJ: Princeton University Press, 1994).

60. Given a regular attendance of seventy-five Tohono O'odham students, the government refused to pay for three teachers, demoting one of the sisters to the position of housekeeper. Sister M. Aquinas, February 7, 1910; Director to Sister M. Aquinas, February 17, 1910; Director to Henry Granjon, February 17, 1910; and Henry McQuigg to Ketcham, July 4, 1910, folder 22, series 1, box 66, BCIM/SC/Marquette.

61. McQuigg to Ketcham, December 7, 1910, folder 22, series 1, box 66; Henry Granjon to Ketcham, January 10, 1911, folder 1, series 1, box 72, BCIM/SC/Marquette.

62. Director to McQuigg, January 17, 1911; McQuigg to Ketcham, March 23, 1911; Director to Benedict Schmidt, O.F.M., May 19, 1911; Director to McQuigg, May 19, 1911; James Cardinal Gibbons to My Dear Bishop [Granjon], May 22, 1911; Granjon to the Cardinal, May 30, 1911; and Henry Granjon to Ketcham, June 7, 1911, folder 1, series 1, box 72, BCIM/SC/Marquette.

63. Mathias Rechsteiner, O.F.M., to Granjon, June 7, 1911; Director to His Excellency Most Reverend Diomede Falconio, D.D., Apostolic Delegate, June 9, 1911; McQuigg to Ketcham, June 16, 1911; and Ketcham to Doctor E. R. Dyer, S.S., Bureau of Catholic Indian Missions, November 11, 1911, folder 1, series 1, box 72, BCIM/SC/Marquette.

64. Father Bonaventure Oblasser to Mr. Thackery, March 31, 1912; Bonaventure to Very Rev. Benedict Smith, April 5, 1912; and McQuigg to Father Nichols, October 11, 1915, folder 1, AZ 554, Bonaventure Oblasser, SC/UA.

65. Sister Mary Aquinas to Ketcham, February 14, 1912, folder 23, series 1, box 77, BCIM/SC/Marquette.

66. Booth, "Creation of a Nation," 114.

67. Ibid., 114–116.

68. Bonaventure to Ketcham, June 8, 1912; Bonaventure to Victoriano Chico, June 9, 1912, folder 1, AZ 554, Bonaventure Oblasser, SC/UA. McQuigg to Ketcham, June 8, 1912, folder 23, series 1, box 77, BCIM/SC/Marquette. Lewis, *Neither Wolf nor Dog*, 143. McQuigg pushed to relieve a field matron assigned to the day school in Tucson of her duties, in part because she had been previously employed by La Escuela. McQuigg to Mrs. Lillie McCoy, Indian Office, May 29, 1913, folder 19, series 1, box 83, BCIM/SC/Marquette. When the treasurer of the Good Government League tried to push for the establishment of a government boarding school in Indian Oasis (Sells) in 1912, he was threatened with recall and backed off. Superintendent McQuigg to Commissioner of Indian Affairs, June 5, 1912, Commissioner of Indian Affairs, 1912, Subject Files of the Superintendent, Henry J. McQuigg, SIA-RG75-NARA/PR/LN. Oblasser would eventually ally himself with a collection of Tohono O'odham

chiefs to create the League of Papago Chiefs, which attempted to defeat some of the Good Government League's priorities. Meeks, *Border Citizens*, 135–136.

69. Booth, "Creation of a Nation," 130–132.

70. Father Bonaventure to Father Nicholas, April 28, 1916, folder 1, AZ 554, Bonaventure Oblasser, SC/UA.

71. Cato Sells to Frank A. Thackery (emphasis in original), February 6, 1914, folder 1, AZ 554, Bonaventure Oblasser, SC/UA.

72. *The Thirty-First Annual Report of the Executive Committee of the Indian Rights Association* (Philadelphia: Office of the Indian Rights Association, 1914), 60–63 (quote from 62).

73. Sheridan, *Arizona: A History* (Tucson: University of Arizona Press, 1995), 162.

74. "The 'Committee of Eight,'" n.d., folder 4, AZ 554, Bonaventure Oblasser, SC/UA.

75. Dobyns, *The Papago People*, 51.

76. "The 'Committee of Eight,'" n.d.; "Merits of the Reservation Case," *Tucson Citizen*, January 10, 1917, folder 4, AZ 554, Bonaventure Oblasser, SC/UA. F. S. Herndon to Superintendent Frank A. Thackery, December 14, 1916; "New Papago Indian Reservation Complaints and Investigation," by A. P. Martin, president, Tucson Chamber of Commerce, Sam Barclay, State School-Land Office, J. M. Rodstadt, Postmaster, Tucson, Mr. Goetz, County Engineer, John F. Meyer, Secretary, Tucson Chamber of Commerce, D. C. Cochran, County Board of Supervisors, John Nelson, County Board of Supervisors, J. W. Bogan, county assessor, R. E. Fishburn, councilman at large, and Allen B. Jaymes, editor, *Tucson Citizen*, January 22, 1917, Land—New Papago Reservation, Complaints Against, Subject Files of the Superintendent, Henry J. McQuigg, SIA-RG75-NARA/PR/LN. "No Violation of Indians Rights Is Asked, but Only Fair Play," *El Paso Herald*, January 18, 1917, Subject Files of the Superintendent Jewell D. Martin, SIA-RG75-NARA/PR/LN. Fontana, "The Papago Indians," part 2, 161–162.

77. Minutes of Council with Papago Indians at Indian Oasis, September 21, 1916, Minutes of Council with Papago, 1916, Subject Files of the Superintendent, Jewell D. Martin, SIA-RG75-NARA/PR/LN.

78. Fontana, "The Papago Indians," part 2, 162.

79. Ibid., 163.

80. Lewis, *Neither Wolf nor Dog*, 148; Spicer, *Cycles of Conquest*, 141–142.

81. Fontana, "History of the Papago," 145.

82. Peter Nabokov, *A Forest of Time: American Indian Ways of History* (Cambridge: Cambridge University Press, 2002); Vine Deloria Jr., *God Is Red* (New York: Grosset and Dunlap, 1973), 138; Alfonzo Ortiz, "Some Concerns Central to the Writing of 'Indian' History," *Indian Historian* (Winter 1977): 20.

83. Bernard Fontana, *Of Earth and Little Rain*, 19.

84. PI 163, Entry 570, Records Concerning Papago Land Case, box 2, RG75-NARA/NA/DC.

85. Minutes of Council with Papago Indians at Indian Oasis, September 21, 1916, Minutes of Council with Papago, 1916, Subject Files of the Superintendent, Jewell D. Martin, SIA-RG75-NARA/PR/LN.

86. Felix Chico, "An Indian Story My Grandfather Told Me," March 1942, series 1-1, box F1, Correspondence by Native Authors; A–I, BCIM/SC/Marquette.

Chapter 2

Author note: Portions of the chapter were adapted from *Smugglers, Brothels, and Twine,* edited by Elaine Carey and Andrae Marak, © 2011 The Arizona Board of Regents. Reprinted by permission of the University of Arizona Press; and from "Los vicios transnacionales de los Tohono O'odham a principios del siglo XX," by Andrae Marak and Laura Tuennerman, in *En la encrucijada: Historia, marginalidad y delito en America Latina y los Estados Unidos de Norteamerica, siglos XIX y XX* (University of Guadalajara, 2010).

1. There is some dispute as to whether the Tohono O'odham ceremony caused the rains to come or simply "located and predicted it." Some scholars have noted that "the wine feast is not to start the rain, but to keep it raining, for it usually rains during the picking season." See Frances Densmore, *Papago Music,* Smithsonian Institution, Bureau of American Ethnology, Bulletin 90 (Washington DC: US Government Printing Office, 1929), 148–163; Ruth M. Underhill et al., *Rainhouse and Ocean: Speeches for the Papago Year* (Tucson: University of Arizona Press, 1979), 21.

2. We want to avoid suggesting here that the arrival of Anglos to the region introduced the Tohono O'odham to markets, though it clearly resulted in meaningful cultural changes. Mauricio Tenorio-Trillo has argued that borderlands Mexicans "had a long history of migration and adaptation, starting especially in the late eighteenth century" that integrated them into regional markets. Eric V. Meeks has made a similar argument about the Tohono O'odham, demonstrating that they tapped into labor markets outside of their ancestral homeland as a means of engaging in "resistant adaptation." See Mauricio Tenorio-Trillo, "On *La Fontera* and Cultures of Consumption: An Essay of Images," in *Land of Necessity: Consumer Culture in the United States–Mexico Borderlands,* ed. Alexis McCrossen (Durham, NC: Duke University Press, 2009), 339; Meeks, "The Tohono O'odham."

3. Ruth Underhill, *Papago Woman* (1936; New York: Holt, Rinehart and Winston, 1979), 74. For a critical discussion of this work as a primary source, see Margaret Connell Szasz, introduction to *Between Indian and White Worlds: The Cultural Broker,* ed. Margaret Connell Szasz (Norman: University of Oklahoma Press, 1994), 9–10.

4. This good behavior did include vomiting cactus wine, symbolic "sympathy with the clouds that they hope to attract." Because the wine made the men drunk, the god Siuuhu made sure that the cactus fruit would only be ripe once per year. See Donald Bahr, Juan Smith, William Smith Allison, and Julian Hayden, *The Short, Swift Time of Gods on Earth: The Hohokam Chronicles* (Berkeley and Los Angeles: University of California Press, 1994), 123 and 130. For a detailed account of the ritual, see Ruth M. Underhill, *Papago Indian Religion* (New York: Columbia University Press, 1946), 41–67.

5. Densmore, "Papago Music," 153.

6. Peter Blaine Sr., AZ 0362, Arizona Historical Society (hereafter AZ/0362/AHS).

7. James McCarthy, *A Papago Traveler: The Memories of James McCarthy,* ed. John Westover (Tucson: University of Arizona Press, 1985), 156. See also 155.

8. Jewell D. Martin to Commissioner of Indian Affairs, July 23, 1917, Commissioner of Indian Affairs, June–September 1917, Jewell D. Martin to Commissioner of Indian Affairs, SIA-RG75-NARA/PR/LN.

9. Janette Woodruff, Report on the Working Girls for the Quarter Ending December 31, 1919, Field Matron Correspondence, Janette Woodruff, 1919–1920, SIA-RG75-NARA/PR/LN.

10. Annual Report, Narrative and Statistical, 1923, Subject Files of the Superintendent, Thomas F. McCormick, SIA-RG75-NARA/PR/LN.

11. Mrs. Libbie C. Light to J. W. Elliot, October 9, 1930, Field Matron, Libbie C. Light, Correspondence, 1929–1930, Reports of the Field Matrons, 1910–1932, SIA-RG75-NARA/PR/LN.

12. Superintendent to Commissioner of Indian Affairs, May 16, 1913, Field Matron, Lydia A. Gibbs, 1911–1919, Reports of the Field Matrons, 1910–1932, SIA-RG75-NARA/PR/LN.

13. Bederman, *Manliness and Civilization*, 25.

14. Annual Report, Narrative and Statistical, 1923, Subject Files of the Superintendent, Thomas F. McCormick, SIA-RG75-NARA/PR/LN.

15. Robert Buffington, "Prohibition in the Borderlands: National Government-Border Community Relations," *Pacific Historical Review* 63, no. 1 (February 1994): 22.

16. Peter Andreas and Ethan Adelman, speaking about drugs and alcohol, though their argument is more generalizable, argue that moral entrepreneurs and advocacy networks spend much of their transnational efforts "toward persuading foreign audiences (especially foreign elites)" that the adoption of their preferred code of conduct "reflects not merely the peculiar moral code of one society but a more widely shared, even universal, moral sense." Peter Andreas and Ethan Nadelmann, *Policing the Globe: Criminalization and Crime Control in International Relations* (Oxford: Oxford University Press, 2006), 19. For a discussion of white supremacy, civilization, and gender, see also Bederman, *Manliness and Civilization*, chap. 4.

17. Regina Kunzel, *Fallen Women, Problem Girls: Unmarried Mothers and the Professionalization of Social Work, 1890–1945* (New Haven, CT: Yale University Press, 1993), 57–58; Alan Dawley, *Struggles for Justice: Social Responsibility and the Liberal State* (Cambridge: Harvard University Press, 1991), 93; and John D'Emilio and Estelle Friedman, *Intimate Matters: A History of Sexuality in America* (New York: Harper-Row, 1988). For a similar discussion in a different imperial setting, see Philippa Levine, "Sexuality and Empire," in *At Home with the Empire: Metropolitan Culture and the Imperial World*, ed. Catherine Hall and Sonya O. Rose (Cambridge: Cambridge University Press, 2006), 130.

18. Janette Woodruff and Cecil Dryden, *Indian Oasis* (Caldwell, ID: Caxton Printers, 1939), 290.

19. Robert Perez notes that while Anglos first "introduced Indians to what in many cases became, and remains, a deadly trade in alcohol," their response to colonial oppression through the smuggling of livestock, peyote, and other ceremonial hallucinogenic plants set them up well to take advantage of alcohol smuggling during Prohibition. This was especially true because many public officials could not tell the difference between Mexicans and Native Americans when the Native Americans were off of their reservation. Although we have no direct evidence that Tohono O'odham took part in alcohol smuggling, common sense suggests that some members did so. See Robert Perez, "Confined to the Margins: Smuggling among Native Peoples of the Borderlands," in *Land of Necessity: Consumer Culture in the United States–Mexico Borderlands*, ed. Alexis McCrossen (Durham, NC: Duke University Press, 2010), 256–263.

20. Mexican officials also feared the impact that alcohol could have on its lower classes, but settled on public health policies that promoted education campaigns and taxation instead of prohibition. See Buffington, "Prohibition in the Borderlands," 24–25; Emilio Portes Gil, "La campaña contra el alcoholismo: Iniciativa presidential," *Boletín de la Sociedad Mexicana de Geografía y Estadística* 40 (April 1930): 5; Gabriela Recio, "Drugs and Alcohol: US Prohibition and the Origins of the Drug Trade in Mexico, 1910–1930," *Journal of Latin American Studies* 34, no. 1 (February 2002): 33.

21. Booth, "Creation of a Nation," 125–126.

22. Minutes of Council with Papago Indians at Indian Oasis, September 21, 1916, Minutes of Council with Papago, 1916, Subject Files of the Superintendent, Jewell D. Martin, SIA-RG75-NARA/PR/LN.

23. For a description of the movement from personal moral failings to the investigation and focus on societal/environmental causes of poverty and vice, see Trattner, *From Poor Law to Welfare State*, 94–97; Wiebe, *Search for Order*, chap. 6.

24. Erika Lee, *At America's Gates: Chinese Immigration during the Exclusion Era, 1882–1943* (Chapel Hill: University of North Carolina Press, 2003); and Ronald Takaki, *Iron Cages: Race and Culture in Nineteenth-Century America* (New York: Knopf, 1979).

25. This does not mean that reformers were not heavily influenced by eugenics. The rise of neo-Lamarckism, which "posited that environmental forces, both favorable and unfavorable, could alter human heredity and be transmitted down the familial line," was at the root of many of the hygiene programs adopted for the Tohono O'odham. See Alexandra Minna Stern, *Eugenic Nation: Faults and Frontiers of Better Breeding in Modern America* (Berkeley and Los Angeles: University of California Press, 2005), 14.

26. M. L. Girton, superintendent, to Dear Friend, March 20, 1936, folder 1, box 19, subseries 28, Tucson Indian Training School Correspondence, 1910–1948, Series 5: Educational and Medical Institutions/Agencies, 1867–1986, Health, Education, and Welfare, RG 301.8, Presbyterian Archives (hereafter 1/28/V/301.8 PHS).

27. Haddington Brown, preface to "Historical Circular of Indian Training School—Tucson, Arizona" (Tucson, AZ: Citizen Printing and Publishing Co. 1905), Historical Sketches, folder 31, box 1, series II—Historical, Promotional, and Student Materials, Tucson Indian Training School Records, 1889–1963, RG 103, Presbyterian Archives (hereafter 103/PHS).

28. Woodruff and Dryden, *Indian Oasis*, 290. See also Minnie M. Estabrook to Honorable Cato Sells, October 13, 1914, Field Matron Correspondence, Minnie M. Estabrook, 1914–1916, Reports of the Field Matrons, 1910–1932, SIA-RG75-NARA/PR/LN.

29. Janette Woodruff, Annual Report on the Working Girls Ending June 30, 1928, Field Matron's Weekly Reports, Janette Woodruff, 1927–1929, Reports of the Field Matrons, 1910–1932, SIA-RG75-NARA/PR/LN.

30. Peggy Pascoe, *Relations of Rescue: The Search for Female Moral Authority in the American West, 1874–1939* (New York: Oxford University Press, 1990), 115.

31. Ibid., 117.

32. Catherine Culman, secretary of the school, to J. E. Crowder, Presbyterian Archives, Miscellaneous Correspondence, 1909, 1924, 1941–1961, n.d., folder 13, series I, Administrative Correspondence and Records, 103/PHS.

33. Dr. Herndon's address, "A Glimpse of the Past," 1926, 31/II/103.8/PHS.

34. Quoted in Hoxie, *Final Promise*, 75.

35. Meeks, *Border Citizens*, 17 and 37. This was especially true for indigenous people, Asians, and people of Asian descent, whose claims to citizenship on both sides of the border were contested. See, for example, Delgado, "At Exclusion's Southern Gate."

36. Mark Anderson, "'What's to Be Done with 'Em?' Images of Mexican Cultural Backwardness, Racial Limitations, and Moral Decrepitude in the United States Press, 1913–1915," *Mexican Studies/Estudios Mexicanos* 14, no. 1 (Winter 1998): 23–70.

37. Alan Dawley, *Changing the World: American Progressives in War and Revolution* (Princeton, NJ: Princeton University Press, 2003), 81.

38. Susan Yohn, *A Contest of Faiths: Missionary Women and Pluralism in the American Southwest* (Ithaca, NY: Cornell University Press, 1995), 146.

39. Evelyn Nakano Glenn, *Unequal Freedom: How Race and Gender Shaped American Citizenship and Labor* (Cambridge: Harvard University Press, 2002); Findlay, "Love in the Tropics." Margaret D. Jacobs also notes that "much of the education Indian children received revolved around training them for such menial positions, a process officials often characterized as making them 'useful.'" See Jacobs, "Working on the Domestic Frontier," 166.

40. Marsha Weisiger, *Dreaming of Sheep*, 228–244 (quotation on 229).

41. Several autobiographies described serious gambling among tribal members that led to the loss of livestock, homes, and other worldly possessions. The gambling reported, however, seems to have remained entirely within the tribe and perhaps for that reason went unnoticed by reformers. This is suggestive of just how little (in some ways) outsiders were able to penetrate Tohono O'odham culture and practices. See Underhill, *Papago Woman*, 55–56 and 66, and McCarthy, *Papago Traveler*, 21.

42. Cato Sells quoted in M. K. Sniffen, "A Man and His Opportunity" (Philadelphia: Indian Rights Association, 1914), 11, Commissioner Cato Sells Scrapbook, 1913–1920, Records of the Office of the Commissioner of Indian Affairs, SIA-RG75-NARA, National Archives Building, Washington DC (hereafter RG75-NARA/NA/DC).

43. A. M. Philipson to T. F. McCormick, June 3, 1924. For other examples, see A. M. Philipson to J. W. Elliot, February 11, 1931; J. W. Elliot to A. M. Philipson, September 29, 1931; A. M. Philipson, Weekly Report of Farm Agent, April 15, 1933; A. M. Philipson, Weekly Report of Farm Agent, July 1, 1933; Farmer, A. M. Philipson, 1924–1926; Reports of the Agency Farmers and Stockmen, 1910–1934, SIA-RG75-NARA/PR/LN. Janette Woodruff to J. D. Martin, July 15, 1917, Field Matron, Janette Woodruff, 1915–1918, Reports of the Field Matrons, 1910–1932, SIA-RG75-NARA/PR/LN. Superintendent to Commissioner of Indian Affairs, May 14, 1920, Office of Commissioner of Indian Affairs, January–June 1920, Subject Files of the Superintendent, Thomas F. McCormick, SIA-RG75-NARA/PR/LN.

44. Janette Woodruff, Quarterly Report on the Outing Girls, September 30, 1924, Field Matron Weekly Reports, Janette Woodruff, 1925–1926, Reports of the Field Matrons, 1910–1932, SIA-RG75-NARA/PR/LN.

45. Scholarship letter, M. L. Girton to Friend, October 30, 1934, 13, I/103/PHS.

46. A. M. Philipson to Mr. McCormick, October 12, 1922, Farmer, A. M. Philipson, 1921–1922, Reports of the Agency Farmers and Stockmen, 1910–1934, SIA-RG75-NARA/PR/LN.

47. A. M. Philipson to E. S. Stewart, March 3, 1928, Farmer, A. M. Philipson, 1927–1929, Reports of the Agency Farmers and Stockmen, 1910–1934, SIA-RG75-NARA/PR/LN.

48. Superintendent to Mr. Philipson, July 7, 1920, Farmer, A. M. Philipson, 1920, Reports of the Agency Farmers and Stockmen, 1910–1934, SIA-RG75-NARA/PR/LN.

49. Superintendent to Commissioner of Indian Affairs, May 14, 1920, Office of Commissioner of Indian Affairs, January–June 1920, Subject Files of the Superintendent, Thomas F. McCormick, SIA-RG75-NARA/PR/LN.

50. Quotation from S. Deborah Kang, "Crossing the Line: The INS and the Federal Regulation of the Mexican Border," in *Bridging National Borders in North America: Transnational and Comparative Histories*, ed. Benjamin H. Johnson and Andrew R. Graybill (Durham, NC: Duke University Press, 2010), 167.

51. Report on the Sells Indian Agency, Arizona, by Karl Y. Henderson, April 20, 1931, vol. 9, 432, Records of the Board of Indian Commissioners, Special Reports, 1915–1933, Records of the Board of Indian Commissioners, Special Reports, box 5, RG 75-NARA/NA/DC.

52. E. B. Meritt, Assistant Commissioner to Mr. Jewell D. Martin, March 26, 1917, Commissioner of Indian Affairs, January–June 1917, Subject Files of the Superintendent, Jewell D. Martin, SIA-RG75-NARA/PR/LN.

53. Perez, "Confined to the Margins," 260. Complaints about the Tohono O'odham use of alcohol for religious ceremonies date from the arrival of Catholic missionaries in San Xavier. See Salpointe, *Soldiers of the Cross*, 184.

54. Superintendent to Mr. Philipson, July 7, 1920, Reports of the Agency Farmers and Stockmen, 1910–1934, Farmer, A. M. Philipson, 1920, and A. M. Philipson to Mr. McCormick, October, 18, 1921, Reports of the Agency Farmers and Stockmen, 1910–1934, Farmer, A. M. Philipson, 1921, SIA-RG75-NARA/PR/LN.

55. A. M. Philipson to E. S. Stewart, December 31, 1928, Farmer, A. M. Philipson, 1927–1929, Reports of the Agency Farmers and Stockmen, 1910–1934, SIA-RG75-NARA/PR/LN.

56. A. M. Philipson, Weekly Report of Farm Agent, October 15, 1932, Farmer, A. M. Philipson, 1932, Reports of the Agency Farmers and Stockmen, 1910–1934, SIA-RG75-NARA/PR/LN. More information on the same case can be found in A. M. Philipson, Weekly Report of Farm Agent, October 14, 1932, Reports of the Agency Farmers and Stockmen, 1910–1934, SIA-RG75-NARA/PR/LN.

57. Underhill, *Papago Woman*, 25–27.

58. Underhill, *Papago Woman*, 40. For a modern-day account of cactus wine that is strikingly similar to reports from the 1930s, see Gary Paul Nabhan, *The Desert Smells Like Rain: A Naturalist in Papago Indian Country*, chap. 2.

59. Blaine, AZ/0362/AHS.

60. Blaine, AZ/0362/AHS.

61. Hamilton, "History of the Presbyterian Work," 124.

Chapter 3

Author note: Portions of this chapter were adapted from "Los vicios transnacionales de los Tohono O'odham a principios del siglo XX," by Andrae Marak and Laura Tuennerman, in *En la encrucijada: Historia, marginalidad y delito en America Latina y los Estados Unidos de Norteamerica, siglos XIX y XX* (University of Guadalajara, 2010).

1. Underhill, *Papago Woman*, 62.
2. Ruth M. Underhill, *The Papago (Tohono O'odham) and Pima Indians of Arizona* (Palmer Lake, CO: Filter Press, 2000), 47–48; Ruth Underhill, *The People of the Crimson Evening* (Palmer Lake, CO: Filter Press, 1982), 97–100.
3. Underhill, *The Papago and Pima*, 47–48; Underhill, *People of the Crimson Evening*, 97–100.
4. Underhill, *Papago Woman*, 78.
5. See, for example, Blaine, *Papagos and Politics*, 31.
6. McCarthy, *Papago Traveler*, 146–147.
7. Underhill, *Papago Woman*, 62.
8. Underhill, *Papago Woman*, 64. This in-between gender, the berdache, was noted by scholars of the Papago and Pima in the 1930s and 1940s, but went unremarked upon by OIA officials as well as religious reformers. See W. W. Hill, "Note on the Pima Berdache," *American Anthropologist* 40, no. 2 (April–June, 1938): 338–340; Charles Callender and Lee M. Kochems, "The North American Berdache," *Cultural Anthropology* 24, no. 4 (August–October, 1983): 445.
9. Booth highlights the Tohono O'odham "stress on kinship and community cohesion," resulting in a focus on gender-specific "responsibilities to the group" in each stage of the life cycle. See Booth, "Creation of a Nation," 11–21 (quotation on 13).
10. Thomas F. McCormick, Annual Report, Narrative and Statistical, 1923, Subject Files of the Superintendent, Thomas F. McCormick, SIA-RG75-NARA/PR/LN. This statement is nearly identical to that of Archbishop J. B. Salpointe, who served in his position from 1885 to 1894. See Salpointe, *Soldiers of the Cross*, 184.
11. Janette Woodruff to T. F. McCormick, July 1, 1920, Field Matron Correspondence, Janette Woodruff, 1919–1920, Reports of the Field Matrons, 1910–1932, SIA-RG75-NARA/PR/LN.
12. Nancy Cott, *Public Vows: A History of Marriage and the Nation* (Cambridge: Harvard University Press, 2000), 121.
13. For a full discussion of definitions of marriage, see Sarah Carter, *The Importance of Being Monogamous: Marriage and Nation Building in Western Canada to 1915* (Edmonton: University of Alberta Press, 2008), 4–5.
14. Cott, *Public Vows*, 3.
15. Cott, *Public Vows*, 25.
16. Field matron to Miss Mary Stewart, Field Officer, Indian Service, April 14, 1932, Field Matron, Libbie C. Light, Correspondence, 1931–1932, Reports of the Field Matrons, 1910–1932, SIA-RG75-NARA/PR/LN.
17. Stoler, *Carnal Knowledge*, 1.
18. Carter, *Importance of Being Monogamous*, 11. Similarly, Cott suggests that "the federal government consistently encouraged or forced Indians to adopt Christian-model monogamy as the *sine qua non* of civilization and morality." Cott, *Public Vows*, 26, and Jacobs, *Engendered Encounters: Feminism and Pueblo Cultures, 1879–1934* (Lincoln: University of Nebraska Press, 1999), cover similar issues.
19. For a full discussion of anthropologists on this issue in the 1870s, see Carter, *Importance of Being Monogamous*, 28.

20. W. J. McGee, "Piratical Acculturation," *American Anthropologist* 11, no. 8 (August 1898): 243–249.

21. Dawley, *Struggles for Justice,* 266. This was also a main focus of the WNIA and other reform organizations who worked to convince the BIA to transform Indian women into the middle-class ideal of the "true woman." Jacobs, introduction to *Engendered Encounters.*

22. Elizabeth Jameson, "Women as Workers, Women as Civilizers: True Womanhood in the American West," *Frontiers: A Journal of Women Studies* 7, no. 3 (1984): 1.

23. Nancy Cott, *The Grounding of Modern Feminism* (New Haven, CT: Yale University Press, 1987).

24. Field Matron to E. S. Stewart, March 10, 1930, Field Matron, Libbie C. Light, Correspondence, Superintendent E. S. Stewart, Reports of the Field Matrons, 1910–1932, SIA-RG75-NARA/PR/LN.

25. Janette Woodruff to Mr. Martin, July 27, 1917, Field Matron, Janette Woodruff, 1915–1918, Reports of the Field Matrons, 1910–1932, SIA-RG75-NARA/PR/LN.

26. Field Matron to E. S. Stewart, June 19, 1929, Field Matron, Libbie C. Light, Correspondence, Superintendent E. S. Stewart, Reports of the Field Matrons, 1910–1932, SIA-RG75-NARA/PR/LN.

27. Woodruff and Dryden, *Indian Oasis,* 245.

28. Ibid., 245.

29. Hamilton, "History of the Presbyterian Work," 125–126.

30. Field Matron to E. S. Stewart, May 31, 1930, Field Matron, Libbie C. Light, Correspondence, 1931–1932, Reports of the Field Matrons, 1910–1932, SIA-RG75-NARA/PR/LN. See also Field Matron to Superintendent S. T. Elliott, April 26, 1931, Field Matron, Libbie C. Light, Correspondence, 1931–1932, Reports of the Field Matrons, 1910–1932, SIA-RG75-NARA/PR/LN.

31. Woodruff and Dryden, *Indian Oasis,* 265.

32. Mary Doyle to T. F. McCormick, February 14, 1920, Field Matron's Weekly Reports, Mary Doyle, 1916–1919, Reports of the Field Matrons, 1910–1932, SIA-RG75-NARA/PR/LN.

33. Superintendent to M. M. Estabrook, June 17, 1915, and Minnie M. Estabrook to H. J. McQuigg, May 24, 1915, Field Matron Correspondence, Minnie M. Estabrook, 1914–1916, Reports of the Field Matrons, 1910–1932, SIA-RG75-NARA/PR/LN.

34. Doyle to T. F. McCormick, July 3, 1920; Mary Doyle to J. D. Martin, May 16, 1917; and Mary Doyle to T. F. McCormick, Annual Report, July 1919, Field Matron's Weekly Reports, Mary Doyle, 1916–1919, and Janette Woodruff, 1921–1922, Janette Woodruff to T. F. McCormick, June 30, 1922, Reports of the Field Matrons, 1910–1932, SIA-RG75-NARA/PR/LN.

35. Jewell D. Martin to Commissioner of Indian Affairs, July 23, 1917, and E. B. Meritt, Assistant Commissioner, to Mr. Jewell D. Martin, July 18, 1917, Commissioner of Indian Affairs, June–September 1917, Jewell D. Martin to Commissioner of Indian Affairs, Subject Files of the Superintendent, Jewell D. Martin, SIA-RG75-NARA/PR/LN.

36. Superintendent to Commissioner of Indian Affairs, July 24, 1917, Commissioner of Indian Affairs, January–June 1917, Subject Files of the Superintendent, Jewell D. Martin, SIA-RG75-NARA/PR/LN.

37. Janette Woodruff to T. F. McCormick, April 23, 1920, and May 5, 1920, Field Matron Correspondence, 1919–1920, Reports of the Field Matrons, 1910–1932, SIA-RG75-NARA/PR/LN.

38. A. M. Philipson to E. S. Stewart, January 27, 1927, Farmer, A. M. Philipson, 1927–1929, Reports of the Agency Farmers and Stockmen, 1910–1934; Field Matron to Miss Mary Stewart, Field Officer, Indian Service, April 14, 1932, Field Matron, Libbie C. Light, Correspondence, 1931–1932, Reports of the Field Matrons, 1910–1932, SIA-RG75-NARA/PR/LN.

39. For a similar discussion of the disinterest in, or even shunning of, civil marriage in Puerto Rico at the turn of the century, see Eileen Findlay, "Love in the Tropics."

40. A. M. Philipson, report, n.d., Farmer, A. M. Philipson, 1923, Reports of the Agency Farmers and Stockmen, 1910–1934, SIA-RG75-NARA/PR/LN.

41. Minnie M. Estabrook to H. J. McQuigg, August 29, 1914, Field Matron Correspondence, Minnie M. Estabrook, 1914–1916, Reports of the Field Matrons, 1910–1932, SIA-RG75-NARA/PR/LN.

42. Janette Woodruff to T. F. McCormick, October 2, 1917, Field Matron, Janette Woodruff, 1915–1918, Reports of the Field Matrons, 1910–1932, SIA-RG75-NARA/PR/LN.

43. A. M. Philipson to E. S. Stewart, January 27, 1927, Farmer, A. M. Philipson, 1927–1929, Reports of the Agency Farmers and Stockmen, 1910–1934, SIA-RG75-NARA/PR/LN.

44. Superintendent to Mrs. J. J. Anderson [from the Crescent Ranch, née Miss Regna Hendrickson], February 15, 1917, Law and Order, 1916–1917, Subject Files of the Superintendent, Jewell D. Martin, SIA-RG75-NARA/PR/LN.

45. Unknown [but probably McQuigg] to Commissioner of Indian Affairs, September 13, 1913, Field Matron, Lydia A. Gibbs, 1911–1919, Reports of the Field Matrons, 1910–1932, SIA-RG75-NARA/PR/LN.

46. Wiebe, *Search for Order*, 149–150; Kunzel, *Fallen Women*.

47. It is worth reiterating that in this regard state and private interests vis-à-vis Native Americans often coincided with and served to buttress state power. See Novak, "Myth of the 'Weak' American State."

48. Susan Yohn, *A Contest of Faiths: Missionary Women and Pluralism in the American Southwest* (Ithaca, NY: Cornell University Press, 1995); Michael Katz, *In the Shadow of the Poorhouse* (New York: Basic Books, 1986).

49. Doyle to J. D. Martin, May 16, 1917, Field Matron's Weekly Reports, Mary Doyle, 1916–1919, Reports of the Field Matrons, 1910–1932, SIA-RG75-NARA/PR/LN.

50. See, for example, Light to J. W. Elliot, October 9, 1930, Field Matron, Libbie C. Light, Correspondence, 1929–1930; Frances D. Hall, Senior Placement Matron, to Mrs. Libbie C. Light, May 16, 1931, and Field Matron to J. W. Elliott, November 11, 1931, Field Matron, Libbie C. Light, Correspondence, 1931–1932, Reports of Field Matrons, 1910–1932, SIA-RG75-NARA/PR/LN.

51. Levine, "Sexuality and Empire," 123.

52. Matron to Antonio Moreno, San Xavier Village, November 5, 1931, Field Matron, Libbie C. Light, Correspondence, 1931–1932, Reports of the Field Matrons, 1910–1932, SIA-RG75-NARA/PR/LN.

53. Field Matron to J. W. Elliot, November 11, 1931, Field Matron, Libbie C. Light, Correspondence, 1931–1932, Reports of the Field Matrons, 1910–1932, SIA-RG75-NARA/PR/LN.

54. Cato Sells to Janette Woodruff, February 23, 1917, Field Matron, Janette Woodruff, 1915–1918, Reports of the Field Matrons, 1910–1932, SIA-RG75-NARA/PR/LN.

55. Robert Trennert, "Educating Indian Girls at Nonreservation Boarding Schools, 1878–1920," *Western Historical Quarterly* 13, no. 3 (July 1982): 283; Woodruff to T. F. McCormick, July 1, 1918, Field Matron, Janette Woodruff, 1915–1918, Reports of the Field Matrons, 1910–1932, SIA-RG75-NARA/PR/LN.

56. Janette Woodruff, Annual Report on the Working Girls ending June 30, 1927, Field Matron's Weekly Reports, Janette Woodruff, 1927–1929, Reports of the Field Matrons, 1910–1932, SIA-RG75-NARA/PR/LN.

57. Marie Chico to Mrs. J. J. McGrath, November 3, 1925, folder C, series 1-1, box F1, Facsimiles, Correspondence by Native Authors, A–I, Bureau of Catholic Indian Missions, Marquette University Archives and Special Collections.

58. Superintendent to Mrs. Janette Woodruff, February 16, 1915, Field Matron, Janette Woodruff, 1915–1918, Reports of the Field Matrons, 1910–1932, SIA-RG75-NARA/PR/LN.

59. Kunzel, *Fallen Women*, 58.

60. A. M. Philipson to Mr. McCormick, May 8, 1923, Reports of the Agency Farmers and Stockmen, 1910–1934, Farmer, A. M. Philipson, 1923, SIA-RG75-NARA/PR/LN.

61. A. M. Philipson, report, n.d.; A. M. Philipson to Mr. McCormick, August 23, 1923, Reports of the Agency Farmers and Stockmen, 1910–1934, Farmer, A. M. Philipson, 1923, SIA-RG75-NARA/PR/LN.

62. Underhill, *Papago Woman*, 55.

63. Ibid., 55.

64. Ibid., 56.

65. Ibid., 85.

66. Unknown to Miss Amanda M. Chingren, Outing Matron, October 25, 1913, Field Matron, Lydia A. Gibbs, 1911–1919, Reports of the Field Matrons, 1910–1932, SIA-RG75-NARA/PR/LN.

67. George O. Hilzinger, County Attorney, to H. J. McQuigg, September 14, 1913, Field Matron, Lydia A. Gibbs, 1911–1919, Reports of the Field Matrons, 1910–1932, SIA-RG75-NARA/PR/LN.

68. A. M. Philipson, Weekly Report of Farm Agent, December 3, 1933, Farmer, A. M. Philipson, 1932, Reports of the Agency Farmers and Stockmen, 1910–1934, SIA-RG75-NARA/PR/LN.

69. Superintendent to Mrs. J. J. Anderson [from the Crescent Ranch, née Miss Regna Hendrickson], February 15, 1917, Law and Order, 1916–1917, Subject Files of the Superintendent, Jewell D. Martin, SIA-RG75-NARA/PR/LN.

70. A. M. Philipson to T. F. McCormick, March 21, 1920, Farmer, A. M. Philipson, 1920, Reports of the Agency Farmers and Stockmen, 1910–1934, SIA-RG75-NARA/PR/LN.

71. Janette Woodruff to T. F. McCormick, April 6, 1918, Field Matron, Janette Woodruff, 1915–1918, Reports of the Field Matrons, 1910–1932, SIA-RG75-NARA/PR/LN.

72. Jacobs, *Engendered Encounters*, 43.

73. Findlay, "Love in the Tropics," 150.

74. Minnie M. Estabrook to H. J. McQuigg, February 6, 1915, Field Matron Correspondence, Minnie M. Estabrook, 1914–1916, Reports of the Field Matrons, 1910–1932, SIA-RG75-NARA/PR/LN.

75. Annual Report—Narrative Section, 1917, Jewell D. Martin to Commissioner of Indian Affairs, Subject Files of the Superintendent, Jewell D. Martin, SIA-RG75-NARA/PR/LN. The 1865 statute was revised in 1901 to include the word "decedents." See *The Revised Statutes of Arizona Territory* (Columbia, MO: Press of E. W. Stephens, 1901), 3092 (sec. 6), 809. Meeks also discusses this issue. See Meeks, *Border Citizens*, 80–88.

76. Annual Report—Narrative Section, 1917, Jewell D. Martin to Commissioner of Indian Affairs, Subject Files of the Superintendent, Jewell D. Martin, SIA-RG75-NARA/PR/LN.

77. For more on the Yaqui and their place in borderlands society, see Brenden Rensink, "The Transnational Immigrant-Refugee Experience of Mexican Yaquis and Canadian Chippewa-Crees in Arizona and Montana," *Journal of the West* 48, no. 3 (Summer 2009): 12–19.

78. Underhill, *Social Organization;* W. J. McGee, *Trails to Tiburón: The 1894 and 1895 Field Diaries of W. J. McGee* (Tucson: University of Arizona Press, 2000), 106–107.

79. Robert Perez, "Confined to the Margins," 262–263. Reuben V. Naranjo Jr. has found in his research on this subject that US Customs officials routinely categorized tribal members under different racial categories depending on the agent and the circumstances of the visit. Personal communication with author, July 2010.

80. McCarthy, *Papago Traveler*, 106 and 147.

81. Reuben V. Naranjo Jr., personal communication with author, July 2010.

82. Malcolm M. McDowell, Secretary, to Thomas F. McCormick, March 8, 1920.

83. This begs the question of to what extent OIA officials were impacted by debates over Indigenismo and racial mixing in Mexico. See Carlos Salomon, "Indigenismo across Borders," *Journal of the West* 48, no. 3 (Summer 2009): 48–52.

84. E. B. Meritt to Mr. H. J. McQuigg, March 9, 1915, Commissioner of Indian Affairs, January–June 1915, Subject Files of the Superintendent, Henry J. McQuigg, SIA-RG75-NARA/PR/LN.

85. Special collections, Bonaventure Oblasser to Rev. Wm. Hughes, October 14, 1923, box 1, AZ 300, Bonaventure Oblasser, 1885–1967, Papers, 1908–1972, AHS.

86. Report on the Papago Indians, Arizona, Malcolm McDowell, April 8, 19, pp. 260–261, RG 75, Records of the Board of Indian Commissioners, Special Reports, 1915–1933, vol. 2, 1918–1919, Bound copies of reports. Vol. 1, 1915–1918, Entry 1388, Records of the Board of Indian Commissioners, Special Reports, 1915–1933, RG75-NARA/NA/DC.

87. Stoler, *Carnal Knowledge*, 41.

88. Jacobs, *Engendered Encounters*, 26. See also Peggy Pascoe, *Relations of Rescue: The Search for Female Moral Authority in the American West, 1874–1939* (New York: Oxford University Press, 1990) for a general discussion of women reformers in the West and an excellent bibliography on the subject.

89. Jacobs, Engendered Encounters, 26.

90. Blaine, AZ/0362/AHS.

91. Lewis Meriam et al., *The Problem of Indian Administration; Report of a Survey Made at the Request of Honorable Hubert Work, Secretary of the Interior* (Baltimore: Johns Hopkins Press, 1928), 16. See also 449 for a discussion of weaknesses in the program.

92. Ibid., 569.

93. Ibid., 572.

94. Carter, *Importance of Being Monogamous*, 277.

Chapter 4

1. McCarthy, *Papago Traveler*, 5.

2. See ibid., 8, 28, and 30. For another discussion of the hair cutting issue, see Ostler, *Plains Sioux*, 152.

3. McCarthy, *Papago Traveler*, 38–39, 41.

4. K. Tsianina Lomawaima, "Domesticity in the Federal Indian Schools: The Power of Authority over Mind and Body," *American Ethnologist* 20, no. 2 (May 1993): 227.

5. Lisa Emmerich, "'Save the Babies!': American Indian Women, Assimilation Policy, and Scientific Motherhood, 1912–1918," in *Writing the Range: Race, Class, and Culture in the Women's West*, ed. Elizabeth Jameson and Susan Armitage (Norman: University of Oklahoma Press, 1997), 396.

6. There is a solid literature focused directly on Indian schools, much of which is listed in the bibliography. Of specific interest to the discussion of the inculcation of Anglo values, see the following: on educating girls at nonreservation boarding schools, see Trennert, "Educating Indian Girls," 271–290, 271, and 283; Hoxie, *Final Promise*, 66–67; and Ostler, *Plains Sioux*, 152–159. For discussions of day school and boarding school options, see Evelyn Adams, *American Indian Education: Government Schools and Economic Progress* (Morningside Heights, NY: King's Crown Press, 1946), chaps. 4 and 5. See also Valerie Sherer Mathes, "Nineteenth Century Women and Reform: The Women's National Indian Association," *American Indian Quarterly* 14, no. 1 (Winter 1990): 6, for a discussion of WNIA and IRA using "public pressure to bring general education" to native children in order to Christianize and civilize them. See also Hoxie, *Final Promise*, 11-12, and Fontana, *Of Earth and Little Rain*, 76–77, for the chronology of Papago-specific schools; and Mihesuah, *Cultivating the Rosebuds*, 2, for a discussion of issues related to the exclusion of native culture in a school founded by the Cherokees themselves.

7. Ostler, *Plains Sioux*, 150. See his note 3 on that page for an excellent, if somewhat dated, list of sources on assimilation.

8. Vicki Ruiz, *From Out of the Shadows: Mexican Women in Twentieth-Century America* (Oxford: Oxford University Press, 1998), 33.

9. Superintendent to Philipson, July 20, 1921; A. M. Philipson to Mr. T. F. McCormick, November 17, 1921; Superintendent to Mr. Philipson, August 4, 1921; and A. M. Philipson to Mr. McCormick, July 25, 1921; Farmer, A. M. Philipson, 1921–1922, Reports of the Agency Farmers and Stockmen, 1910–1934, SIA-RG75-NARA/PR/LN.

10. A. M. Philipson to Mr. McCormick, September 9, 1922, Farmer, A. M. Philipson, 1922, Reports of the Agency Farmers and Stockmen, 1910–1934, SIA-RG75-NARA/PR/LN.

11. Father Bonaventure to Father Praeses, May 18, 1914, AZ 554, Bonaventure Oblasser, SC/UA.

12. A. M. Philipson to Mr. Jewell D. Martin, August 2, 1916, Subject Files of the Superintendent, Jewell D. Martin, Education: Tucson Day School, Teacher, A. M. Philipson, SIA-RG75-NARA/PR/LN.

13. George W. P. Hunt, Governor of Arizona, to Hon. Carl Hayden, House of Representatives, March 30, 1914, Pima Indian Agency, Frank A. Thackery's File, Subject Files of the Superintendent, Henry J. McQuigg, SIA-RG75-NARA/PR/LN/.

14. Haddington Brown, preface to "Historical Circular of Indian Training School—Tucson, Arizona" (Tucson, AZ: Citizen Printing and Publishing Co., 1905), 103/PHS.

15. Of course, the Jesuits had set up a series of missions in the seventeenth and eighteenth centuries in what would later become Arizona Territory and then the state of Arizona. The earliest mission of Guevavi was established by 1690. Later missions were established in Tucson, San Xavier, Tubac, and Tumacacuri. Archbishop Salpointe notes that a number of Tohono O'odham were already attached to and receiving an education from the San Xavier mission in 1866. See Salpointe, *Soldiers of the Cross*, 180–185.

16. Special Agent to Commissioner of Indian Affairs, March 31, 1873, AZ 344, SC/US. See also interview of Nicolas Perschi by Bernard Fontana, AZ 396, Nicolas Perschi: Reminiscences of a Franciscan in Papagueria, SC/UA. Father Perschi discusses the Sisters of St. Joseph who taught the Tohono O'odham under government supervision.

17. For a description of Tucson at the time, see Thomas Sheridan, *Los Tucsonenses: The Mexican Community in Tucson, 1854–1941* (Tucson: University of Arizona Press, 1997), chaps. 3, 4, and 5.

18. Annual Report, 1874, folder 12, box 1, AZ 565, R. A. Wilbur Papers, SC/UA.

19. Ibid.

20. Salpointe, *Soldiers of the Cross*, 183.

21. Annual Report, 1874, folder 12, box 1, AZ 565, R. A. Wilbur Papers, SC/UA.

22. Ibid.

23. Hoxie, *Final Promise*, 53.

24. Francis Paul Prucha, *The Churches and the Indian Schools, 1888–1912* (Lincoln: University of Nebraska Press, 1979), 4.

25. Anonymous, "High School Girls' Home," typewritten report, 1939, folder 1, box 1, II/103/PHS, and Hamilton, "History of the Presbyterian Work."

26. Fontana, *Of Earth and Little Rain*, 76.

27. Hamilton, "History of the Presbyterian Work," 160.

28. Prucha, *Churches and the Indian Schools*, x. See also chap. 5.

29. Memo, February 18, 1871, and Appointments, 1871, folder 1, box 1, AZ 565, R. A. Wilbur Papers, 1840–1882, SC/UA. Archbishop Salpointe to R. A. Wilbur, November 11, 1873, folder 11, box 1, AZ 565, R. A. Wilbur Papers, 1840–1882, SC/UA.

30. "Education in Papago Country," AZ 554, Bonaventure Oblasser, SC/UA. Father Bonaventure Oblasser to Mr. Thackery, March 31, 1912, and Bonaventure to Very Rev.

Benedict Schmidt, April 5, 1912, AZ 554, Bonaventure Oblasser, SC/UA, also discuss brokering deals between the Presbyterians, Catholics, and the government to provide schools without duplicating efforts. Also worthy of mention is the fact that state, federal, Catholic, and Presbyterian officials worked as a team with Tohono O'odham leaders to create the Papago (now Tohono O'odham) Reservation. See "The 'Committee of Eight,'" folder 4, AZ 554, Bonaventure Oblasser, SC/UA.

31. Bureau of C.J.M. to Bonaventure, December 19, 1914; Bureau of C.J.M. Charles Lusk to Bonaventure, January 30, 1915; Ketcham to Bonaventure, March 26, 1915; McQuigg to Father Nichols, October 11, 1915; and Father Bonaventure to Father Nicholas, April 28, 1916, folder 1, AZ 554, Bonaventure Oblasser, SC/UA.

32. Bonaventure to Victoriano Chico, June 9, 1912, folder 1, AZ 554, Bonaventure Oblasser, SC/UA. Underline in the original.

33. Transcript of an interview by Bernard Fontana, 1959, AZ 397, Bonaventure Oblasser, SC/UA.

34. See, for example, a report of 1925 enrollments that suggests there are 183 students and could easily be 100 more. Anonymous, n.d., and three typed pages, "Chronology of dates," folder 31, box 1, II/103/PHS.

35. Bonaventure to Charles Burke, Commissioner of Indian Affairs, August 7, 1924, box 2, AZ 300, Bonaventure Oblasser, 1885–1967, papers, 1908–1972, SC/UA.

36. Bonaventure to Rev. William J. Hughes, August 7, 1924, box 2, AZ 300, Bonaventure Oblasser, 1885–1967, papers, 1908–1972, SC/UA.

37. Bonaventure to Rev. William Hughes, December 1, 1924, and Bonaventure to Hughes, October 10, 1925, box 2, AZ 300, Bonaventure Oblasser, 1885–1967, papers, 1908–1972, SC/UA. For a discussion of quotas at other schools, see, for example, Ostler, *Plains Sioux,* 164–166.

38. Rev. William Hughes to Rev. Bonaventure, August 11, 1924, and Bonaventure to Hughes, October 18, 1925, box 2, AZ 300, Bonaventure Oblasser, 1885–1967, papers, 1908–1972, SC/UA.

39. Blaine, *Papagos and Politics,* 15.

40. Prucha, *Churches and the Indian Schools,* Appendix C, 214–216. Prucha also points to legal battles over this issue, describing the Browning Ruling, which found that the government could transfer Indian students to government schools, even against the wishes of the parents, and the overturning of this ruling as tribes fought to gain control, through funding, of school choice for their children. Prucha, 59 and chaps. 7–11. It is also worth noting that as Catholic schools struggled for funding, the issue of saving souls was utilized in their fund-raising efforts. See, for example, the newspaper clipping and photo of Tohono O'odham children whose caption reads, "Six Small Day Schools in the Arizona Desert Must be Kept Open or the Little Indian Children of that Vast District Will Never Know Christ," box 2, AZ 300, Bonaventure Oblasser, 1885–1967, papers, 1908–1972, SC/UA.

41. Dr. Herndon, "A Glimpse of the Past," 1926, folder 31, box 1, II/103/PHS.

42. Antonia Garcia, "Holy Week Devils," sometime in the 1930s, folder G, series 1-1, box F1, facsimiles, Correspondence by Native Authors A–J, BCIM/SC/Marquette.

43. H. B. Peairs, Chief Supervisor of Education, to All Superintendents, July 28, 1924, Field Matron's Weekly Reports, Mary Doyle, 1922–1924, Reports of the Field Matrons, 1910–1932, SIA-RG75-NARA/PR/LN.

44. Annual Report—Narrative Section, 1916, Annual Narrative Report, Subject Files of the Superintendent, Henry J. McQuigg, SIA-RG75-NARA/PR/LN.

45. Catherine Culman, secretary of the school, to J. E. Crowder, Presbyterian archives, folder 13, box 1, SIA-RG75-NARA/PR/LN.

46. Matilda Ramon to Dear Father, November 27, 1946, folder R, series 1-1, box F2, facsimiles, Correspondence by Native Authors J–Z, BCIM/SC/Marquette.

47. Malcolm McDowell, Annual report of the Phoenix Indian Vocational School, April 27, 1925, 277, Records of the Board of Indian Commissioners, Special Reports, 1915–1933, vol. 5, RG75-NARA/NA/DC.

48. Ibid., 283.

49. For a similar discussion of this issue, see Jacobs, *Engendered Encounters,* 11.

50. Trennert, "Educating Indian Girls," 271.

51. Osburn, *Southern Ute Women,* 45–46.

52. J. O. Barnd to unknown, August 23, 1919, Education: Day School Inspector, J. O. Barnd, Subject Files of the Superintendent, Thomas F. McCormick, SIA-RG75-NARA/PR/LN.

53. Letter to Mr. Malcolm McDowell, April 12, 1922, from McCormick, Board of Indian Commissioners, Subject Files of the Superintendent, Thomas F. McCormick, SIA-RG75-NARA/PR/LN.

54. Letter to Mr. Malcolm McDowell, April 12, 1922, from McCormick, Board of Indian Commissioners, Subject Files of the Superintendent, Thomas F. McCormick, SIA-RG75-NARA/PR/LN.

55. Letter to Mr. Malcolm McDowell, April 12, 1922, from McCormick, Board of Indian Commissioners, Subject Files of the Superintendent, Thomas F. McCormick, SIA-RG75-NARA/PR/LN. In AZ 396, Nicolas Perschi: Reminiscences of a Franciscan in the Papaguera, interview by Bernard Fontana, Father Perschi also describes a domestic curriculum in the schools run by the Sisters of St. Joseph. Other sources also suggest that natives did not feel the pressure to work that whites felt, and thus were less likely to be successful after school. Responses from Superintendents (anonymous) to "Returned Student Survey," October 1917, Education: Report of Returned Students, Subject Files of the Superintendent, Thomas F. McCormick, SIA-RG75-NARA/PR/LN.

56. Underhill, *Papago Woman,* 90.

57. Meeting minutes from Teacher Convention, October 12 and 14, 1919. Inspector Barnd, "The Foundation of Successful Teaching among the Indians," Subject Files of the Superintendent, Thomas F. McCormick, SIA-RG75-NARA/PR/LN.

58. For a more complete discussion of this trend toward training wage-based industrial workers at Indian schools, see Hoxie, *Final Promise.*

59. Meeting minutes from Teacher Convention, October 13 and 14, 1919, Inspector Barnd's lecture on "The Foundation of Successful Teaching among the Indians," Education: Day School Inspector, J. O. Barnd, Subject Files of the Superintendent, Thomas F. McCormick, SIA-RG75-NARA/PR/LN.

60. J. O. Barnd to F. A. Broomfield, October 27, 1919, Education: Sells Day School, Teacher—Florian Broomfield, Subject Files of the Superintendent, Thomas F. McCormick, SIA-RG75-NARA/PR/LN.

61. Underhill tells of similar training in "classic" childhood stories in a humorous passage where she writes about a girl Vela who talks about singing a song at

school: "I love lil' pussy, her coat so warm." Underhill's response was to point out to the girl that the tribe did not even have cats. *Papago Woman*, 18.

62. Program, Closing Exercises of the San Xavier Day School, May 31, 1917, San Xavier Day School, Subject Files of the Superintendent, Thomas F. McCormick, SIA-RG75-NARA/PR/LN.

63. Not only was this "pre-citizenship" training at best, many Tohono O'odham who served in World Wars I and II have either been denied US citizenship or are unable to prove their US citizenship and are subject to deportation. For example, see the case of the Domingo family in Castillo and Cowan, *It Is Not Our Fault*, 27–28. In general, Native American support for the war was considerable. About one in four eligible adult Native American men served in World War I. In addition, Native Americans purchased an average of $75 worth of war bonds each. See Frederick E. Hoxie, ed., *Talking Back to Civilization: Indian Voices from the Progressive Era* (Boston: Bedford/St. Martin's, 2001), 123–124.

64. Outline of Tucson Indian Training School Development, ca. 1937, folder 31, box 1, II/103/PA.

65. Anonymous, "A Glimpse Then and Now of the Tucson Indian Training School, Escuela, Arizona," 1933, folder 31, box 1, II/103/PA.

66. Two major leagues vied for control of Tohono O'odham leadership, the aforementioned Papago Good Government League and the League of Papago Chiefs. The latter was formed in 1925 with the assistance of Father Bonaventure and the support of Catholics from San Xavier and the northern parts of the reservation. See Lewis, *Neither Wolf nor Dog*, 154–155.

67. J. O. Barnd to unknown, August 23, 1919, Education: Day School Inspector, J. O. Barnd, Subject Files of the Superintendent, Thomas F. McCormick, SIA-RG75-NARA/PR/LN.

68. J. O. Barnd to Commissioner, May 1, 1920, Education: Day School Inspector, J. O. Barnd, Subject Files of the Superintendent, Thomas F. McCormick, SIA-RG75-NARA/PR/LN.

69. A. A. Graham, Secretary of the Ohio Historical Society, "Pimas and Papagos: A Visit to the Indian School at Tucson, Arizona," ca. 1890, folder 31, box 1, II/103/PA.

70. Day School Inspector to Commissioner, March 3, 1920, Education: Day School Inspector, J. O. Barnd, Subject Files of the Superintendent, Thomas F. McCormick, SIA-RG75-NARA/PR/LN.

71. Common training in English at boarding schools along with the mixing of Native Americans from a wide range of tribes also provided the underpinnings for later pan-Indian movements.

72. Hoxie, *Final Promise*, 68; Blaine, AZ/0362/AHS.

73. Superintendent to Mr. Hammond, September 13, 1921, Education: District Supervisor of Indian Education, E. H. Hammond, Subject Files of the Superintendent, Thomas F. McCormick, SIA-RG75-NARA/PR/LN. That same year the records of Santa Rosa Day School contain discussions of the serious lack of school clothing for day school students and a plan to give them clothing to wear only while at school. Unknown to Mr. Wilton, April 7, 1921, Education: Santa Rosa Day School, Teacher, Joseph Wilton, Subject Files of the Superintendent, Thomas F. McCormick, SIA-RG75-NARA/PR/LN.

74. RG 75, Sells Indian Agency, E. H. Hammond to R. McCormick, n.d., Education: District Supervisor of Indian Education, E. H. Hammond, Subject Files of the Superintendent, Thomas F. McCormick, SIA-RG75-NARA/PR/LN.

75. Commissioner Cato Sells argued about cotton in the Salt River Valley:

> It appears that other sources of labor are so uncertain from several points of view as to place this new and very important industry in danger unless some plan be devised whereby the growers may depend upon Indian pickers and be reasonably sure of securing help when needed. . . . In order to create a proper and necessary local market for this product, it appears essential that we cooperate with the white growers in stabilizing labor to the extent of giving the growers and commercial interest sufficient encouragement and incentive, so that they will put forth the effort and capital necessary to place this industry on a sound and substantial basis. . . . It is therefore thought advisable that the Office designate some representative in that immediate locality to take direct charge and supervision of the Indian labor questions involved, in order that he may co-operate with the growers and others interested in the final success of this important industry.

See Cato Sells to Mr. H. J. McQuigg, March 26, 1914, Commissioner of Indian Affairs, January–June 1914, Subject Files of the Superintendent, Henry J. McQuigg, SIA-RG75-NARA/PR/LN.

76. Jean O. Barnd to Commissioner, November 1, 1920, Education: Day School Inspector, J. O. Barnd, Subject Files of the Superintendent, Thomas F. McCormick, SIA-RG75-NARA/PR/LN. McQuigg to Commissioner, April 27, 1916, Commissioner of Indian Affairs, Subject Files of the Supervisor-in-Charge, Charles McChesney, 1916, SIA-RG75-NARA/PR/LN. A similar problem of low school attendance owing to work in the cotton fields and copper mines was noted in Malcolm McDowell, "Report on the Papago Indians, Arizona," April 8, 1919, 256, Records of the Board of Indian Commissioners, Special Reports, 1915–1933, vol. 2, RG75-NARA/NA/DC.

77. 1903 Report, J. M. Berger to BIA, November 25, 1903, Annual Reports, 1897, 1903, 1905, 1907, San Xavier Reservation, Subject Files of the Farmer-in-Charge, John M. Berger, 1898–1910, SIA-RG75-NARA/PR/LN.

78. Superintendent to Commissioner, September 23, 1915, Commissioner of Indian Affairs, July–December 1915, Subject Files of the Superintendent, Henry J. McQuigg, SIA-RG75-NARA/PR/LN. Superintendent to Commissioner, March 15, 1912, Commissioner of Indian Affairs, 1912, Subject Files of the Superintendent, Henry J. McQuigg, SIA-RG75-NARA/PR/LN.

79. Cato Sells to Mr. H. J. McQuigg, November 15, 1915, Commissioner of Indian Affairs, July–December 1915, Subject Files of the Superintendent, Henry J. McQuigg, SIA-RG75-NARA/PR/LN.

80. Superintendent to Commissioner, November 10, 1920, Office of Commissioner of Indian Affairs, July–December, 1920, Subject Files of the Superintendent, Thomas F. McCormick, SIA-RG75-NARA/PR/LN; E. B. Meritt to Thomas F. McCormick, August 20, 1921, and Superintendent to Commissioner, July 20, 1921, Office of Commissioner of Indian Affairs, July–December, 1921, Subject Files of the Superintendent, Thomas F. McCormick, SIA-RG75-NARA/PR/LN.

81. Blaine, *Papagos and Politics*, 31.

82. A. M. Philipson to Mr. McCormick, January 26, 1923, Farmer, A. M. Philipson, 1923, Reports of the Agency Farmers and Stockmen, 1910–1934, SIA-RG75-NARA/PR/LN. See also A. M. Philipson to Mr. McCormick, January 25, 1923, Farmer, A. M. Philipson, 1924–1926, Reports of the Agency Farmers and Stockmen, 1910–1934, SIA-RG75-NARA/PR/LN.

83. Good Government League Petition, 1912, quoted in *The Thirtieth Annual Report of the Executive Committee of the Indian Rights Association* (Philadelphia: Office of the Indian Rights Association, 1912), 26–27.

84. Meriam et al., *Problem of Indian Administration*, 16.

85. Ibid., 15.

Chapter 5

Author note: Portions of this chapter were originally published in *Journal of the West* 48, no. 3 (Summer 2009). Copyright ABC-CLIO, LLC ©2009, reprinted with permission of ABC–CLIO.

1. For details, see Ruth M. Underhill et al., *Rainhouse and Ocean.*

2. Fontana, *Of Earth and Little Rain*, 43.

3. The Tohono O'odham were able to cultivate some ten thousand acres of land using this method in 1913; by the 1980s, less than a hundred acres were cultivated in this manner. See Nabhan, *The Desert Smells Like Rain*, 47.

4. Lewis notes that this work was not strictly communal in nature and would be better described as reciprocal, since land, although owned communally, was controlled individually. See Lewis, *Neither Wolf nor Dog*, 127.

5. Underhill, *People of the Crimson Evening*, 57.

6. Fontana, *Of Earth and Little Rain*, 43.

7. Ibid.

8. Lewis, *Neither Wolf nor Dog*, 125.

9. Underhill, *People of the Crimson Evening*, 59–60.

10. Fontana, *Of Earth and Little Rain*, 45.

11. Blaine, AZ/0362/AHS.

12. Eric Meeks covers this in great detail. See Meeks, "The Tohono O'odham," 468–489.

13. Blaine, AZ/0362/AHS.

14. Men were also likely to have accompanied the women. They could find jobs working in the mines or for the railroad.

15. Naranjo, "Tohono O'odham Potters in Tombstone and Bisbee, Arizona, 1890–1920," MA thesis, University of Arizona, chap. 3.

16. "Justification," January 22, 1917, Jewell D. Martin, Agriculture, Subject Files of the Superintendent, SIA-RG75-NARA/PR/LN.

17. Ibid.

18. For an excellent discussion of the connection between allotment and citizenship, see Frederick Hoxie, *The Final Promise*, 74–78.

19. Osburn, *Southern Ute Women*, chap. 3, especially p. 37.

20. Susan Sleeper-Smith, *Indian Women and French Men: Rethinking Cultural Encounter in the Western Great Lakes* (Amherst: University of Massachusetts, 2001), 96.

21. Newspaper clipping, "Forming the Papago Reservation: Ownership of Papago Lands," n.d., folder 1, AZ 554, Bonaventure Oblasser, SC/UA. Bonaventure quotes Alan B. Jaynes, *Tucson Citizen*, January 10, 1917, the *Arizona Republican*, June 14, 1916, and Carl Hayden, "Merits of the Reservation Case," *Tucson Citizen*, January 10, 1917, in "The 'Committee of Eight,'" folder 4, AZ 554, Bonaventure Oblasser, UA/SC. See also Lewis, *Neither Wolf nor Dog*, 148.

22. George W. P. Hunt to Mr. Thackery, April 7, 1914, Pima Indian Agency, Frank A. Thackery's File, Subject Files of the Superintendent, Henry J. McQuigg, SIA-RG75-NARA/PR/LN.

23. Response from Superintendents, Returned Student Survey, October 10, 1917, Education: Report of Returned Students, Subject Files of the Superintendent, Thomas F. McCormick, SIA-RG75-NARA/PR/LN.

24. Hamilton, "History of the Presbyterian Work," 167.

25. Cott, *Public Vows*, 25.

26. David Peterson del Mar, *Environmentalism* (Harlow, England: Pearson-Longman, 2006), 31–60.

27. Lewis, *Neither Wolf nor Dog*, 9. A Presbyterian among the Tohono O'odham made this exact connection between lack of sustained agriculture and lack of social development when he wrote of students going "back to their 'wickey-up,' and to their lazy, nomadic life." A. A. Graham, Secretary of the Ohio Historical Society, "Pimas and Papagos: A Visit to the Indian School at Tucson, Arizona," ca. 1890, folder 31, box 1, II/103/PHS.

28. Gary Paul Nabhan, *Enduring Seeds: Native American Agriculture and Wild Plant Conservation* (New York: North Point Press, 1989), 61–62.

29. Evelyn Nakano Glenn provides an interesting description of these roles as they apply to larger ideas about the labor market in her work *Unequal Freedom*, 74–75.

30. Lewis, *Neither Wolf nor Dog*, 11.

31. "Report on the San Xavier Agency—Papago Reservation Arizona," by Commissioner Eliot, Board of Indian Commissioners, May 21, 1917, 265–266, Special Reports, 1915–1933, vol. 1, 1915–1918, Records of the Board of Indian Commissioners, RG75-NARA/NA/DC.

32. Ibid., 332.

33. Fontana, *Papago Indians*, part 3, 183.

34. Sheridan, *Arizona*, 215.

35. The Camino Real and Mesilla corridors had long been part of the seasonal migratory pattern of Mexican agriculturalists. The shift from seasonal work in mines to seasonal agricultural work in the cotton sector was a natural transition. See Rodolfo F. Acuña, *Corridors of Migration: The Odyssey of Mexican Laborers, 1600–1933* (Tucson: University of Arizona Press, 2007), 2–3.

36. Even R. A. Wilbur, the special agent assigned to the Tohono O'odham in 1871, focused primarily on farming, even though he was a rancher and doctor and had originally been assigned to them as an attending physician. He hired an agency farmer to assist him shortly after his arrival. See Special Agent to Superintendent, October 1, 1872, AZ 344, SC/UA.

37. Lewis, *Neither Wolf nor Dog*, 17–18. Lewis notes both the hiring of farmers and also their counterparts, field matrons. As such he is perhaps the leading historian to group these two positions together in the same way that we do.

38. Wilbert H. Ahern notes that the employment of Native Americans in the Indian Service as a means of assimilation ended shortly after the turn of the century. Thereafter, Native Americans were hired in roles that were "most obviously subordinate to the authority of the agent." See Ahern, "An Experiment Aborted: Returned Indian Students in the Indian School Service, 1881–1908," *Ethnohistory* 44, no. 2 (Spring 1997): 267.

39. Meeks notes that the average herd consisted of 25 to 30 head of cattle, but that most Tohono O'odham had only a few head, while some, such as José X. Pablo (250 head) and the Toros family (2,000 head), owned much more. See Meeks, *Border Citizens*, 135.

40. Ibid.

41. Iverson, *When Indians Became Cowboys*, 93.

42. Ibid., 95.

43. Booth, "Creation of a Nation," 385–400.

44. Jewell D. Martin to Commissioner of Indian Affairs, Annual Report, Narrative Section, 1917, Subject Files of the Superintendent, Jewell D. Martin, SIA-RG75-NARA/PR/LN.

45. Superintendent to Commissioner, March 17, 1914, Commissioner of Indian Affairs, January–June 1914, Subject Files of the Superintendent, Henry J. McQuigg, SIA-RG75-NARA/PR/LN.

46. Superintendent to Commissioner, March 17, 1914, Commissioner of Indian Affairs, January–June 1914, Subject Files of the Superintendent, Henry J. McQuigg, SIA-RG75-NARA/PR/LN.

47. Catherine Culman, secretary of the school, to J. E. Crowd, folder 13, box 1, SIA-RG75-NARA/PR/LN.

48. See, for example, Annual Report, Statistical, 1917, Subject Files of the Superintendent, Jewell D. Martin, SIA-RG75-NARA/PR/LN.

49. "List of Indians Submitted by José X. Pablo Who Are Likely to Succeed in the Cattle Business with a Little Help from the Reimbursable Fund," n.d., José X. Pablo, Stockman, Reports of the Agency Farmers and Stockmen, 1910–1934, SIA-RG75-NARA/PR/LN.

50. Sadly, this style of farming was not functional in a desert and led to long-term declines in production. See David Rich Lewis, "Native Americans and the Environment: A Survey of Twentieth-Century Issues," *American Indian Quarterly* 19, no. 3 (Summer 1995): 424–425, and Nabhan, *Enduring Seeds*, 46–65. Not all men were trained to be farmers or livestock herders. The OIA also sent a few Tohono O'odham to Ohio and Michigan to work in automobile factories. See, for example, E. B. Merritt, Assistant Commissioner, to Mr. Jewell D. Martin, August 8, 1916, Commissioner of Indian Affairs, 1916, Subject Files of the Superintendent, Jewell D. Martin, SIA-RG75-NARA/PR/LN.

51. A. M. Philipson to Mr. T. F. McCormick, Superintendent, February 6, 1918, and A. M. Philipson to J. B. Brown, Superintendent of Phoenix Indian School, February 14, 1918, Reports of the Agency Farmers and Stockmen, 1910–1934, Farmer, A. M. Philipson, 1919, SIA-RG75-NARA/PR/LN.

52. Lewis, "Native Americans and the Environment," 425–426.

53. Iverson, *When Indians Became Cowboys*, 93.

54. Superintendent to Commissioner, February 23, 1917, José X. Pablo, Stockman, Reports of the Agency Farmers and Stockmen, 1910–1934, SIA-RG75-NARA/PR/LN.

55. Sonny Chico, St. Anthony's School, Topawa, Arizona, probably in 1942, folder C, series 1-1, box F1, facsimiles, Correspondence by Native Authors, A–I, BCIM/SC/Marquette.

56. Lewis, "Native Americans and the Environment," 425–426.

57. Jewell D. Martin to BIA, January 22, 1917, Agriculture, Subject Files of the Superintendent, Jewell D. Martin, SIA-RG75-NARA/PR/LN.

58. Vocational training extended beyond farming and ranching. Catholic day schools, for example, taught boys painting, interior decorating, paperhanging, and construction, as well as how to be a good altar boy. See "What Men Catholic Day Schools Make of Papago Boys," *Indian Sentinel* 12, no. 1 (1930–31): 37.

59. B. Brown to Jewell D. Martin, June 11, 1917, Education: Phoenix Indian School, Superintendent John B. Brown, Subject Files of the Superintendent, Jewell D. Martin, SIA-RG75-NARA/PR/LN.

60. The mineral claims were perfectly legal.

61. Letter to Cato Sells, February 6, 1916, Employee Record, Farmer, Wilbert O. Hodgson, Subject Files of the Superintendent, Jewell D. Martin, SIA-RG75-NARA/PR/LN.

62. That is, until he was fired for "taking kickbacks from cattle buyers" in 1935. Even then, he maintained a strong following among the Tohono O'odham. See Booth, "Creation of a Nation," 386–387.

63. A. M. Philipson, Farmer, 1919–1934, Reports of the Agency Farmers and Stockmen, 1910–1934, SIA-RG75-NARA/PR/LN.

64. T. F. McCormick to Commissioner of Indian Affairs, October 24, 1918, Office of Commissioner of Indian Affairs, July–December 1918, Subject Files of the Superintendent Thomas F. McCormick, SIA-RG75-NARA/PR/LN.

65. Technically, in the OIA there were both field matrons, working with women on reservations, and outing matrons, working with job placements in the cities. However, in the case of the Tohono O'odham there were only field matrons, who did both jobs. For background on the field matron program, see Lisa Emmerich, "'To Respect and Love and Seek the Ways of White Women': Field Matrons, the Office of Indian Affairs, and Civilization Policy, 1890–1938," PhD diss., University of Maryland, 1987, and Jacobs, *Engendered Encounters*, who describes the founding of the program as such: "Together with the Quakers and other religious denominations, the WNIA encouraged the OIA to institutionalize this 'women's work for women' into a field matron program. Responding to their pressure, the OIA created the position of field matron in the 1890s 'in order that Indian women may be influenced in their home life and duties, and may have done for them in their sphere what farmers and mechanics are supposed to do for Indian men in their sphere'" (26).

66. Thomas J. Morgan to Secretary of the Interior, April 19, 1890, Letters Received 1890/12481, RG75-NARA/NA/DC, cited in Lisa Emmerich, "To Respect and Love."

67. For a full discussion of the establishment and the development of the field matron program, see Emmerich, "To Respect and Love," the most comprehensive

work available on the subject. For similar attitudes in the settlement house movement, see Ruiz, *From Out of the Shadows*. As Ruiz points out, "Like the proponents of Americanization programs in California, settlement workers believed that women held a special guardianship over their families' welfare. As head nurse Millie Rickford explained, 'If we can teach her [the mother to be] the modern methods of cooking and preparing foods and simple hygiene habits for herself and her family, we have gained a stride'" (38).

68. For numbers of matrons by year, see Lisa Emmerich, "'Right in the Midst of My Own People': Native American Women and the Field Matron Program," *American Indian Quarterly* 15, no. 2 (Spring 1991): appendix 1, 212.

69. For an interestingly detailed account of Woodruff's career, see Woodruff and Dryden, *Indian Oasis*.

70. William was a Mason and a Republican; the family was a member of the Congregational Church. *Commemorative Biographical Record of the Upper Lake Region* (Chicago: J. H. Beers and Company, 1905), 12.

71. Mary Doyle to T. F. McCormick, February 14, 1920, Field Matron's Weekly Reports, Mary Doyle, 1916–1919, Reports of the Field Matrons, 1910–1932, SIA-RG75-NARA/PR/LN.

72. Mary Doyle to T. F. McCormick, Annual Report, July 1919, Field Matron's Weekly Reports, Mary Doyle, 1916–1919, Reports of the Field Matrons, 1910–1932, SIA-RG75-NARA/PR/LN.

73. Report on the Papago Indians, Arizona, Malcolm McDowell, April 8, 1919, 253, vol. 2, 1918–1919, Special Reports, 1915–1933, Records of the Board of Indian Commissioners, RG75-NARA/NA/DC.

74. Lewis, *Neither Wolf nor Dog*, 140–141. Even when the OIA (and others) did pay attention to areas outside of the reservation's southeast, they often faced heavy resistance. See Meeks, *Border Citizens*, 135–140, and Booth, "Creation of a Nation," 229–237.

75. Woodruff and Dryden, *Indian Oasis*, 264.

76. See, for example, Light to J. W. Elliot, October 9, 1930, Frances D. Hall, Senior Placement matron to Mrs. Libbie C. Light, May 16, 1931, and Field Matron to J. W. Elliott, November 11, 1931. Field Matron, Libbie C. Light, Correspondence, 1931–1932, Reports of the Field Matrons, 1910–1932, RG75/NARA/PR/LN.

77. Woodruff and Dryden, *Indian Oasis*, 241.

78. For an interesting variation on this theme, it is worth considering Tohono O'odham women who manufactured and sold household items. For an exploration of this process as it relates to potters, see Naranjo, "Tohono O'odham Potters."

79. Janette Woodruff, Field Matron Report for April 1917, Field Matron, Janette Woodruff, 1915, 1918, Reports of Field Matrons, 1910-1932, RG75-NARA/PR/LN.

80. For an excellent discussion of female "gendered" work in the Anglo and Mexican community, see Glenn, *Unequal Freedom*, 155–156. Note that Native women fell more closely in line with Mexican women: they were allowed to take on both "feminine" domestic work and some more physical jobs in agriculture.

81. Woodruff and Dryden, *Indian Oasis*, 290.

82. Hamilton, "History of the Presbyterian Work," 125.

83. Janette Woodruff, Annual Report on the Working Girls Ending June 30, 1928, Field Matron Weekly Reports, Janette Woodruff, 1925–1926, Reports of the Field Matrons, 1910–1932, SIA-RG75-NARA/PR/LN.

84. Mary Doyle to T. F. McCormick, October 2, 1920, Field Matron's Weekly Reports, Mary Doyle, 1916–1919, Reports of the Field Matrons, 1910–1932, SIA-RG75-NARA/PR/LN.

85. Woodruff and Dryden, *Indian Oasis*, 241.

86. Woodruff to Mr. Martin, November 11, 1916, Field Matron, Janette Woodruff, 1915–1918, Reports of the Field Matrons, 1910–1932, SIA-RG75-NARA/PR/LN.

87. Lewis, *Neither Wolf nor Dog*, 169.

88. Meeks, *Border Citizens*, 218–220.

89. Newspaper clipping, March 15, 1915, Field Matron Correspondence, Minnie M. Estabrook, 1914–1916, Reports of the Field Matrons, 1910–1932, SIA-RG75-NARA/PR/LN.

90. J. W. Elliot to Gentlemen, December 16, 1931, Field Matron, Libbie C. Light, Correspondence, 1931–1932, Reports of the Field Matrons, 1910–1932, SIA-RG75-NARA/PR/LN. See also Field Matron to Superintendent P. W. Daniels, Mescalero, New Mexico, July 15, 1931, Field Matron, Libbie C. Light, Correspondence, 1931–1932, Reports of the Field Matrons, 1910–1932, SIA-RG75-NARA/PR/LN, which discusses retraining as a secretary for one Tohono O'odham girl in hopes of finding paying employment.

91. McCarthy, *Papago Traveler*, 151–153. On the popularity of the CCC-ID, see Booth, "Creation of a Nation," 388.

Chapter 6

1. Michael C. Coleman argues that "despite their ethnocentric assimilationist policies and practices, the BIA and missionary schools . . . may have done more good than harm." See Coleman, "Counterfactuals I'd Rather Not Contemplate: What If Government Schooling Campaigns (1820s–1920s) to Americanize the Indians and to Anglicize the Irish Had Never Taken Place?" *Irish Journal of American Studies* 2 (June 2010), http://www.ijasonline.com/Michael-Coleman.html, accessed January 14, 2012. We find his argument to be interesting but not compelling. He is not wrong that there were some benefits to schooling, but he asks the wrong questions. It was not a "do this or do nothing." The BIA could have approached things differently, but Coleman does not offer this as an option.

2. Paul K. Eiss, "Deconstructing Indians, Reconstructing *Patria:* Indigenous Education in Yucatan from the *Porfiriato* to the Mexican Revolution," *Journal of Latin American Anthropology* 9, no. 1 (Spring 2004): 120–121, and Rick A. López, *Crafting Mexico: Intellectuals, Artisans, and the State after the Revolution* (Durham, NC: Duke University Press, 2010), 8–9.

3. It should be noted, however, that Mexico's Education Ministry tried to assimilate both rural and indigenous folks (obviously overlapping groups of people), as they thought that neither group was quite ready for full citizenship. See Mary Kay Vaughan, "Modernizing Patriarchy: State Policies, Rural Households, and Women in Mexico, 1930–1940," in *Hidden Histories of Gender and the State in Latin America*, ed. Elizabeth Dore and Maxine Molyneux (Durham, NC: Duke University Press, 2000), 194–214. José Angel Hernández argues that long before the creation of the Education Ministry in 1921, Mexico used its immigration policy to "incorporate the majority of

the indigenous populace into the larger 'Mexican family,' . . . [and] as a way to 'Mexicanize' communities outside of state control." See Hernández, "From Conquest to Colonization: *Indios* and Colonization Policies after Mexican Independence," *Mexican Studies/Estudios Mexicanos* 26, no. 2 (Summer 2010): 291–322.

4. Elizabeth Dore, "One Step Forward, Two Steps Back: Gender and the State in the Long Nineteenth Century," in *Hidden Histories of Gender and the State in Latin America,* ed. Dore and Molyneux (Durham, NC: Duke University Press, 2000), 3–32; Paul Gillingham, *Cuauhtémoc's Bones: Forging National Identity in Modern Mexico* (Albuquerque: University of New Mexico Press, 2011), 99–102; Emilio Kourí, "Interpreting the Expropriation of Indian Pueblo Lands in Porfirian Mexico: The Unexamined Legacies of Andrés Molina Enríquez," *Hispanic American Historical Review* 82, no. 1 (February 2002): 87; and Emilio Kourí, "Los pueblos indígenas, el Porfiriato y la revolución: Etnología y politicas públicas," paper delivered at the XIII Reunión de Historiadores de México, Estados Unidos, y Canadá, Queretaro, Mexico, October 29, 2010.

5. Sam Truett emphasizes this in "Neighbors by Nature: Rethinking Region, Nation, and Environmental History in the U.S.–Mexico Borderlands," *Environmental History* 2, no. 2 (April 1997): 160–178. See also Mario T. García, *Desert Immigrants: The Mexicans of El Paso, 1880–1920* (New Haven, CT: Yale University Press, 1981), 9–10, and Tim Loreck, "All Along the Borderline: The El Paso and Southwestern Railroad's Effect on Natural and Human Environments in Southwest New Mexico," paper delivered at the annual meeting of the Rocky Mountain Council for Latin American Studies, April 2011, Santa Fe, NM. On the dominance of US capital in Mexican economic development during this period, see John Mason Hart, *Empire and Revolution: The Americans in Mexico since the Civil War* (Berkeley and Los Angeles: University of California Press, 2002), 71–267, and Thomas E. Sheridan, *Arizona: A History* (Tucson: University of Arizona Press, 1995), 123.

6. Salas, *In the Shadow of the Eagles,* 4–12. Jürgen Buchenau argues that Sonora's "location on the border made the state a keystone of efforts to link the Mexican and US economies." See Buchenau, *The Last Caudillo: Alvaro Obregón and the Mexican Revolution* (Malden, MA: Wiley-Blackwell, 2011), 25. Many elite families solidified transnational connections through marriage and god-parentage. For example, see *Borderman: Memoirs of Federico José María Rondstadt,* ed. Edward Ronstadt (Albuquerque: University of New Mexico Press, 1993), 55, and Bernard L. Fontana, epilogue to *Borderman,* 131–137.

7. Citation in Mario García, *Desert Immigrants: The Mexicans of El Paso, 1880–1920* (New Haven, CT: Yale University Press, 1981), 34. See also John H. Coatsworth, "Measuring Influence: The United States and Mexican Peasantry," in *Rural Revolt in Mexico: U.S. Intervention and the Domain of Subaltern Politics,* ed. Daniel Nugent (Durham, NC: Duke University Press, 1998), 68. Kourí argues that a lot of work on disentailment of indigenous lands during the Porfiriato still needs to be done. See Kourí, "Interpreting the Expropriation," 69–117.

8. Dore, "One Step Forward," 17–21.

9. For details, see Júrgen Buchenau, *Plutarco Elías Calles and the Mexican Revolution* (Lanham, MD: Rowman and Littlefield, 2007), 7–8, and Alonso, *Thread of Blood.*

10. Kouri, "Interpreting the Expropriation," 87.

11. Jocelyn Olcott, *Revolutionary Women in Postrevolutionary Mexico* (Durham, NC: Duke University Press, 2005), 6.

12. Alonso, *Thread of Blood*, 87.

13. Quotation from Alonso, *Thread of Blood*, 83. Olcott, *Revolutionary Women*, 15–17.

14. Deborah Cohen, *Braceros: Migrant Citizenship and Transnational Subjects in the Postwar United States and Mexico* (Chapel Hill: University of North Carolina Press, 2011), 74.

15. Friedrich Katz, "The Liberal Republic and the Porfiriato, 1867–1910," in *Mexico since Independence*, ed. Leslie Bethel (Cambridge: Cambridge University Press, 1991), 90–94.

16. The attempt to recruit European immigrants largely failed, and many Chinese migrants used Mexico as a means of bypassing US immigration restrictions. See Roberto Chao Romero, *The Chinese in Mexico, 1882–1940* (Tucson: University of Arizona Press, 2010); Romero, "Chinese Immigrants Smuggling"; Delgado, "At Exclusion's Southern Gate"; and Samantha Huang, "Chinese Smuggling across the U.S.–Mexico Border: Migratory Knowledge and Networks," *World History Bulletin* 27, no. 1 (Spring 2011): 32–44.

17. Hernández, "From Conquest to Colonization."

18. The Reform Laws of 1867 had already decreed that primary education was to be not only free but obligatory, but the federal government was unable to fund primary education outside of central Mexico until after the Mexican Revolution. See Luz Elena Galván de Terraza, *Los maestros y la educación pública en México: Un studio histórico* (Hidalgo y Matamoros, Tlalpan: Centro de Investigaciones y Estudios Superiores en Antropología Social, 1985), 27; Mary Kay Vaughan, *The State, Education, and Social Class in Mexico, 1880–1928* (DeKalb: Northern Illinois University Press, 1982), 50; and T. G. Powell, "Mexican Intellectuals and the Indian Question, 1876–1911," *Hispanic American Historical Review* 48, no. 1 (February 1968): 21–23.

19. Andrae M Marak, "Federalization of Education in Chihuahua," *Paedagogica Historica* 41, no. 3 (June 2005): 357–375; Marak, *From Many, One*, 29–46; and Dawson, *Indian and Nation*, xxi.

20. Alan Knight, "Cardenismo: Juggernaut or Jalopy," *Journal of Latin American Studies* 26, no. 1 (February 1994): 73–107; Joel Migdal, *Strong Societies and Weak States: State-Society Relations and State Capabilities in the Third World* (Princeton, NJ: Princeton University Press, 1988).

21. John J. Dwyer, for example, argues that the federal government was able to move successfully against foreign capital only when subaltern actors were highly coordinated and mobilized. John J. Dwyer, *The Agrarian Dispute: The Expropriation of American-Owned Rural Land in Postrevolutionary Mexico* (Durham, NC: Duke University Press, 2008). Linda B. Hall warns us against underestimating the capacity of the postrevolutionary government's ability to negotiate equitable deals vis-à-vis American capital, but the Calles administration (1924–1928) immediately reopened the agreement struck by the Obregón administration (1920–1924), suggesting that the original deal may not have been all that satisfactory. See Linda B. Hall, *Oil, Politics, and Banks: The United States and Postrevolutionary Mexico, 1917–1924* (Austin: University of Texas Press, 1995).

22. The establishment of the Education Ministry (SEP) in 1921 under president Álvaro Obregón and the intervention of the National Agrarian Commission (CNA) on behalf of the Tohono O'odham under president Plutarco Elías Calles in 1928

were building blocks for the eventual expansion of federal power/intervention under Cárdenas in 1938. Superintendent to Commissioner, February 28, 1923, Office of the Commissioner of Indian Affairs, Subject Files of the Superintendent, Thomas F. McCormick, SIA-RG75-NARA/PR/LN.

23. Kenneth Dean Madsen, "A Nation across Nations," 87.

24. Meeks, "The Tohono O'odham," citation from 470.

25. Worster was talking about the entry of capital into the US West, but his argument better fits the Mexican northwest. Donald Worster, *Rivers of Empire: Water, Aridity, and the Growth of the American West* (New York: Oxford University Press, 1992), 51. Worster covers the Salt River project outside of Phoenix on 171–174.

26. Fontana, *Of Earth and Little Rain*, 85. Vaughan argues that the "incorporation of the indigenous through education was seen as a prerequisite for political stability"—in other words, as a means of avoiding military conflict. But the federal government and the state of Sonora did not reach out to the Tohono O'odham with offers of schooling until the 1920s. Mary Kay Vaughan, *Cultural Politics in Revolution* (Tucson: University of Arizona Press, 1997), 50.

27. On the Yaqui use of military force to defend their ancestral lands, see John J. Dwyer, "It's about Time: The Restitution of Yaqui Indian Land and the Idea of Time," *Journal of the West: American Indians and the Borderlands of the West*, ed. Andrae Marak and Laura Tuennerman, 48, no. 3 (Summer 2009): 28–30.

28. The Díaz regime moved the Tohono O'odham off of their lands to make room for additional Mexican settlers between 1905 and 1908. Fontana, "History of the Papago," 141. The practice of forcing the Tohono O'odham off their lands and then conscripting them predates the twentieth century. See Lumholtz, *New Trails in Mexico*, 75; W. J. McGee, *The Seri Indians* (Seventeenth Annual Report of the Bureau of American Ethnology, 1898), 120; and Jack D. Forbes, "Historical Survey of the Indians of Sonora, 1821–1910," *Ethnohistory* 4, no. 4 (Autumn 1957): 350.

29. It is worth noting that although they refused to recognize the Tohono O'odham as a tribal group in a legal sense, Sonoran officials kept separate records on them as a tribal group and treated them as if their leaders spoke on behalf of all tribal members, a dubious assumption given the local nature of tribal leadership.

30. Robert H. Holden has argued that the survey companies did not undermine peasant landholdings; but his work fails to account for land ownership by corporate groups like the Tohono O'odham who often did not have legal title to lands. See Robert H. Holden, *Mexico and the Survey of Public Lands: The Management of Modernization, 1876–1911* (DeKalb: Northern Illinois University Press, 1994).

31. Cited in Alonso, *Thread of Blood*, 127–128.

32. Marak, *From Many, One*, 112–114.

33. Alan Knight notes that in spite of the anti-American rhetoric of the revolution, the US direct investment actually increased in the 1920s. Knight, "The United States and the Mexican Peasantry," 40.

34. Antonio L. Bustamante to Governor of Sonora, June 25, 1921, Governor to Consulate of Mexico, San Fernando, Arizona, July 4, 1921, Archivo Historico General del Estado de Sonora (hereafter AHGES), Tribus/Papagos, tomo 3411. Jesus M. Zepeda to Governor of Sonora, October 3, 1921; Mose Drachman to Governor of Sonora, October 3, 1921; Governor to Jesus M. Zepeda, October 7, 1921; Mose Drachman to Governor of Sonora, October 17, 1921; Governor to Municipal President of

Altar, October 24, 1921; Municipal President of Altar to Governor, November 1, 1921; Antonio L. Bustamante, December 12, 1921; Governor to Antonio L. Bustamante, December 31, 1921; Governor of Sonora to Comisión Nacional Agraria, December 31, 1921; Secretary General of Sonora to Governor of Sonora, January 23, 1922; José Angel Baviche, Luis Lopéz, and Antonio L. Bustamante to Governor of Sonora, February 13, 1923; Governor to José Angel Baviche, April 7, 1923; El Oficial Primero E. del D. to Lucas Segundo, Lucas Campillo, and José Ventura, July 20, 1923; Local Agrarian Commission to Governor of Sonora, July 25, 1923; and José Angel Baviche and Rafael Ortiz to Governor of Sonora, June 20, 1923, AHGES, Tribus/Papagos, tomo 3472. Municipal President of Saric to Secretary of Government, July 14, 1922, and Secretary of Government to Antonio L. Bustamante, March 2, 1922, AHGES, Tribus/Papagos, tomo 3546. Raúl Hernández León, Police Commander, to Don Alejo Bay, Governor, April 22, 1925, and Jesus Siqueros to Governor, May 8, 1925, AHGES, Tribus/Papagos, tomo 3814. See also Buchenau, *Plutarco Elías Calles*, 20.

35. "Sáric, Estado de Sonora," *Enciclopedia de los municipios de México*, http://www.e-local.gob.mx/work/templates/enciclo/sonora/municipios/26060a.htm, accessed March 11, 2011; and Fontana, "History of the Papago," 141.

36. Galland, "La etnicidad O'otham," 116. Federal and state policies continued to favor mestizo ranchers and farmers through the 1950s and beyond. See Castillo Ramírez, "Las veredas," 15.

37. Not surprisingly, Castillo Ramírez found in his study that later Tohono O'odham rural-to-urban migrations made use of social networks already established by earlier Tohono O'odham migrants. See Castillo Ramírez, "Las veredas," 325–332.

38. Fontana, *Of Earth and Little Rain*, 85.

39. Martin S. Stabb, "Indigenism and Racism in Mexican Thought: 1857–1911, *Journal of Inter-American Studies* 1, no. 4 (October 1959): 405–423.

40. Allan J. McIntyre and the Arizona Historical Society, *Images of the Tohono O'odham and Pimeria Alta* (Charleston, SC: Arcadia Publishing, 2008), 89.

41. Galland explores the multiple ways in which the Tohono O'odham identify themselves, for political reasons and otherwise, as indigenous. See Galland, "La etnicidad O'otham," 116–158.

42. Forbes, "Historical Survey," 358.

43. Gustavo A. Serrano to Ezequiel Padilla, Sonora, July 18, 1929, *Archivo Historico de la Secretaria de Eduación Pública–Educación Rural* (hereafter AHSEP-ER), box 8420, exp. 6.

44. Marak, *From Many, One*, 116–129.

45. Ibid., 94–102.

46. Madsen, "A Nation across Nations," 76–79.

47. Castillo Ramírez, "Las veredas," 28–29 and 322–337 (quotations from 323 and 325).

48. Quoted in Vaughan, *Cultural Politics in Revolution*, 134. See also Engracia Loyo, *Gobiernos revolucionarios y eduación popular en México, 1911–1928* (México: El Colegio de México, 1999), 137–160; Josefina Zoraida Vázquez, *Nacionalismo y eduación en México* (México: El Colegio de México, 2005), 156–160; Guillermo de la Peña, "Educación y cultura en el México del siglo XX," in *Un siglo de educación en México*, vol. 1, ed. Pablo Latapí Sarre (México: Consejo Nacional para la Cultura y las Artes, Fondo de Cultura Económica, 1998), 50–64; and Stephen E. Lewis, "The

Nation, Education, and the 'Indian Problem' in Mexico, 1920–1940," in *The Eagle and the Virgin: Nation and Cultural Revolution in Mexico, 1920–1940*, ed. Mary Kay Vaughan and Stephen E. Lewis (Durham, NC: Duke University Press), 176–182.

49. Superintendent to Commissioner, February 28, 1923, Office of the Commissioner of Indian Affairs, Subject Files of the Superintendent, Thomas F. McCormick, SIA-RG75-NARA/PR/LN.

50. Given the claims made by McCormick that the Mexican government had set aside lands at Pozo Verde in 1923, one wonders if he was informed by José X. Pablo about the establishment of the school there.

51. Estado Unidos de Mexico, Censo de Poblacion, Estado de Sonora, 1930, Municipio de Caborca y sus anexos, Papago (O'odham) populations, exp. 667, Archivo General de la Nación; Fernando F. Dworak to SEP, May 25, 1928, Sonora, AHSEP-ER, box 8420, exp. 6.

52. Fernando F. Dworak to SEP, May 25, 1928, Sonora, AHSEP-ER, box 8420, exp. 6.

53. David Torres Orozco to Fernando F. Dworak, June 15, 1928, Sonora, AHSEP-ER, box 8433, exp. 2.

54. Ibid.

55. Gustavo A. Serrano to Ezequil Padilla, Sonora, July 18, 1929, AHSEP-ER, box 8420, exp. 6.

56. Castillo Ramírez, "Las veredas," 328. Castillo Ramírez also lists a second factor, the death of many tribal leaders such as Bustamante during the 1940s and 1950s.

57. Rafael Ramírez, the head of the rural education department located in the SEP headquarters in Mexico City, told his Sonoran colleagues that they needed to engage in an "intense labor" on behalf of the Tohono O'odham, specifically because of their connections with the United States and his fear that Mexico would lose their allegiance. His entreaties had little effect. Rafael Ramírez to Ramón R. Reyes, October 4, 1932, Sonora, AHSEP-ER, box 8433, exp. IV/100 (04)(IV-4)(721.5).

58. In 1932, Vicente Ochoa, the mestizo police chief of Pozo Verde, petitioned the Education Ministry to open a school on the Tohono O'odham's behalf. Proposal, Pozo Verde, Municipio Saric, Pápago, August 31, 1932, Sonora, AHSEP-ER, box 8415, exp. IV/161 (IV-14)/19194. On the attempted recruitment for the Mexico City boarding school, see Dip. Fernando P. Serrano, Com. Vicente Ochoa, Com. Anselmo Figueroa, Insp. De Caza y Pesca Ygnacio Mendoz, Prof. Insp. Ramón R. Reyes, report, February 2, 1932, Sonora, AHSEP-ER, box 8433, exp. 4.

59. When education official Ramón G. Bonfil suggested that the SEP accede to Tohono O'odham demands and pay for and build a school on their behalf, his request was denied. Ramón G. Bonfil to SEP, Sonora, November 5, 1929, AHSEP-ER, box 8420, exp. 6.

60. Elpidio López, Monthly Report, March 25, 1933, Sonora, AHSEP-ER, box 8446, exp. 21.

61. Spicer, *Cycles of Conquest*, 144; Juan Antony Kachiica to Commissioner of Sonoyta, June 30, 1939, AHGES, Tribus/Papagos, tomo 214.4.

62. Madsen, "A Nation across Nations," 70–95.

63. The Gadsden Purchase guaranteed the Tohono O'odham their rights to their titled land and the right to continue their religious practices, including their pilgrimage to Magdalena, but only Tohono O'odham who are US citizens are allowed to

freely cross the border. Although it was not until the mid-1980s that the Border Patrol officially prevented Sonoran Tohono O'odham from crossing the border, the fact that many Mexican O'odham lack birth certificates often prevented them from crossing even prior to this time. See "Indigenous Peoples' Human Rights Initiative," http://www.hrusa.org/indig/reports/Tohono.shtm, accessed May 24, 2011. Jeremy Adelman and Stephen Aron, "From Borderlands to Borders"; Alexandra Minna Stern, "Nationalism on the Line: Masculinity, Race, and the Creation of the U.S. Border Patrol, 1910–1940," in *Continental Crossroads: Remapping U.S.–Mexico Borderlands History*, ed. Truett and Young (Durham, NC: Duke University Press, 2004), 299–301; Mae M. Ngai, *Impossible Subjects: Illegal Aliens and the Making of Modern America* (Princeton, NJ: Princeton University Press, 2004). Julian Dodson rightly notes that the US federal government, through the Bureau of Investigation, was already paying close attention to border issues prior to the creation of the Border Patrol. See Julian Dodson, "The Revolt of the Losers: General Enrique Estrada's Failed Rebellion on the California–Mexico Border," paper delivered at the annual conference of the Rocky Mountain Council for Latin American Studies, Santa Fe, April 2001.

64. Castillo Ramírez, "Las veredas," 82 (our translation); Castillo and Cowan, *It Is Not Our Fault*, 10; and Madsen, "A Nation across Nations," 79–80.

65. Fontana, *Of Earth and Little Rain*, 90–91.

66. See Thomas E. Sheridan, "The O'odham (Pimas and Papagos): The World Would Burn without Rain," in *Paths of Life: American Indians of the Southwest and Northern Mexico*, ed. Thomas E. Sheridan and Nancy J. Parezo (Tucson: University of Arizona Press, 1996), 126–133, and Perez, "Confined to the Margins," 264–266.

67. Meeks, *Border Citizens*, 227–228; Castillo and Cowan, *It Is Not Our Fault*; and Rachel Rose Starks, Jen McCormack, and Stephen Cornell, *Native Nations and U.S. Borders: Challenges to Indigenous Culture, Citizenship, and Security* (Tucson: Udall Center for Studies in Public Policy, University of Arizona, 2011), 36.

Selected Bibliography

Archival Sources

Archivo General de la Nación
Archivo Historico de la Secretaria de Eduación Pública–Educación Rural
Archivo Historico General del Estado de Sonora
Arizona Historical Society
Arizona State Museum Library
Fideicomiso Archivos Plutarco Elías Calles y Fernando Torreblanca
Library of Congress
Marquette, Bureau of Catholic Indian Mission Records, Department of Special Collections and University Archives, Marquette University
National Archives and Records Administration, District of Columbia
National Archives and Records Administration, Pacific Region, Laguna Niguel
Presbyterian Historical Society
Unidad de Información de Pueblos Indigenas, Hermosillo, Sonora
University of Arizona, Special Collections

Sources

Acuña, Rodolfo F. *Corridors of Migration: The Odyssey of Mexican Laborers, 1600–1933*. Tucson: University of Arizona Press, 2007.

Adams, Evelyn. *American Indian Education: Government Schools and Economic Progress*. Morningside Heights, NY: King's Crown Press, 1946.

Adelman, Jeremy, and Stephen Aron. "From Borderlands to Borders: Empires, Nation-States, and the Peoples in between in North American History." *American Historical Review* 104, no. 3 (June 1999): 814–841.

Ahern, Wilbert H. "An Experiment Aborted: Returned Indian Students in the Indian School Service, 1881–1908." *Ethnohistory* 44, no. 2 (Spring 1997): 263–304.

Albers, Patricia, and Beatrice Medicine, eds. *The Hidden Half: Studies of Plains Indian Women.* Lanham, MD: University Press of America, 1983.

Albers, Patricia, and William James. "Illusion and Illumination: Visual Images of American Indian Women in the West." In *The Woman's West,* edited by Susan Armitage and Elizabeth Jameson, 35–50. Norman: University of Oklahoma Press, 1987.

Alonso, Ana María. *Thread of Blood: Colonialism, Revolution, and Gender on Mexico's Northern Frontier.* Tucson: University of Arizona Press, 1995.

Anderson, Benedict. *Imagined Communities.* London: Verso, 1991.

Anderson, Douglass Firth. "'More Conscience Than Force': U.S. Indian Inspector William Vandever, Grant's Peace Policy, and Protestant Whiteness." *Journal of the Gilded Age and the Progressive Era* 9, no. 2 (April 2010): 167–196.

Anderson, Mark C. "'What's to Be Done with 'Em?' Images of Mexican Cultural Backwardness, Racial Limitations, and Moral Decrepitude in the United States Press, 1913–1915." *Mexican Studies/Estudios Mexicanos* 14, no. 1 (Winter 1998): 23–70.

Andreas, Peter, and Ethan Nadelmann. *Policing the Globe: Criminalization and Crime Control in International Relations.* Oxford: Oxford University Press, 2006.

Arnove, Robert, ed. *Philanthropy and Cultural Imperialism: The Foundations at Home and Abroad.* Boston: G. K. Hall, 1980.

Arreola, Daniel D. "The Fence and Gates of Ambos Nogales: A Postcard Landscape Exploration." In *On the Border: Society and Culture between the United States and Mexico,* edited by Andrew Grant Wood, 43–49. Lanham, MD: SR Books, 2001.

Axtel, James. *Beyond 1492: Encounters in Colonial North America.* New York: Oxford University Press, 1992.

Bahr, Donald. "Pima-Papago Christianity." *Journal of the Southwest* 3, no. 2 (1988): 133–147.

Bahr, Donald, Juan Smith, William Smith Allison, and Julian Hayden. *The Short, Swift Time of Gods on Earth: The Hohokam Chronicles.* Berkeley and Los Angeles: University of California Press, 1994.

Banner, Stuart. *How the Indians Lost Their Land: Law and Power on the Frontier.* Cambridge: Harvard University Press, 2005.

Bederman, Gail. *Manliness and Civilization: A Cultural History of Gender and Race in the United States, 1880–1917.* Chicago: University of Chicago Press, 1995.

Blackhawk, Ned. *Violence over the Land: Indians and Empires in the Early American West.* Cambridge: Harvard University Press, 2006.

Blaine, Peter, Sr. *Papagos and Politics.* As told to Michael Adams. Tucson: Arizona Historical Society, 1981.

Blum, Ann S. "Speaking of Work and Family: Reciprocity, Child Labor, and Social Reproduction, Mexico City, 1920–1940." *Hispanic American Historical Review* 91, no. 1 (February 2011): 63–66.

Booth, Peter Macmillan. "Creation of a Nation: The Tohono O'odham Political Culture, 1900–1937." PhD diss., Purdue University, 2000.

Bordewich, Fergus M. *Killing the White Man's Indian: Reinventing Native Americans at the End of the Twentieth Century.* New York: Anchor Books, 1996.

Boyer, Paul. *Urban Masses and Moral Order in America, 1820–1920.* Cambridge: Harvard University Press, 1978.

Brown, Haddington. Preface to "Historical Circular of Indian Training School—Tucson, Arizona." Tucson, AZ: Citizen Printing and Publishing Co., 1905.

Buchenau, Jürgen. *The Last Caudillo: Alvaro Obregón and the Mexican Revolution.* Malden, MA: Wiley-Blackwell, 2011.

——. *Plutarco Elías Calles and the Mexican Revolution.* Lanham, MD: Rowman and Littlefield, 2007.

Buffington, Robert. "Prohibition in the Borderlands: National Government–Border Community Relations." *Pacific Historical Review* 63, no. 1 (February 1994): 19–38.

Callender, Charles, and Lee M. Kochems. "The North American Berdache." *Cultural Anthropology* 24, no. 4 (August–October 1983): 443–470.

Campbell, Howard, and Josiah McCheyman. "The Study of Borderlands Consumption: Potentials and Precautions." In *Land of Necessity: Consumer Culture in the United States–Mexico Borderlands,* edited by Alexis McCrossen, 325–332. Durham, NC: Duke University Press, 2009.

Canaday, Margot. *The Straight State: Sexuality and Citizenship in Twentieth-Century America.* Princeton, NJ: Princeton University Press, 2009.

Carey, Elaine, and Andrae Marak. Introduction to *Smugglers, Brothels, and Twine: Historical Perspectives on Contraband and Vice in North America's Borderlands,* edited by Carey and Marak. Tucson: University of Arizona Press, 2011.

Carter, Sarah. *The Importance of Being Monogamous: Marriage and Nation Building in Western Canada to 1913.* Alberta: University of Alberta Press, 2008.

Castillo, Guadalupe, and Margo Cowan. *It Is Not Our Fault: The Case for Amending Current Nationality Law to Make All Members of the Tohono O'odham Nation United States Citizens, Now and Forever.* Sells, AZ: Tohono O'odham Nation, Executive Branch, 2001.

Castillo Ramírez, Guillermo. "Las veredas entre el desierto y la ciudad: Reconfiguracion de la identidad en el proceso historic do cambio de los Tohono O'odham." PhD diss., Universidad Nacional Autonoma de Mexico, 2010.

Chambers, Clarke. *Seedtime of Reform: American Social Service and Social Action 1918–1933.* Minneapolis: University of Minnesota Press, 1963.

Coatsworth, John H. "Measuring Influence: The United States and Mexican Peasantry." In *Rural Revolt in Mexico: U.S. Intervention and the Domain of Subaltern Politics,* edited by Daniel Nugent, 64–71. Durham, NC: Duke University Press, 1998.

Coben, Stanley. "The Assault on Victorianism in the Twentieth Century." *American Quarterly* 27, no. 5 (December 1975): 604–625.

Cohen, Deborah. *Braceros: Migrant Citizenship and Transnational Subjects in the Postwar United States and Mexico.* Chapel Hill: University of North Carolina Press, 2011.

Coleman, Michael. "Counterfactuals I'd Rather Not Contemplate: What If Government Schooling Campaigns (1820s–1920s) to Americanize the Indians and to Anglicize the Irish Had Never Taken Place?" *Irish Journal of American Studies* 2 (June 2010). http://www.ijasonline.com/Michael-Coleman.html, accessed January 14, 2012.

Commemorative Biographical Record of the Upper Lake Region. Chicago: J. H. Beers and Company, 1905.

Corrigan, Philip, and Derek Sayer. *The Great Arch: English State Formation as Cultural Revolution.* Oxford: Basil Blackwell, 1985.

Cott, Nancy. *The Grounding of Modern Feminism.* New Haven, CT: Yale University Press, 1987.

———. *Public Vows: A History of Marriage and the Nation.* Cambridge: Harvard University Press, 2000.

Crawford, Matthew B. *Shop Class as Soulcraft: An Inquiry into the Value of Work.* New York: Penguin Books, 2009.

Davis, Allen. *Spearheads for Reform: The Social Settlements and the Progressive Movement, 1890–1914.* New York: Oxford University Press, 1967.

Dawson, Alexander S. "From Models for the Nation to Model Citizens: Indigenismo and the 'Revindication' of the Mexican Indian, 1920–40." *Journal of Latin American Studies* 30, no. 2 (May 1998): 279–308.

———. *Indian and Nation in Revolutionary Mexico.* Tucson: University of Arizona Press, 2004.

Dawley, Alan. *Changing the World: American Progressives in War and Revolution.* Princeton, NJ: Princeton University Press, 2003.

———. *Struggles for Justice: Social Responsibility and the Liberal State.* Cambridge: Harvard University Press, 1991.

Deeds, Susan. *Defiance and Deference in Mexico's Colonial North: Indians under Spanish Rule in Nueva Vizcaya.* Austin: University of Texas Press, 2003.

De la Peña, Guillermo. "Educación y cultura en el México del siglo XX." In *Un siglo de educación en México,* vol. 1, edited by Pablo Latapí Sarre, 50–64. México: Consejo Nacional para la Cultura y las Artes, Fondo de Cultura Económica, 1998.

Delgado, Grace Peña. "At Exclusion's Southern Gate: Categories of Race and Class among Chinese *Fronterizos,* 1882–1904." In *Continental Crossroads: Remapping U.S.–Mexico Borderlands History,* edited by Samuel Truett and Elliot Young. Durham, NC: Duke University Press, 2004.

Deloria, Vine, Jr. *God Is Red.* New York: Grosset and Dunlap, 1973.

D'Emilio, John, and Estelle Friedman. *Intimate Matters: A History of Sexuality in America.* New York: Harper and Row, 1988.

Densmore, Frances. "Papago Music." Smithsonian Institution Bureau of American Ethnology, Bulletin 90. Washington, DC: US Government Printing Office, 1929.

Deutsch, Sarah. *No Separate Refuge: Culture, Class, and Gender on an Anglo-Hispanic Frontier in the American Southwest, 1880–1940.* New York: Oxford University Press, 1987.

Dobyns, Henry. *The Papago People.* Phoenix: Indian Tribal Series, 1972.

Dodson, Julian. "The Revolt of the Losers: General Enrique Estrada's Failed Rebellion on the California–Mexico Border." Paper presented at the Rocky Mountain Council for Latin American Studies annual conference, Santa Fe, April 2001.

Dore, Elizabeth. "One Step Forward, Two Steps Back: Gender and the State in the Long Nineteenth Century." In *Hidden Histories of Gender and the State in Latin America,* edited by Elizabeth Dore and Maxine Molyneux, 3–32. Durham, NC: Duke University Press, 2000.

Dwyer, John J. *The Agrarian Dispute: The Expropriation of American-Owned Rural Land in Postrevolutionary Mexico.* Durham, NC: Duke University Press, 2008.

———. "It's about Time: The Restitution of Yaqui Indian Land and the Idea of Time." *Journal of the West: American Indians and the Borderlands of the West,* edited by Andrae Marak and Laura Tuennerman, 48, no. 3 (Summer 2009): 28–30.

Eiss, Paul. "Deconstructing Indians, Reconstructing *Patria:* Indigenous Education in Yucatan from the *Porfiriato* to the Mexican Revolution." *Journal of Latin American Anthropology* 9, no. 1 (Spring 2004): 120–121.

Emmerich, Lisa. "'Civilization' and Transculturation: The Field Matron Program and Cross-Cultural Contact." *American Indian Culture and Research Journal* 15, no. 4 (1991): 33–48.

———. "Marguerite Laflesche Diddock: Office of Indian Affairs Field Matron." *Great Plains Quarterly* 13 (Summer 1993): 162–171.

———. "'Right in the Midst of My Own People': Native American Women and the Field Matron Program." *American Indian Quarterly* 15, no. 2 (Spring 1991): 201–216.

———. "'Save the Babies!': American Indian Women, Assimilation Policy, and Scientific Motherhood, 1912–1918." In *Writing the Range: Race, Class, and Culture in the Women's West,* edited by Elizabeth Jameson and Susan Armitage, 393–411. Norman: University of Oklahoma Press, 1997.

———. "'To Respect and Love and Seek the Ways of White Women': Field Matrons, the Office of Indian Affairs, and Civilization Policy, 1890–1938." PhD diss., University of Maryland, 1987.

Farmer, Edward. "Un Nacionalismo Pragmático: El Gobierno Callista en Sonora y el Capital Extranjero." *Boletín* 31 (May–August 1999): 1–23.

Findlay, Eileen. "Love in the Tropics: Marriage, Divorce, and the Construction of Benevolent Colonialism in Puerto Rico, 1898–1910." In *Close Encounters of Empire: Writing the Cultural History of U.S.–Latin American Relations,* edited by Gilbert Joseph, Catherine Legrand, et al., 139–172. Durham, NC: Duke University Press, 1998.

Fontana, Bernard. "History of the Papago." In *Handbook of North American Indians,* vol. 10, edited by William C. Sturtevant (gen. ed.) and Alfonso Ortiz (vol. editor), 137–148. Washington DC: Smithsonian Institution, 1983.

———. *Of Earth and Little Rain.* Tucson: University of Arizona Press, 1986.

———. *The Papago Indians.* Parts 1–3. Arizona State Museum Library, University of Arizona, Tucson, 1964–1966.

Forbes, Jack D. "Historical Survey of the Indians of Sonora, 1821–1910." *Ethnohistory* 4, no. 4 (Autumn 1957): 335–368.

Fowler, Will. *Santa Anna of Mexico.* Lincoln: University of Nebraska Press, 2007.

Frankel, Noralee, and Nancy Dye. *Gender. Class, Race, and Reform in the Progressive Era.* Lexington: University Press of Kentucky, 1991.

French, William E. A *Peaceful and Working People: Manners, Morals, and Class Formation in Northern Mexico.* Albuquerque: University of New Mexico Press, 1996.

Gaillard, D. D. "The Papago of Arizona and Sonora." *American Anthropologist* 7, no. 3 (July 1894): 293–296.

Galland, Karyn. "La etnicidad O'otham como estrategia politica: Ensayo antropológico sobre la otredad étnica." MA thesis, Universidad Nacional Autónoma de México, 2006.

Galván de Terraza, Luz Elena. *Los maestros y la educación pública en México: Un studio historic.* Hidalgo y Matamoros, Tlalpan: Centro de Investigaciones y Estudios Superiores en Antropología Social, 1985.

García, Mario T. *Desert Immigrants: The Mexicans of El Paso, 1880–1920.* New Haven, CT: Yale University Press, 1981.

Gerstle, Gary. "A State Both Strong and Weak." *American Historical Review* 115, no. 3 (June 2010): 779–785.

Gillingham, Paul. *Cuauhtémoc's Bones: Forging National Identity in Modern Mexico.* Albuquerque: University of New Mexico Press, 2011.

Glenn, Evelyn Nakano. *Unequal Freedom: How Race and Gender Shaped American Citizenship and Labor.* Cambridge: Harvard University Press, 2002.

Greenberg, Amy S. "Domesticating the Border: Manifest Destiny and the 'Comforts of Life' in the U.S.–Mexico Boundary Commission and Gadsden Purchase, 1848–1854." In *Land of Necessity: Consumer Culture in the United States–Mexico Borderlands,* edited by Alexis McCrossen, 83–112. Durham, NC: Duke University Press, 2009.

Griffith, James S. *A Shared Space: Folklife in the Arizona-Sonora Borderlands.* Logan: Utah State University Press, 1995.

Hagan, William T. "Kiowas, Comanches, and Cattlemen, 1867–1906: A Case Study of the Failure of U.S. Reservation Policy." *Pacific Historical Review* 40, no. 3 (August 1971): 333–355.

Hall, Catherine. *Civilizing Subjects: Metropole and Colony in the English Imagination, 1830–1867.* Chicago: University of Chicago Press, 2002.

Hall, Catherine, and Sonya Rose, eds. *At Home with the Empire: Metropolitan Culture and the Imperial World.* Cambridge: Cambridge University Press, 2006.

Hall, Linda B. *Oil, Politics, and Banks: The United States and Postrevolutionary Mexico, 1917–1924.* Austin: University of Texas Press, 1995.

Hämäläinen, Pekka. *The Comanche Empire.* New Haven, CT: Yale University Press, 2008.

Hamilton, John M. "A History of the Presbyterian Work among the Pima and Papago Indians of Arizona." MA thesis, University of Arizona, 1948.

Hart, John Mason. *Empire and Revolution: The Americans in Mexico since the Civil War.* Berkeley and Los Angeles: University of California Press, 2002.

——. *Revolutionary Mexico: The Coming and Process of the Mexican Revolution.* Berkeley and Los Angeles: University of California Press, 1988.

Hernández, José Angel. "From Conquest to Colonization: *Indios* and Colonization Policies after Mexican Independence." *Mexican Studies/Estudios Mexicanos* 26, no. 2 (Summer 2010): 291–322.

Hill, W. W. "Note on the Pima Berdache." *American Anthropologist* 40, no. 2 (April–June 1938): 338–340.

Holden, Robert H. *Mexico and the Survey of Public Lands: The Management of Modernization, 1876–1911.* DeKalb: Northern Illinois University Press, 1994.

Hoxie, Frederick. *A Final Promise: The Campaign to Assimilate the Indians, 1880–1920.* Lincoln: University of Nebraska Press, 2001.

——, ed. *Talking Back to Civilization: Indian Voices from the Progressive Era.* Boston: Bedford/St. Martin's, 2001.

Huang, Samantha. "Chinese Smuggling across the U.S.–Mexico Border: Migratory Knowledge and Networks." *World History Bulletin* 27, no. 1 (Spring 2011): 32–44.

"Indigenous Peoples' Human Rights Initiative." http://www.hrusa.org/indig/reports/Tohono.shtm, accessed May 24, 2011.

Iverson, Peter. *When Indians Became Cowboys: Native Peoples and Cattle Ranching in the American West.* Norman: University of Oklahoma Press, 1994.

Jacobs, Margaret. *Engendered Encounters: Feminism and Pueblo Cultures, 1879–1934.* Lincoln: University of Nebraska Press, 1999.

———. "Working on the Domestic Frontier: American Indian Domestic Servants in White Women's Households in the San Francisco Bay Area, 1920–1940." *Frontiers: A Journal of Women's Studies* 28, nos. 1 and 2 (2007): 165–199.

Jameson, Elizabeth. "Women as Workers, Women as Civilizers: True Womanhood in the American West." *Frontiers: A Journal of Women Studies* 7, no. 3 (1984): 1–8.

Jameson, Elizabeth, and Susan Armitage, eds. *Writing the Range: Race, Class, and Culture in the Women's West.* Norman: University of Oklahoma Press, 1997.

Johnson, Benjamin H., and Andrew R. Graybill. "Borders and Their Historians in North America." In *Bridging National Borders in North America: Transnational and Comparative Histories,* edited by Johnson and Graybill, 1–29. Durham, NC: Duke University Press, 2010.

Joseph, Gilbert. "Close Encounters: Toward a New Cultural History of U.S.–Latin American Relations." In *Close Encounters of Empire: Writing the Cultural History of U.S.–Latin American Relations,* edited by Gilbert Joseph, Catherine Legrand, et al., 3–46. Durham, NC: Duke University Press, 1998.

Kang, S. Deborah. "Crossing the Line: The INS and the Federal Regulation of the Mexican Border." In *Bridging National Borders in North America: Transnational and Comparative Histories,* edited by Benjamin H. Johnson and Andrew R. Graybill, 167–198. Durham, NC: Duke University Press, 2010.

Karras, Alan L. *Smuggling: Contraband and Corruption in World History.* Lanham, MD: Rowman and Littlefield, 2010.

Katz, Friedrich. "The Liberal Republic and the Porfiriato, 1867–1910." In *Mexico since Independence,* edited by Leslie Bethell, 49–124. Cambridge: Cambridge University Press, 1991.

———. *The Life and Times of Pancho Villa.* Stanford, CA: Stanford University Press, 1998.

Katz, Michael. *In the Shadow of the Poorhouse.* New York: Basic Books, 1986.

Katzman, David. *Seven Days a Week: Women and Domestic Service in Industrializing America.* New York: Oxford University Press, 1978.

Kessler-Harris, Alice. *In Pursuit of Equity: Women, Men, and the Quest for Economic Citizenship in Twentieth-Century America.* New York: Oxford University Press, 2001.

Knack, Martha. "Philene T. Hall, Bureau of Indian Affairs Field Matron: Planned Culture Change of Washakie Shoshone Women." *Prologue* 22, no. 2 (Summer 1990): 150–167.

Knight, Alan. "Cardenismo: Juggernaut or Jalopy." *Journal of Latin American Studies* 26, no. 1 (February 1994): 73–107.

———. "The United States and the Mexican Peasantry, circa 1880–1940." In *Rural Revolt in Mexico: U.S. Intervention and the Domain of Subaltern Politics,* edited by Daniel Nugent, 25–63. Durham, NC: Duke University Press, 1998.

Kourí, Emilio. "Interpreting the Expropriation of Indian Pueblo Lands in Porfirian Mexico: The Unexamined Legacies of Andrés Molina Enríquez." *Hispanic American Historical Review* 82, no. 1 (February 2002): 69–117.

———."Los pueblos indígenas, el Porfiriato y la revolución: Etnología y politicas públicas." Paper delivered at the XIII Reunión de Historiadores de México, Estados Unidos, y Canadá, Queretaro, Mexico, October 29, 2010.

Kroeber, Henriette Rothschild. "Traditions of the Papago Indians." *Journal of American Folk-lore* 25, no. 96 (April–June 1912): 95–105.

Kunzel, Regina G. *Fallen Women, Problem Girls: Unmarried Mothers and the Professionalization of Social Work, 1890–1945*. New Haven, CT: Yale University Press, 1993.

Kusmer, Kenneth. *A Ghetto Takes Shape: Black Cleveland, 1870–1930*. Urbana: University of Illinois Press, 1976.

Labaree, David F. *The Making of an American High School: The Credentials Market and the Central High School of Philadelphia, 1838–1939*. New Haven, CT: Yale University Press, 1988.

Lasch-Quinn, Elizabeth. *Black Neighbors: Race and the Limits of Reform in the American Settlement House Movement, 1890–1945*. Chapel Hill: University of North Carolina Press, 1993.

Lee, Erika. *At America's Gates: Chinese Immigration during the Exclusion Era, 1882–1943*. Chapel Hill: University of North Carolina Press, 2003.

Levine, Philippa. "Sexuality and Empire." In *At Home with the Empire: Metropolitan Culture and the Imperial World*, edited by Catherine Hall and Sonya O. Rose. 122–142. Cambridge: Cambridge University Press, 2006.

Lewis, David Rich. "Native Americans and the Environment: A Survey of Twentieth-Century Issues." *American Indian Quarterly* 19, no. 3 (Summer 1995): 423–450.

———. *Neither Wolf nor Dog: American Indians, Environment, and Agrarian Change*. New York: Oxford University Press, 1994.

Lewis, Stephen E. "The Nation, Education, and the 'Indian Problem' in Mexico, 1920–1940." In *The Eagle and the Virgin: Nation and Cultural Revolution in Mexico, 1920–1940*, edited by Mary Kay Vaughan and Stephen E. Lewis, 176–195. Durham, NC: Duke University Press, 2006.

Lomawaima, K. Tsianina. "Domesticity in the Federal Indian Schools: The Power of Authority over Mind and Body." *American Ethnologist* 20, no. 2 (May 1993): 227–240.

Lomnitz, Claudio. *Deep Mexico, Silent Mexico: An Anthropology of Nationalism*. Minneapolis: University of Minnesota Press, 2001.

López, Rick A. *Crafting Mexico: Intellectuals, Artisans, and the State after the Revolution*. Durham, NC: Duke University Press, 2010.

Loreck, Tim. "All Along the Borderline: The El Paso and Southwestern Railroad's Effect on Natural and Human Environments in Southwest New Mexico." Paper presented at the annual meeting of the Rocky Mountain Council for Latin American Studies, Santa Fe, NM, April 2011.

Loyo, Engracia. *Gobiernos revolucionarios y eduación popular en México, 1911–1928*. México: El Colegio de México, 1999.

Lubove, Roy. *The Progressive and the Slums*. Pittsburgh: University of Pittsburgh Press, 1962.

Lugo, Alejandro. *Fragmented Lives, Assembled Parts: Culture, Capitalism, and Conquest at the U.S.–Mexico Border*. Austin: University of Texas Press, 2008.

Lumholtz, Carl. *New Trails in Mexico: An Account of One Year's Exploration in North-Western Sonora, Mexico, and South-Western Arizona, 1909–1910*. Tucson: University of Arizona Press, 1990.

Madley, Benjamin. "California's Yuki Indians: Defining Genocide in Native American History." *Western Historical Quarterly* 39, no. 3 (Autumn 2008): 303–332.

Madsen, Kenneth Dean. "A Nation across Nations: The Tohono O'odham and the United States–Mexico Border." PhD diss., Arizona State University, 2005.

Marak, Andrae M. "Federalization of Education in Chihuahua." *Paedagogica Historica* 41, no. 3 (June 2005): 357–375.

———. "Forging Identity: Mexican Federal Frontier Schools, 1924–1935." *New Mexico Historical Review* 80, no. 2 (Spring 2005): 163–188.

———. *From Many, One: Indians, Peasants, Borders, and Education in Callista Mexico, 1924–1935.* Calgary, AB: University of Calgary Press, 2009.

Markstorm, Carol. *Empowerment of North American Indian Girls, Ritual Expressions at Puberty.* Lincoln: University of Nebraska Press, 2008.

Martínez, Oscar J. *Border Boom Town: Ciudad Juárez since 1848.* Austin: University of Texas Press, 1975.

———. *Troublesome Border.* Tucson: University of Arizona Press, 1988.

Mathes, Valerie Sherer. "Nineteenth Century Women and Reform: The Women's National Indian Association." *American Indian Quarterly* 14, no. 1 (Winter 1990): 1–18.

McCarthy, James. *A Papago Traveler: The Memories of James McCarthy*, edited by John Westover. Tucson: University of Arizona Press, 1985.

McCrossen, Alexis, ed. *Land of Necessity: Consumer Culture in the United States–Mexico Borderlands.* Durham, NC: Duke University Press, 2009.

McDonnell, Janet A. *The Dispossession of the American Indian, 1887–1934.* Bloomington: Indiana University Press, 1991.

McGee, W. J. "Piratical Acculturation." *American Anthropologist* 11, no. 8 (August 1898): 243–249.

———. *The Seri Indians: Seventeenth Annual Report of the Bureau of American Ethnology.* Washington DC: US Government Printing Office, 1898.

———. *Trails to Tiburón: The 1894 and 1895 Field Diaries of W. J. McGee.* Tucson: University of Arizona Press, 2000.

McGuire, Randall H. *Archaeology as Political Action.* Berkeley and Los Angeles: University of California Press, 2008.

McIntyre, Allan, and the Arizona Historical Society. *The Tohono O'odham and Pimeria Alta.* Charleston, SC: Arcadia Publishing, 2008.

Meeks, Eric. *Border Citizens: The Making of Indians, Mexicans, and Anglos in Arizona.* Austin: University of Texas Press, 2007.

———. "The Tohono O'odham, Wage Labor, and Resistant Adaptation, 1900–1930." *Western Historical Quarterly* 34, no. 4 (Winter 2003): 468–489.

Meriam, Lewis, et al. *The Problem of Indian Administration: Report of a Survey Made at the Request of Honorable Hubert Work, Secretary of the Interior.* Baltimore: Johns Hopkins Press, 1928.

Meyer, Michael C., William L. Sherman, and Susan M. Deeds. *The Course of Mexican History.* 7th ed. New York: Oxford University Press, 2003.

Migdal, Joel. *Strong Societies and Weak States: State-Society Relations and State Capabilities in the Third World.* Princeton, NJ: Princeton University Press, 1988.

Mihesuah, Devon. *Cultivating the Rosebuds: The Education of Women at the Cherokee Female Seminary 1851–1909.* Urbana: University of Illinois Press, 1993.

———. *Indigenous American Women: Decolonization, Empowerment, Activism.* Lincoln: University of Nebraska Press, 2003.

Nabhan, Gary Paul. *The Desert Smells Like Rain: A Naturalist in Papago Indian Country*. New York: Farrar, Straus and Giroux, 1999. First published 1982 by North Point Press.

———. *Enduring Seeds: Native American Agriculture and Wild Plant Conservation*. New York: North Point Press, 1989.

Nabokov, Peter. *A Forest of Time: American Indian Ways of History*. Cambridge: Cambridge University Press, 2002.

Naranjo, Reuben, Jr. "Tohono O'odham Potters in Tombstone and Bisbee, Arizona, 1890–1920." MA thesis, University of Arizona, 2000.

Ngai, Mae M. *Impossible Subjects: Illegal Aliens and the Making of Modern America*. Princeton, NJ: Princeton University Press, 2004.

Novak, William J. "The Myth of the 'Weak' American State." *American Historical Review* 113, no. 3 (June 2008): 752–772.

Olcott, Jocelyn. *Revolutionary Women in Postrevolutionary Mexico*. Durham, NC: Duke University Press, 2005.

Ortiz, Alfonso, ed. *Handbook of North American Indians: Southwest*. Vol. 10. Washington DC: Smithsonian Institution, 1983.

———. "Some Concerns Central to the Writing of 'Indian' History." *Indian Historian* 10, no. 1 (Winter 1977): 17–22.

Osburn, Katherine. *Southern Ute Women: Autonomy and Assimilation on the Reservation, 1887–1934*. Lincoln: University of Nebraska Press, 2008.

Ostler, Jeffrey. *The Plains Sioux and U.S. Colonialism from Lewis and Clark to Wounded Knee*. Cambridge: Cambridge University Press, 2004.

Pascoe, Peggy. *Relations of Rescue: The Search for Female Moral Authority in the American West, 1874–1939*. New York: Oxford University Press, 1990.

Perez, Robert. "Confined to the Margins: Smuggling among Native Peoples of the Borderlands." In *Land of Necessity: Consumer Culture in the United States–Mexico Borderlands*, edited by Alexis McCrossen, 248–273. Durham, NC: Duke University Press, 2010.

Perry, Adele. *On the Edge of the Empire: Gender, Race, and the Making of British Columbia, 1849–1871*. Toronto: University of Toronto Press, 2001.

Peterson del Mar, David. *Environmentalism*. Harlow, England: Pearson-Longman, 2006.

Portes Gil, Emilio. "La campaña contra el alcoholismo: Iniciativa presidencial." *Boletín de la Sociedad Mexicana de Geografía y Estadística* 40 (April 1930): 5–7.

Powell, T. G. "Mexican Intellectuals and the Indian Question, 1876–1911." *Hispanic American Historical Review* 48, no. 1 (February 1968): 21–23.

Prucha, Francis Paul. *The Churches and the Indian Schools, 1888–1912*. Lincoln: University of Nebraska Press, 1979.

Quinn, Elizabeth Lasch Quinn. *Black Neighbors: Race at the Limits of Reform in the American Settlement House Movement, 1890–1945*. Chapel Hill: University of North Carolina Press, 1993.

Radding, Cynthia. *Wandering Peoples: Colonialism, Ethnic Spaces, and Ecological Frontiers in Northwestern Mexico, 1700–1850*. Durham, NC: Duke University Press, 1997.

Radding de Murrieta, Cynthia. "The Function of the Market in Changing Economic Structures in Mission Communities of Pimería Alta, 1768–1821." *The Americas* 34, no. 2 (October 1977): 155–170.

Ramos, Raúl. *Beyond the Alamo: Forging Mexican Ethnicity in San Antonio, 1821–1861*. Chapel Hill: University of North Carolina Press, 2008.

Recio, Gabriela. "Drugs and Alcohol: US Prohibition and the Origins of the Drug Trade in Mexico, 1910–1930." *Journal of Latin American Studies* 34, no. 1 (February 2002): 21–42.

Reina, Leticia. "Local Elections and Regime Crises: The Political Culture of Indigenous Peoples." In *Cycles of Conflict, Centuries of Chaos: Crisis, Reform, and Revolution in Mexico*, edited by Elisa Servín, Leticia Reina, and John Tutino, 91–125. Durham, NC: Duke University Press, 2007.

Rensink, Brenden. "The Transnational Immigrant-Refugee Experience of Mexican Yaquis and Canadian Chippewa-Crees in Arizona and Montana." *Journal of the West* 48, no. 3 (Summer 2009): 12–19.

Reséndez, Andrés. *Changing National Identities at the Frontier: Texas and New Mexico, 1800–1850*. New York: Cambridge University Press, 2005.

Restall, Matthew. *Seven Myths of the Spanish Conquest*. New York: Oxford University Press, 2003.

Rodgers, Daniel. "In Search of Progressivism." *Reviews in American History* 10, no. 4 (December 1982): 113–132.

Rollins, Judith. *Between Women: Domestics and Their Employers*. Philadelphia: Temple University Press, 1985.

Romero, Robert Chao. "Chinese Immigrants Smuggling to the United States via Mexico and Cuba, 1882–1916." In *Smugglers, Brothels, and Twine: Historical Perspectives on Contraband and Vice in North America's Borderlands*, edited by Elaine Carey and Andrae M. Marak, 13–23. Tucson: University of Arizona Press, 2011.

———. *The Chinese in Mexico, 1882–1940*. Tucson: University of Arizona Press, 2010.

Ronstadt, Edward F., ed. *Borderman: Memoirs of Federico José María Rondstadt*. Albuquerque: University of New Mexico Press, 1993.

Ruiz, Ramón Eduardo. *On the Rim of Mexico: Encounters of the Rich and Poor*. Boulder, CO: Westview Press, 1998.

Ruiz, Vicki. "Dead Ends or Gold Mines?: Using Missionary Records in Mexican-American Women's History." *Frontiers: A Journal of Women's Studies* 12, no. 1 (1991): 33–56.

———. *From Out of the Shadows: Mexican Women in Twentieth-Century America*. Oxford: Oxford University Press, 1998.

Salas Tinker, Miguel. *In the Shadow of the Eagles: Sonora and the Transformation of the Border during the Porfiriato*. Berkeley and Los Angeles: University of California Press, 1997.

Salomon, Carlos. "*Indigenismo* across Borders." *Journal of the West* 48, no. 3 (Summer 2009): 48–52.

Salpointe, J. B. *Soldiers of the Cross: Notes on the Ecclesiastical Period of New Mexico, Arizona, and Colorado*. Whitefish, MT: Kessinger, 2006.

"Sáric, Estado de Sonora." *Enciclopedia de los municipios de México*. http://www.e-local.gob.mx/work/templates/enciclo/sonora/municipios/26060a.htm, accessed March 11, 2011.

Schmidt, Joel. "'Until the Mothers are Reached': Field Matrons on the Cheyenne and Arapaho Reservations." *Chronicles of Oklahoma* 74, no. 4: 436–445.

Scott, James C. *Seeing Like a State: How Certain Schemes to Improve the Human Condition Have Failed.* New Haven, CT: Yale University Press, 1998.

Sheridan, Thomas. *Arizona: A History*. Tucson: University of Arizona Press, 1995.

——. *Landscapes of Fraud: Mission Tumacácori, the Baca Float, and the Betrayal of the O'odham.* Tucson: University of Arizona Press, 2006.

——. *Los Tucsonenses: The Mexican Community in Tucson, 1854–1941.* Tucson: University of Arizona Press, 1997.

——. "The O'odham (Pimas and Papagos): The World Would Burn without Rain." In *Paths of Life: American Indians of the Southwest and Northern Mexico,* edited by Thomas E. Sheridan and Nancy J. Parezo, 115–140. Tucson: University of Arizona Press, 1996.

——. *Where the Dove Calls: The Political Ecology of a Peasant Corporate Community in Northwestern Mexico.* Tucson: University of Arizona Press, 1988.

Sheridan, Thomas, and Gary Nabhan. "Living with a River: Traditional Farmers of the Río San Miguel." *Journal of Arizona History* 19, no. 1 (Spring 1978): 1–16.

Sheridan, Thomas, and Nancy Parezo, eds. *Paths of Life: American Indians of the Southwest and Northern Mexico.* Tucson: University of Arizona Press, 1996.

Silverblatt, Irene. *Modern Inquisitions: Peru and the Colonial Origins of the Civilized World.* Durham, NC: Duke University Press, 2004.

Simonsen, Jane. "'Object Lessons': Domesticity and Display in Native American Assimilation." *American Studies* 43, no. 1 (Spring 2002): 75–99.

Singal, Daniel Joseph. "Towards a Definition of American Modernism." *American Quarterly* 39, no. 1 (Spring 1987): 7–26.

Sleeper-Smith, Susan. *Indian Women and French Men: Rethinking Cultural Encounter in the Western Great Lakes.* Amherst: University of Massachusetts Press, 2001.

Spicer, Edward H. *Cycles of Conquest: The Impact of Spain, Mexico, and the United States on the Indians of the Southwest, 1533–1960.* Tucson: University of Arizona Press, 1962.

Spratt, Margaret. "To Be Separate or One: The Issue of Race in the History of the Pittsburgh and Cleveland YWCAs, 1920–1946." In *Men and Women Adrift: The YMCA and the YWCA in the City,* edited by Nina Mjagkij and Margaret Spratt, 188–205. New York: New York University Press, 1997.

Stabb, Martin S. "Indigenism and Racism in Mexican Thought: 1857–1911." *Journal of Inter-American Studies* 1, no. 4 (October 1959): 405–423.

Stadum, Beverly. *Poor Women and Their Families: Hard Working Charity Cases, 1900–1930.* Albany: State University of New York Press, 1992.

Stanley, Amy Dru. *From Bondage to Contract: Wage Labor, Marriage, and the Market in the Age of Slave Emancipation.* Cambridge: Cambridge University Press, 1998.

Starks, Rachel Rose, Jen McCormakc, and Stephen Cornell. *Native Nations and U.S. Borders: Challenges to Indigenous Culture, Citizenship, and Security.* Tucson: Udall Center for Studies in Public Policy, University of Arizona, 2011.

Stern, Alexandra Minna. *Eugenic Nation: Faults and Frontiers of Better Breeding in Modern America.* Berkeley and Los Angeles: University of California Press, 2005.

——. "Nationalism on the Line: Masculinity, Race, and the Creation of the U.S. Border Patrol, 1910–1940." In *Continental Crossroads: Remapping U.S.–Mexico Borderlands History,* edited by Samuel Truett and Elliott Young, 299–323. Durham, NC: Duke University Press, 2004.

Stoler, Ann Laura. *Carnal Knowledge and Imperial Power: Race and the Intimate in Colonial Rule*. Berkeley and Los Angeles: University of California Press, 2002.

———. "Making Empire Respectable: The Politics of Race and Sexual Morality in 20th-Century Colonial Cultures." *American Ethnologist* 16, no. 4 (November 1989): 634–660.

Szasz, Margaret Connell, ed. *Between Indian and White Worlds: The Cultural Broker*. Norman: University of Oklahoma Press, 1994.

Takaki, Ronald. *Iron Cages: Race and Culture in Nineteenth-Century America*. New York: Knopf, 1979.

Tenorio-Trillo, Mauricio. "On *La Frontera* and Cultures of Consumption: An Essay of Images." In *Land of Necessity: Consumer Culture in the United States–Mexico Borderland*, edited by Alexis McCrossen, 333–354. Durham, NC: Duke University Press, 2009.

The Thirtieth Annual Report of the Executive Committee of the Indian Rights Association. Philadelphia: Office of the Indian Rights Association, 1912.

The Thirty-First Annual Report of the Executive Committee of the Indian Rights Association. Philadelphia: Office of the Indian Rights Association, 1914.

Torfing, Jacob. *New Theories of Discourse: Laclau, Mouffe, and Zizek*. London: Blackwell, 1999.

Trattner, Walter. *From Poor Law to Welfare State: A History of Social Welfare in America*. 4th ed. New York: Free Press, 1989.

Trennert, Robert. "Educating Indian Girls at Nonreservation Boarding Schools, 1878–1920." *Western Historical Quarterly* 13, no. 3 (July 1982): 271–290.

———. "Victorian Morality and the Supervision of Indian Women Working in Phoenix, 1906–1930." *Journal of Social History* 22, no. 1 (Autumn 1988): 113–128.

Truett, Samuel. "Neighbors by Nature: Rethinking Region, Nation, and Environmental History in the U.S.–Mexico Borderlands." *Environmental History* 2, no. 2 (April 1997): 160–178.

Truett, Samuel, and Elliott Young, eds. *Continental Crossroads: Remapping U.S.–Mexico Borderlands History*. Durham, NC: Duke University Press, 2004.

Turner, John Kenneth. *Barbarous Mexico*. Austin: University of Texas Press, 1969.

Underhill, Ruth. *The Papago (Tohono O'odham) and Pima Indians of Arizona*. Palmer Lake, CO: Filter Press, 2000.

———. *Papago Indian Religion*. New York: Columbia University Press, 1946.

———. *Papago Woman*. New York: Holt, Rinehart and Winston, 1979. First published 1936.

———. *People of the Crimson Evening*. Palmer Lake, CO: Filter Press, 1982.

———. *Social Organization of the Papago Indians*. New York: AMS Press, 1969.

Underhill, Ruth, Donald M. Bahr, Baptisto Lopez, Jose Pancho, and David Lopez. *Rainhouse and Ocean: Speeches for the Papago Year*. Tucson: University of Arizona Press, 1979.

Vanderwood, Paul. *Disorder and Progress: Bandits, Police, and Mexican Development*. Wilmington, DE: Scholarly Resources, 1992.

Vaughan, Mary Kay. *Cultural Politics in Revolution*. Tucson: University of Arizona Press, 1997.

———. "Modernizing Patriarchy: State Policies, Rural Households, and Women in Mexico, 1930–1940." In *Hidden Histories of Gender and the State in Latin America*, edited by Elizabeth Dore and Maxine Molyneux, 194–214. Durham, NC: Duke University Press, 2000.

———. *The State, Education, and Social Class in Mexico, 1880–1928*. DeKalb: Northern Illinois University Press, 1982.

Voss, Stuart F. *On the Periphery of Nineteenth-Century Mexico: Sonora and Sinaloa, 1810–1877*. Tucson: University of Arizona Press, 1982.

Wall, Wendy. *Inventing the "American Way": The Politics of Consensus from the New Deal to the Civil Rights Movement*. Oxford: Oxford University Press, 2008.

Weisiger, Marsha L. *Dreaming of Sheep in Navajo Country*. Seattle: University of Washington Press, 2009.

White, Richard. *The Middle Ground: Indians, Empires, and Republics in the Great Lakes Region, 1650–1850*. Cambridge: Cambridge University Press, 1991.

Wiebe, Robert. *The Search for Order, 1877–1920*. New York: Hill and Wang, 1967.

Woodruff, Janette, and Cecil Dryden. *Indian Oasis*. Caldwell, ID: Caxton Printers, 1939.

Worster, Donald. *Rivers of Empire: Water, Aridity, and the Growth of the American West*. New York: Oxford University Press, 1992.

Yohn, Susan. *A Contest of Faiths: Missionary Women and Pluralism in the American Southwest*. Ithaca, NY: Cornell University Press, 1995.

Young, Mary E. "Women, Civilization, and the Indian Question." In *Clio Was a Woman: Studies in the History of American Women*, edited by Virginia Purdy, 98–110. Washington DC: Howard University Press, 1980.

Zelizer, Viviana A. *Pricing the Priceless Child: The Changing Social Value of Children*. Princeton, NJ: Princeton University Press, 1994.

Zoraida Vázquez, Josefina. *Nacionalismo y eduación en México*. México: El Colegio de México, 2005.

Index

Page numbers in *italics* refer to illustrations.

About the Authors

Andrae Marak is chair of the Division of Humanities and Social Sciences and a professor of history and political science at Governors State University. He recently coedited *Smugglers, Brothels, and Twine: Historical Perspectives on Contraband and Vice in North America's Borderlands* with Elaine Carey. His book *From Many, One: Indians, Peasants, Borders, and Education in Callista Mexico, 1924–1935* was published by the University of Calgary Press. He earned a PhD from the University of New Mexico.

Laura Tuennerman is chair of the Department of History and Political Science, and a professor of history at California University of Pennsylvania. Her monograph *Helping Others, Helping Ourselves* (Kent State University Press, 2001) merged examination of philanthropy with the study of working-class communities. She earned a PhD in history at the University of Minnesota.

Together the authors have coedited an issue of *Journal of the West* (Summer 2009) focused on borderland history, coauthored multiple papers presented at national and international conferences, and coauthored multiple publications. These include: "Official Government Discourses about Vice and Deviance: The Early 20th Century Tohono O'odham," in *Smugglers, Brothels, and Twine: Historical Perspectives on Contraband and Vice in North America's Borderlands*, ed. Andrae Marak and Elaine Carey (University of Arizona Press, 2011); "Los vicios transnacionales de los Tohono o'odham a principios del siglo XX," in *En la encrucijada: Historia, marginalidad y delito en América Latina y los Estados Unidos de Norteamérica, siglos XIX y XX*, ed. Jorge Alberto Truillo Bretón (University of Guadalajara, 2010); and "'He Don't Show Us Much about Farming': Tohono O'odham Agency and Agricultural Priorities, 1910–1940," *Journal of the West* (Summer 2009).